W9-BDS-343

Bridging Multiple Worlds

Cultures, Identities, and

Pathways to College

Catherine R. Cooper

OXFORD
UNIVERSITY PRESS

Oxford University Press, Inc., publishes works that further Oxford University's objective of excellence in research, scholarship, and education.

Oxford   New York

Auckland   Cape Town   Dar es Salaam   Hong Kong   Karachi Kuala Lumpur
Madrid   Melbourne   Mexico City   Nairobi   New Delhi   Shanghai   Taipei   Toronto

With offices in

Argentina   Austria   Brazil   Chile   Czech Republic   France   Greece   Guatemala   Hungary   Italy
Japan   Poland   Portugal   Singapore   South Korea   Switzerland   Thailand   Turkey   Ukraine
Vietnam

Published by Oxford University Press, Inc.
198 Madison Avenue, New York, New York 10016

www.oup.com
Oxford is a registered trademark of Oxford University Press

ISBN 978-0-19-508020-9

A copy of this book's Cataloging-in-Publication Data is on file with the Library of Congress.

1 2 3 4 5 6 7 8 9

Printed in the United States of America on acid-free paper

Note to Readers

This publication is designed to provide accurate and authoritative information in regard to the subject matter covered. It is based upon sources believed to be accurate and reliable and is intended to be current as of the time it was written. It is sold with the understanding that the publisher is not engaged in rendering legal, accounting, or other professional services. If legal advice or other expert assistance is required, the services of a competent professional person should be sought. Also, to confirm that the information has not been affected or changed by recent developments, traditional legal research techniques should be used, including checking primary sources where appropriate.

(Based on the Declaration of Principles jointly adopted by a Committee of the American Bar Association and a Committee of Publishers and Associations.)

You may order this or any other Oxford University Press publication by visiting the Oxford University Press website at www.oup.com

The author's proceeds from this book will be donated to a fund for college scholarships for culturally diverse youth.

To readers of this book—I hope you find it useful for asking your
own questions and opening pathways worldwide.

To my husband Bob, our son David, and my parents
Chaim and Betty, with deepest thanks.

And to the aspirations of youth and their families
who inspire our shared purpose.

CONTENTS

Appendix 2
Demographic Portraits:
Comparing Home Languages of Language Learners across Schools 142

ACKNOWLEDGMENTS

One day in Amsterdam, as I gave a talk about our work with African American and Latino youth in California, I watched a group of Indian women in bright saris at the top row of the steep auditorium, nodding in agreement at each of my points. Later they told me that the same experiences I had described had happened to them. Such experiences talking about our work around the world motivated me to write this book. In the U.S., Europe, Asia, and Africa, these responses have shown me how many people worldwide are working on access and equity and the enormous potential for synergy in our efforts.

Warm thanks to those whose thoughtful reviews and other support helped this book come to fruition, including Patricia Phelan, Rachel Seginer, Gabriela Chavira, Elizabeth Domínguez, Denise Su, Angélica López, Edward Lopez, Margarita Azmitia, Richard Duran, Barbara Rogoff, Carrol Moran, Jeanette Lawrence, Moin Syed, Bud Mehan, and Judith Langlois. I give special thanks to Bob Cooper for reading so many drafts with such care and insight.

I appreciate the expertise and dedication of Joan Bossert, Sarah Harrington, Jodi Narde, and Karen Kwak at Oxford University Press and Aiswarya Narayanan at Glyph International. Patricia Aslin prepared the helpful index, and anonymous reviewers for Oxford provided valuable insights. Special thanks to Don Rothman, who gave such wise and generous guidance at just the right time, to David Cooper for designing the figures and graphs, and to Sara Stanley and Jenny Chalmers for careful preparation of the references.

The work in this book draws from partnerships among university faculty, staff, and students as well as youth, families, educators, and community program and policy leaders. Because this work has grown from a set of interwoven lines of research, throughout the book I use the words "we" and "our research team" to mean an evolving and vibrant set of such collaborations. I regret that I cannot acknowledge each team member by name here, but I express particular gratitude for collaborations with Hiroshi Azuma, Keiko Kashiwagi, and Per Gjerde in our studies with Japanese, Japanese American, and European American youth; with Harold Grotevant in our studies of family individuality and connectedness in identity development; with Margarita Azmitia in studying family-school-peer linkages among African American, Latino, and European American youth and families; with Yvette Gullatt, Liz Halimah, Winston Doby, Bud Mehan, and Carrol Moran for educational partnerships through the University of California Office of the President and the P-20 Leaders Group; and with the Bridging Multiple Worlds Alliance and their local, national, and international bridging across cultural communities. As part of these collaborations, I welcome readers' comments to C. R. Cooper, Department of Psychology, UC Santa Cruz, Santa Cruz, California 95064 or ccooper@ucsc.edu.

I greatly appreciate the support of our work from the University of California Linguistic Minority Research Institute, University of California Pacific Rim Foundation, University of California Office of the President, U.S. Office of Education, University of California Santa Cruz Educational Partnership Center, the Spencer Foundation, the John D. and Catherine T. MacArthur Foundation, National Institute of Child Health and Human Development, and the W. K. Kellogg Foundation. I wrote parts of this book during a scholarly residency at the Bellagio Center of the Rockefeller Foundation.

Thank you to the Richman and Cooper families for believing in my dream all these years, and to Chaika Stekoll, Linda Lewis Williams, and Sugely Chaidez—may their memories be a blessing.

My royalties from this book are devoted to college scholarships for under-represented students.

CONTRIBUTORS

Margarita Azmitia, Ph.D.
Department of Psychology
University of California
Santa Cruz, California

Gabriela Chavira, Ph.D.
Department of Psychology
California State University
Northridge, California

David Cooper, B.A.
San Francisco State University
San Francisco, California

Robert G. Cooper, Jr., Ph.D.
Department of Psychology
San José State University
San José, California

Elizabeth Domínguez, M.A.
Cabrillo Advancement Program
Cabrillo Community College
Aptos, California

Harold D. Grotevant, Ph.D.
Department of Psychology
University of Massachusetts
Amherst, Massachusetts

Yvette Gullatt, Ph.D.
Division of Academic Affairs
University of California Office of the
    President
Oakland, California

Dolores Mena, Ph.D.
Department of Counselor Education
San José State University
San José, California

Dawn Mikolyski, M.A.
Department of Psychology
San José State University
San José, California

Soledad Rosas, B.A.
San José State University
San José, California

Moin Syed, Ph.D.
Department of Psychology
University of Minnesota
Minneapolis, Minnesota

Bridging Multiple
Worlds

PART ONE

Introduction

1

THE ACADEMIC PIPELINE PROBLEM
A LOCAL, NATIONAL, AND GLOBAL DILEMMA[a]

The voices of youth reveal how they are thinking—with hopes and worries—about their cultural worlds, identities, and pathways to college. These excerpts are drawn from their writing as they took part in studies described in this book.

> My important experiences as an individual are watching my friends in my neighborhood waste their lives and seeing how they end up. I don't want to be stuck in a poor apartment in an unsatisfactory home or stuck on welfare. I've experienced how far college can help you out. Education truly to me is a key to success. I've seen people drop out and all because of children and drugs. That to me is stupidity. I've noticed college life in the [college prep] program and I really like it. College and a good future is for me.
>
> African American high school female

> My mom has influenced me the most. She got her G.E.D. [high school equivalent degree] after getting married at 16. Then went through 3 husbands, and some assistance before realizing it was time to finish her education. She went to [a business technical college] and got her secretarial sciences certificate. So now she works and has her freedom. I want to go to college first so I don't end up like her.
>
> European American high school female

> The major (most important) people are my mother, sister (age 19), and brother (age 27). They have explained to me with examples and words that the best way for me to succeed in a career is to study hard. The most important experience for me did not even happen to me. It happened to my mother. She wanted to go to college and become a professional. She did not accomplish her dream because back then women were born to

---

[a] This chapter draws on discussions of these issues by Cooper (1994); Cooper and Denner (1998); and Cooper and Burciaga (2011).

be housewives, not professionals. Her parents did not pay for her education because of this.

Latino high school male

Many societies embrace the ideals that their children will have equal access to school and advance through their merit. However, worldwide, as children move through primary and secondary school toward college, the numbers of immigrant, ethnic minority, and low-income youth who continue through school shrinks disproportionately, and troubling gender gaps appear (Shavit & Blossfeld, 1993). Figure 1.1 illustrates this *academic pipeline problem* for the United States in the attrition of students in five ethnic groupings between high school and attaining graduate degrees (Gándara, Larson, Mehan, & Rumberger, 1998; Geiser, 1996; U.S. Census Bureau, 2000). In Africa, the narrowing access to higher levels of schooling is called the *academic staircase problem* (Serpell, 1993, 2009). This global dilemma is intensifying as immigrant, refugee, and ethnic minority youth make up growing segments of school enrollments in many nations.

Of course, a college education is not the only definition of success, and academic pipelines extend only to primary schools in some regions of the world and to universities in others. But in each cultural group and in regions worldwide, education is strongly linked to children and adolescents' life opportunities and choices. Those who are denied access to education and its opportunities are at greater risk for marginalized life pathways that are costly for them and their communities.

In this book, I present recent advances in research, practice, and policies, drawn from the work of social scientists, educators, and policymakers who address the academic pipeline problem. This book invites readers to compare viewpoints and

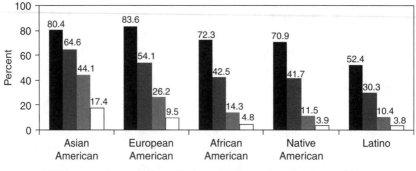

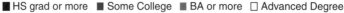

Figure 1.1 *The academic pipeline problem: Percent of students in five ethnic groups who persist through school:* In the U.S., the academic pipeline problem can be seen in five ethnic groups in the declining percent of students who graduate from high school, complete some college, attain a bachelor's degree, and attain advanced degrees. Greater attrition occurs among African American, Native American, and Latino students than Asian American and European American students (U.S. Census Bureau, 2000).

ask their own questions about the roots of this problem and possible remedies for it. Readers will also need to judge how to apply the principles in this book to their own communities, since both differences and parallels across settings are important.

DEFINING CULTURES

Controversies about how to define cultures have come to the forefront of the social sciences, social policy forums, and everyday conversations. These debates have also sparked research addressing the academic pipeline problem. Many analysts have assumed that all nations are culturally homogeneous and stable. However, global demographic, political, and economic changes and massive immigration are challenging these assumptions (Cooper & Denner, 1998).

Recent increases in global migration now challenge the fulfillment of our ideals of inclusiveness and equal access to higher education. In many nations, immigrant and refugee families—both relatively impoverished families and those from relatively impoverished countries—have arrived in great numbers, seeking better lives for their children (Daniels, 1990; Hurrelmann, 1994; Suárez-Orozco, Suárez-Orozco, & Todorova, 2008). For these families, public schools are the "hills of gold." Yet despite their dreams, as immigrant, ethnic minority, and working-class youth move through schools, the academic pipeline problem makes many of these youth expensive social liabilities rather than economic and social assets. In the U.S., educational disparities, once seen as primarily an issue between Black and White students, are now about inclusion in a multicultural society involving more than 100 different linguistic groups in some communities (Cooper & Denner, 1998).

Studies of cultures and human development have often compared individuals from different cultural and national groups on the basis of *individualism* and *collectivism* (Greenfield, 2010; Greenfield, Keller, Fuligni, & Maynard, 2003; Markus & Kitayama, 1991; Triandis & Suh, 2002). These qualities have often been portrayed as mutually exclusive, stable, and uniformly held among people in each cultural group. For example, the U.S. and Europe are considered individualistic societies, while Africa, Asia, and Latin America are considered collectivist. Perhaps because of this binary approach, cultures are viewed separately from measures of variation within groups like age, gender, national origin, occupation, income, education, ethnicity, or race. The limits of this two-category paradigm have prompted scholars in many nations to seek new ways to understand how cultures matter for human development, without overemphasizing or ignoring either societal or psychological levels of analysis (Crystal, Kakinuma, DeBell, Azuma, & Miyashita, 2008; Kagitçibasi, 2007).

Rather than seeing cultural influences either as monolithic societal forces that shape passive individuals or as immutable psychological traits, we are coming to understand cultures and human development as an ongoing interplay among individuals enacting their lives, their social relationships, public and private institutions, and communities (Cooper & Denner, 1998; Rogoff, 2003). Beyond any scholarly goals, the widening gaps between rich and poor and resurgence of worldwide intolerance of ethnic and cultural minority groups have triggered a sense of purpose and urgency for researchers, educators, and policy investors. They seek to understand cultural variation, change, and stability—without stereotyping cultural groups—to contribute to productive actions on behalf of children, youth, and families.

Demographers have long mapped variation within nations by recording people's countries of birth, race, ethnicity, language, income, gender, age, education, and occupation. Responses to surveys are analyzed according to political and geographical units such as census tracts, cities, states, or provinces. The results guide policy decisions in allocating resources; practical decisions about daily life in families, schools, and workplaces; and how far scientists generalize from studies based on samples rather than entire populations. In some nations, new census categories, such as the "multiracial" category in the U.S., illustrate evolving approaches to measuring cultural variation in multicultural societies.

In anthropology, definitions of cultures have long been disputed. Anthropologists have traditionally focused on the shared values and practices that are passed across generations, but some now emphasize cognitive orientations to ideas, beliefs, and knowledge; others focus on values or orientations to technological and environmental features; and still others concentrate on moral themes. Anthropologists increasingly probe the disputed aspects of cultures, such as immigrants' shifting transnational identities and values rather than adopting shared national values (Linger, 2006).

Such advances in thinking about cultural diversity and equity have not only sparked debates about cultural diversity and equity among intellectual and political leaders but also led to important changes in social policy. Examples include the U.S. Civil Rights Act of 1964, for issues of "race, color, and national origin" and later amended to include gender and disability, and the Japanese Equal Employment Opportunity Law of 1985 for gender equity. These policies express ideals about cultural diversity by seeking to increase access to educational and occupational opportunities.

The academic pipeline problem has become such a compelling social and moral focus that an extraordinary range of social scientists are engaged with this problem in the U.S. and worldwide, from senior scholars who have been working for decades to an ongoing influx of newcomers injecting their insights. These scholars often come from different starting points—in sociology, anthropology, social psychology, and developmental psychology, as well as education, law, and demography, with surprisingly little contact across disciplinary and national borders.

Despite this limited contact, global demographic changes have prompted social scientists to reconsider and revise their theories about cultures, identities, and pathways through school. The history of science provides examples of scholars revising what first appeared to be incompatible models of the same phenomena. In the physical sciences, compelling empirical evidence—after significant dispute—eventually led to wide acceptance for viewing light with equal validity as separate particles and as continuous waves, depending on the context in which it is measured. Likewise, social scientists in multicultural nations are increasingly viewing cultures through more than one conceptual lens—as both stable and dynamic, shared by groups and disputed within and across national borders, and operating at multiple levels of analysis.

As part of these efforts, researchers using different theoretical frameworks are productively addressing the academic pipeline problem. Discovering where theories are distinct and complementary is helping to open new dialogues and collaborations in culturally diverse communities. The next step is to align key concepts and recent advances to build a shared language for research, practice, and policy investments about the academic pipeline problem. This book offers a progress report on these efforts.

CAPITAL, ALIENATION, AND CHALLENGE

For some years, researchers, educators, and policymakers who work on the academic pipeline problem have taken one of three viewpoints about its origins and remedies, which we have come to call *capital, alienation,* and *challenge* (Cooper, Domínguez, & Rosas, 2005). Sociologists trace the role of social capital—the networks of resources and relationships among upper- and middle-class families that help children attain their parents' educational and occupational status. Studies in many nations have mapped how families pass social capital across generations through "cultural reproduction," so that youth whose parents have gone to college are more likely to develop college-based career identities than those who have not (Bourdieu & Passeron, 1986; Coleman, 1988; Kao & Rutherford, 2007). Recent research investigates how social capital can be created to enhance access to higher education for culturally diverse and working-class youth (Heath & McLaughlin, 1993; Mehan, 2007; Portes, 1998, 2000). How these families and youth access resources and "community wealth" will be a major theme in this book (Yosso, 2005).

Accounts of youth *alienation* proposed by cultural anthropologists suggest that working-class, immigrant, and ethnic minority parents often hold high hopes for their children's school success and economic advancement. However, their experiences with poverty and discrimination can dim their hopes, while their youth develop "oppositional identities." John Ogbu, a Nigerian immigrant to the U.S., challenged conventional explanations of the school problems of ethnic minority youth that were based on cultural deprivation or genetic inferiority (1993, 1995, 2003). Instead, Ogbu proposed that human competence is defined by the cultural and historical settings in which youth grow up. He argued that some inner-city Black children have academic difficulties not because of their ancestral culture, but because they so often have unequal access to educational opportunities. An ethnographic study by Fordham and Ogbu (1988; Fordham & Ogbu, 1986) with African American high school youth in Washington, DC, revealed that the stress of being successful alongside peers who faced limited opportunities led some students to downplay their racial identity by "acting white" or hiding their academic success by taking the role of "class clown." Recent research analyzes factors that contribute to and reduce such alienation (Gibson & Hidalgo, 2009; Matute-Bianchi, 1991; Vigil, 2004).

In contrast, research on the *challenge* perspective has revealed that under some conditions, the experiences of immigration, poverty, and discrimination can motivate youth to succeed on behalf of their families and cultural communities and thereby foster positive identity formation (Ceja, 2004; Cooper, 1999; Cooper, Brown, Azmitia, & Chavira, 2005; Fuligni, 2007; Kao & Tienda, 1998; Phelan, Davidson, & Yu, 1998). Educational anthropologists Patricia Phelan, Anne Locke Davidson, and Hanh Cao Yu (1991) proposed that all youth in diverse societies experience challenges in navigating among their cultural worlds. Phelan et al. chose the geographical metaphor of *worlds* to refer to "cultural knowledge and behavior found within the boundaries of students' particular families, peer groups, and schools.... Each world contains values and beliefs, expectations, actions, and emotional responses familiar to insiders" (1991, p. 53). Phelan et al. used the metaphor of *navigation* to capture students' actions and experiences as they try to move across the borders among their worlds.

Building on the work of Phelan and her team, my colleagues and I developed the Bridging Multiple Worlds Theory. This theory helps bring researchers, practitioners, and policymakers together to understand how culturally diverse youth navigate across their cultural worlds on pathways toward college and careers. The theory traces five dimensions: *family demographics* of youth who continue through the pipeline and those who leave it; youths' *identity pathways*; their *math and language academic pathways*; *challenges and resources* across their multiple worlds; and *cultural research partnerships* between universities and communities to open the academic pipeline to college.

For almost 40 years, I have worked with university faculty, staff, and students, and with youth, families, and community colleagues in such partnerships. Our partners have included youth and families from many different cultural communities, including multiple-heritage youth and their families. To test and refine the Bridging Multiple Worlds Theory, we have pursued a set of related lines of empirical studies and developed new research methods that I highlight in this book. On a broader level, in concert with other social scientists whose work is featured in this book, I have used capital, alienation, and challenge models to illuminate core issues about the academic pipeline problem.

FIVE CORE QUESTIONS

The academic pipeline problem raises five core questions about cultures, identities, and pathways to college in multicultural societies. I have framed these questions to highlight areas of active scholarly work and progress on the pipeline problem. As we examine each of the questions in a separate chapter, readers will see that their sequence progressively integrates individual, social, institutional, and community levels of analysis (Bronfenbrenner, 1979; Cole, 2010; Lerner &

Steinberg, 2009). Throughout the discussion of these questions, we will also see how the answers can open or constrain opportunities for youth to navigate their pathways through school.

Autonomy or Connections?

The first question asks, what does it mean to grow up? When should we define adolescents' psychological maturity by their growing autonomy and independence from their families and "leaving the nest"? When should we view emerging maturity as developing both autonomy and connections as part of a lifelong intergenerational project? Identity development can be seen in terms of personal exploration and commitment in domains such as careers, gender role, sexuality, political ideology, and religious beliefs, and as part of a collective process of categorizing one's membership in social groups. In addition, societal, institutional, and intergenerational forces can affect identity development. We will examine how defining identity development in terms of both autonomy and connections can offer important insights about the academic pipeline problem.

What Matters for Pathways to College?

What factors lead youth along academic pathways toward or away from college and college-based careers? As noted above, researchers, educators, and policymakers who work on the academic pipeline problem often take one of three viewpoints about its origins and remedies that we have called *capital*, *alienation*, and *challenge*. The second question examines students' pathways through school and how their experiences reflecting capital, alienation, and challenge may shape diverging pathways.

Brokers or Gatekeepers? How Youth Navigate Their Cultural Worlds

The third question examines linkages across adolescents' cultural worlds of their families, peers, schools, and communities. When are these worlds mismatched and competing? When can youth navigate successfully across compatible or even cooperative worlds along their pathways? This issue has a long history in research on the cross-pressures between families and peers and the discontinuities between schools and families of immigrant, ethnic minority, and working-class youth. *Cultural mismatch* or cultural discontinuity models consider immigrant and ethnic minority youth to be at risk for leaving school too early. Scholars are mapping under what conditions youth navigate their multiple worlds, persist in school, and attain their academic and career aspirations by examining how youth confront mismatches and also build connections across their worlds. New studies are revealing when youth encounter *cultural brokers*, who help bridge across worlds, or *gatekeepers*, who create obstacles along their pathways. As shown in Figure 1.2,

Figure 1.2 When Danny Melendez was a college student teaching math in the pre-college bridging program, he also served as a cultural broker for youth. He is now continuing these roles as a math teacher at his former high school. © Catherine Cooper; reprinted with permission from Sage Publications.

young adults can serve as cultural brokers to support younger students building their pathways to college.

From Fragile Bridges to Alliances:
How Can We Open Institutional Opportunities?

The fourth question reconsiders the common view of adolescents' identity development as exploration and choice among opportunities for their future schooling and careers. In the U.S., this idealized "freedom of choice" is particularly inappropriate for youth who encounter ethnic, gender, linguistic, or economic barriers along their pathways (Chisholm, Büchner, Kruger, & Brown, 1990; Hurrelmann, 1994; Yoder, 2000). These youth can become alienated and overrepresented among unemployed and prison populations (Vigil & Yun, 1996). This question reaches beyond social relations or networks to ask how youth build identities as they navigate institutional structures and how bridging institutions can (and actually do) support college pathways. Families, peers, schools, and community programs can serve as bridges along students' pathways, but they can be fragile. For this reason, alliances that span from preschool through graduate school (P–20) and link across multiple worlds hold promise for building and sustaining support for pathways to college.

How Do Multicultural Communities Define Success?

The fifth question asks how communities define successful development for their youth in cultural terms. When do communities see themselves as culturally homogeneous and thus view diversity in terms of deficits or threats to overcome in succeeding along a single successful pathway? When do communities see themselves as multicultural and offer more than one successful pathway for all of their youth?

OVERVIEW OF BOOK

Chapter 1 has introduced the academic pipeline problem and five overarching questions that highlight areas of active scholarly work and progress on this dilemma. In closing Part I, Chapter 2 provides a foundation for mapping progress on the five questions by examining challenges and useful strategies for understanding cultures, identities, and pathways to college. The first challenge arises when we try to use demographic categories in cultural explanations. The second arises when comparisons of majority and minority youth lead to defining minorities as either deficient or as "model minorities". The third challenge arises when youth, families, and other community members mistrust researchers, program staff, and funders as cultural outsiders. I offer strategies for addressing each of these challenges and examples of how they apply in different cultural communities.

In Part II, Chapters 3 through 7 each consider one of the five core questions, with evidence drawn from research across the social sciences. These chapters focus on progress on each issue that has also begun to bridge mutual isolation across disciplines. Readers will see differences within theoretical approaches but also converging evidence across approaches.

In Part III, Chapter 8 brings together recent progress on the academic pipeline problem and considers future work from a global perspective. Finally, the Appendices take a more technical look at tools for advancing cycles of research, practice, and policy. Partnerships often want to know how to support youth and families more effectively, how to make and monitor better investments, and how to build understanding about what conditions support pathways to college and careers. In Appendix 1, I seek to align the five dimensions of the Bridging Multiple Worlds model with those of other theories used to study the academic pipeline problem. These include social capital (McDonough, 2004; Mehan, 2007); ecocultural and sociocultural (Durán, Durán, Perry-Romero, & Sanchez, 2001; Weisner, 2010); overlapping spheres (Epstein et al., 2009); self-efficacy (Chemers, Syed, Goza, Zurbriggen, Bearman, Crosby, et al., 2010); social identity (Azmitia, Syed, & Radmacher, 2008; Orbe, 2008); critical race (Burciaga, 2008); ecological systems (Weiss, Kreider, Lopez, & Chatman-Nelson, 2010); possible selves (Oyserman, Bybee, & Terry, 2006); and resiliency theories (Buriel, Perez, DeMent,

Chavez, & Moran, 1998), among others. The Appendices offer ways for partners to ask their own questions, analyze and communicate findings, and align work across regions, states, and nations.

This book presents what we know about cultures and identities as they influence pathways to college. It also points to gaps where more knowledge is needed to address the academic pipeline problem. The five questions create ways to align contributions from a diverse set of theoretical and empirical approaches. I encourage readers to investigate details of the studies cited in their primary sources.

One sign of the confluence and divergence of viewpoints on the issues of this book can be heard in the many metaphors used by both adults and youth. Besides those about *academic pipelines* and *staircases* and students *navigating and bridging their cultural worlds*, readers will note metaphors about *ladders* (to describe progressions in math, language, and careers), *pathways*, *roads*, *pyramids*, *rivers*, and more. These metaphors often trigger passionate debates as to which better captures the most important features of these issues. I welcome readers into this dynamic and contested conversation.

I have written this book to offer fresh approaches to the academic pipeline problem for science, policy, and practice in the U.S. and other nations. By addressing these goals in one book, I hope to advance partnerships that open academic pipelines in the multicultural communities of which we are all a part.

2

ASKING BETTER QUESTIONS
CHALLENGES AND USEFUL STRATEGIES[a]

What if I'm both Black *and* Japanese?
What do I put under "mother" and "father" if I was raised by my grandmother and never knew my mother or father?
In this survey, I found out [things] that I never even thought about before. I know more about myself and how family, friends and teachers influence me.

This chapter considers three challenges that have confronted researchers, educators, and policymakers in thinking about cultures, identities, and pathways to college. We will examine these challenges and promising strategies for addressing them, with examples drawn from a wide range of cultural communities. They will be useful in discussing the five overarching questions of the book in the chapters that follow.

First, demographic indicators like ethnicity, race, income, and immigrant status are often used to sort youth and families into categories. However, these demographic labels are often treated as explanations rather than descriptions (Helms, Jernigan, & Mascher, 2005). Further, these categories are commonly linked to negative stereotypes rather than assets in adolescents' lives. Students face such negative stereotypes when their communities are equated with being "at risk." How can we move beyond this costly use of demographic categories in work on the academic pipeline problem? This chapter offers some ways to counter these limitations.

A second challenge arises when researchers compare working-class, ethnic minority, or immigrant youth with middle-class, ethnic majority youth. This comparative

---

[a] This chapter draws on discussions of these issues by Cooper, García Coll, Thorne, and Orellana (2005) and Cooper, Jackson, Azmitia, and Lopez (1998).

approach can lead to interpreting differences among groups as deficits from the mainstream norm (McLoyd, 1991, 2005). This design can also confound family income, nationality, ethnicity, and immigrant status. What alternatives are there to such comparative designs?

The third challenge arises when youth, families, and other community members mistrust researchers, program staff, and funders as cultural outsiders (whom youth sometimes call "the suits"), particularly when community members' resources are restricted and their circumstances unstable. They worry about being misrepresented and stereotyped by outsiders and even by insiders. For families with difficult experiences with welfare, immigration, or juvenile justice authorities, revealing information about birthplace, immigration status, or income, or agreeing to be photographed can be sensitive (Liamputtong, 2007). Such mistrust may limit researchers' ability to gather useful information, and prevent youth and families from accessing valuable services.

Three strategies are especially useful for addressing these challenges: *unpackaging demographic categories* to reveal the psychological, social, and institutional processes underlying them; using *parallel research designs* to compare cultural communities without defining one as deficient; and building *cultural research partnerships* to connect university researchers, youth, families, schools, programs, and communities in collaborations marked by safety and mutual respect. These strategies are being adapted across a range of cultural communities. We now consider each challenge and its corresponding strategy more closely.

UNPACKAGING DEMOGRAPHIC CATEGORIES

We often view cultures, ethnicities, social class, and immigration in terms of demographic categories that apply equally to people within a group and remain stable across time and social settings. As mentioned in Chapter 1, Europeans and European Americans are often considered members of *individualistic* or *independent* cultures, and Asians, African Americans, Asian Americans, Latin Americans, and Native Americans as members of *collectivist*, *interdependent*, or *communal* cultures (the validity of this dichotomy is under continuing debate; see Greenfield, 2010; Matsumoto, 1999; Oyserman, Coon, & Kemmerlmeier, 2002; Raeff, 2010).

Demographic categories can be useful for describing samples and monitoring inclusiveness and attrition from the academic pipeline. Some demographic categories, such as high vs. low parental educational attainment, are strongly correlated with children's attainment and well-being (Hernandez, 2004). However, beyond the risks of negative stereotypes and confusing description with explanation that we discussed, using demographic categories may also group together people who see themselves as very different from one another, while ignoring those who see themselves as part of more than one group (Stephan, 1992). These risks are especially relevant for understanding how youth forge their identities and pathways through school in multicultural societies.

Rather than misuse demographic categories by treating them as explanations, the anthropologist Beatrice Whiting (1976) challenged scholars to "unpackage" or "unwrap" their multidimensional meanings to discover the processes and experiences that these concepts summarize. In the same vein, Weisner, Gallimore, and Jordan (1988) warned:

> Culture is not a nominal variable to be attached equally to every child, in the same way that age, height, or sex might be. Treating culture in this way assumes that all children in a cultural group have common natal experiences. In many cases, they do not. The assumption of homogeneity of experience of children within cultures, without empirical evidence, is unwarranted .... A similar error is to treat national or ethnic status as equivalent to a common cultural experience for individuals (1988, p. 328).

The ecocultural model has proven valuable for "unpackaging" demographic categories (Gallimore, Goldenberg, & Weisner, 1993; Tharp & Gallimore, 1988; Weisner, 2005, 2010). Ecocultural researchers start by assuming that all families seek to adapt to the cultural settings where they live through their everyday routines or *activity settings*, such as household chores, mealtimes, homework, or making items for selling at a market. Ecocultural researchers study activity settings in terms of their key *participants*, the *cultural scripts* or expected ways that participants communicate with one another, and their *values, goals,* and *aspirations* (LeVine, 1988; Rogoff, 2003; Rogoff et al., 2006).

For example, in a longitudinal study in Los Angeles of immigrant families from Mexico and Central America, Reese, Gallimore, Goldenberg, and Balzano (1995; Goldenberg et al., 2005) examined immigrant parents' aspirations, values, and scripts in guiding children on their pathways through school. Reese and her team interviewed parents about their views of *el camino de la vida*, the path of life. Parents explained how their educational and occupational aspirations for their children drew on their broader moral values regarding the *buen camino*, or good path. Parents of higher-achieving children guided their children in terms of moral values that in turn led to positive academic results. These parents also worried that their children might slip onto the *mal camino*, or bad path, as they approached adolescence, so they needed protection from and help in resisting bad influences.

In many cultural traditions, older children, adolescents, and adults other than parents are key participants in caring for and guiding children. This reflects families' cultural values, community obligations, and economic realities like parents' work schedules (Azmitia, Cooper, & Brown, 2009; Cooper, Baker, Polichar, & Welsh, 1993; Lowe, Weisner, Geis, & Huston, 2005). Cultural scripts or communication patterns also shift as adolescents start to consider their future education and careers and their political, religious, gender, and ethnic identities.

Thus, it is important to discover cultural meanings by listening to youth, families, and community members describe their experiences rather than relying on demographic categories to summarize and implicitly explain such meanings. For example, it may be tempting to assume that immigrant parents who have little formal education do not guide their children toward higher education. Interview studies with such parents, described in Chapter 5, reveal evidence to the contrary.

In their Students' Multiple Worlds model, Phelan, Davidson, and Yu (1991) used concepts that align with ecocultural approaches to examine how ethnically diverse youth navigate across their family, peer, and school worlds. In their studies of students attending large urban high schools in Northern California, Phelan and her team found that some youth felt that their parents, friends, and teachers held compatible aspirations for them to succeed. They could cross the borders among their worlds relatively smoothly and seemed on track to their career goals. Even so, they sometimes felt overwhelmed by the pressure of these high expectations and isolated from students who were not part of their highly connected worlds. For a second group of students, their families' culture, social class, ethnicities, or religion differed from most of their school peers, but they could manage moving between home and school worlds. Still, they risked criticism from each world for being disloyal and felt they did not fully belong in either world. A third group lived in different worlds and found border crossing difficult. They did well in classes when teachers showed personal interest in them, but "teetered between engagement and withdrawal, whether with family, school, or friends" (1991, p. 84). For a fourth group, moving across worlds was so difficult that they became alienated from school, families, and peers. Some gave up on school, while others hoped to return. In this important study, Phelan and her team showed how many youth face ongoing and daunting issues moving across cultural worlds that in turn shape their pathways through school.

Our research team built on both the ecocultural model and the Students' Multiple Worlds model in studying the academic pipeline problem. In one long-term study that we discuss here and in Chapter 4, we interviewed African American and Latino students in college-preparation programs serving low-income and ethnic minority students (Cooper, Cooper, Azmitia, Chavira, & Gullatt, 2002; Cooper, Jackson, Azmitia, Lopez, & Dunbar, 1995). To learn about students' resources and challenges across their cultural worlds as they built identity pathways to college, we conducted focus group interviews and asked questions like the following (Steward & Shamdasani, 1990):

What are your main worlds?
What things do you usually do in each world?
Who are the main people in each of your worlds?
What kind of person do people in each of your worlds expect you to be?
What kind of person do you want to be?
How do these people help you become what they want you to be?
How do these worlds fit together for you? Which worlds feel separate? Which ones feel like they overlap?
How does being your ethnicity affect your experiences in these worlds?
How does being your gender affect your experiences in these worlds?

As the students sat around a table and ate large quantities of snacks, they discussed each question as a group with the interviewers and with one another. Then they drew and wrote about their worlds. We built on students' answers and suggestions in developing our Bridging Multiple Worlds model and survey (Cooper et al., 2002).

What Are Your Main Worlds?
How Do These Worlds Fit Together for You?

In the focus groups, students readily discussed and drew a wide array of different worlds in their lives, including their families, countries of origin, friends' homes, church youth groups, mosques, pre-college programs, shopping malls, video arcades (reported by most middle school boys and no girls), school math clubs, sports, and even the commuter train they rode from their homes to the university to attend their programs. Over half described more than one family world. Like the students described by Phelan and her team, these youth described how some of their worlds felt like they fit together, while others were in conflict or far apart. Some people served as *cultural brokers,* by helping students to bridge across their worlds, but others were *gatekeepers,* who created obstacles on their pathways. Overall, we were struck with how easily these students could draw and discuss the personal meanings of their worlds and the challenges and resources in each one. Their eloquence and responsiveness encouraged us to continue using these questions to learn more about how students navigate the academic pipeline.

What Is Your Ethnicity or Ethnicities?

In describing themselves and their families, we asked students to describe their ethnicity or ethnicities, rather than "check one box" from a predetermined list of categories. These 120 students listed 38 different ethnicities, including 20 who reported multiple ethnicities, such as Black/Ethiopian, American/Filipino, Black/Chinese, Black/European, American/Italian, Chicano/Native American, Colombian/Italian, Creole/Native American, Filipino/Pakistani, Mexican/Japanese, Mexican/Polish, and Peruvian/Japanese. Some of these labels differed from what students had checked on their program applications, which asked them to "check one box." These differences may indicate, for multiple-heritage youth, that one's most salient ethnic identity can vary across worlds (Stephan, 1992; Teranishi, 1995). Programs that target African American, Latino, and Native American students as underrepresented minorities may prompt youth to highlight those ethnicities on program applications (Syed, 2010). The issues of multiple-heritage youth in the academic pipeline merit our attention (Root, 1992).

Personnel and Cultural Scripts

When our research team asked youth to list their family members, they often included siblings, grandparents, aunts, uncles, and cousins, as well as friends and even pets in their families. When we asked youth who helped them with schoolwork, staying on track to college, being a good person, and other topics, they most often listed their mothers, perhaps because this sample included a large number of mother-headed households. Many students listed their fathers as helping them, although not all students were living with their fathers. Older siblings at the university were mentoring these youth or trying to convince their parents to allow them to come to college. Students described friends in pre-college programs as "like brothers and sisters," and siblings as key resources in school. Unexpectedly, some youth said they were their only sources of help in pursuing math-based careers and that no one else helped them manage their responsibilities. Some listed themselves as causing their own difficulties for many topics. These responses alerted us to the varying breadth and depth of resources that these youth experienced. We also realized that focusing only on resources misses the salience of challenges for these youth.

Expectations in Different Cultural Worlds

When we asked students about the expectations that other people held for them across their different worlds, a number saw their schools and especially their neighborhoods as worlds where people expected them to fail, become pregnant and leave school, or engage in delinquent activities. In contrast, the students perceived their pre-college bridging programs as expecting them to succeed academically and to give back to their communities, such as by working as engineers and helping their younger siblings go to college.

An important finding was that each world can hold both positive and negative expectations. As two middle school students explained:

> When I'm in school, there's no worry. I don't know . . . you just feel more free. So like your parents are at work and you don't have to worry about them watching you do something wrong or something like that, but when I'm at home you have to watch out for that. You have to watch what you say, watch what you do.

> My brother is real good in sports and he thinks he can rap, and his teachers expect him to be ignorant. One day he was absent because they had a field trip that day. When we came back, my teacher saw him walking down the hallway. She thought he was cutting class, and she got mad at him and sent him to the principal's office. And he just got back from the field trip!

Gatekeepers and Cultural Brokers in Navigating the Academic Pipeline

Beyond specific expectations, we were struck by two powerful experiences that students reported as they tried to move across their worlds. First, students were challenged by *gatekeeping*, such as when teachers and counselors discouraged them from taking college-prep math and science classes or tried to place them in non-college tracks (Erickson & Shultz, 1982). In contrast, students also described supportive *cultural brokering* when people spoke up for them at school or with their parents or friends. For example, staff members in the pre-college programs offered to serve as cultural brokers between families and schools when they told parents, "You can trust us with your kids." In addition, the same people could be both brokers and gatekeepers, such as when parents encouraged daughters to attend college but expected them to live at home.

We asked students to describe what experiences, either positive or negative, shaped their identity pathways, based on the interview by Grotevant and Cooper (1981), discussed further in Chapter 3. Students wrote how resources from their families and academically involved friends as well as challenges from the school dropouts, gang identities, and arrests of friends strengthened their motivation to study hard and "prove the gatekeeper wrong."

These youth anticipated working on behalf of their families and communities, but they also felt pressure to succeed to make it easier for future students. One Latino immigrant university student said that he felt the burden of representing his race on his shoulders by having to be smarter, speak with perfect English, and be more polite and more responsible than White students to prove he belonged in college. Many reported that the stress of this burden made it difficult to go to class. Students found a "safe escape" from these pressures in university support programs, where no one questioned their qualifications and they could be themselves. Students also found support in these programs for keeping their academic and career goals and their ties to friends who were not in school or were in gangs (Lopez, Wishard, Gallimore, & Rivera, 2006). These observations show that complex challenges in navigating the pipeline continue through college.

In sum, concepts like cultural worlds, personnel, scripts, and expectations, goals, and values help to "unpackage" demographic categories. These concepts help us understand who are the key personnel, what scripts take place, and in what worlds they happen. The studies that do such unpackaging have yielded valuable surprises and insights. They continue to motivate us to ask students whether there is anything they think we are leaving out and how we can pose better questions. Particularly in individual and group interview settings, students regularly offer valuable suggestions:

Are you going to ask about the ones who are not here?

You ask, "Who helps us?", but you also need to ask, "Who do *we* help?"

BEYOND DEFICIT MODELS AND MODEL MINORITIES: PARALLEL DESIGNS

What happens when we want to compare more than one group, based on their national origins, ethnicities, social class, or cultural communities? How can we understand differences and similarities across and within groups, rather than automatically interpreting differences as deficits? What alternative research designs can we use to avoid negative stereotypes (Helms et al., 2005; McLoyd, 1991, 2005)?

How can we use concepts and measures developed in one cultural community with others?

To address these complex but crucial issues, Sue and Sue (1987) proposed the *parallel research design*. It links two contrasting approaches to understanding culture, known as *emic* and *etic* (Pike, 1990). With the *emic* approach (named for *phonemes*, the smallest meaningful units of language), we can describe a cultural community from the viewpoint of insiders. With this approach, researchers seek to discover rather than impose conceptual categories and to base evaluations on meanings and standards of each community. This approach is also useful for understanding each community's unique history and experiences. With an *etic* approach (as in *phonetics*, the smallest standardized units of sound, seen in the International Phonetic Alphabet), researchers seek to compare communities with standardized criteria as a way to study dimensions that might be universal or at least similar across more than one community. Many scholars specialize in one or the other of these approaches, but parallel designs offer the benefits of both. They also help avoid three common mistakes: assuming cultural communities hold the same developmental goals, misusing constructs and measures derived from one cultural community with others, and interpreting differences among groups as deficits (Gjerde et al., 1995).

Parallel designs involve three steps. First, researchers identify potentially universal or general constructs, such as how older youth or adults guide younger students toward their future school, work, and family roles. In the second step, researchers develop ways to measure these concepts that are appropriate for each cultural community from the viewpoint of community insiders. In this example, researchers might develop ways to measure families' aspirations and guidance for their children in each cultural community they are studying. In the third step, scholars identify variation within cultural communities as well as similarities and differences across them. For example, in communities where older siblings often serve as "the third parent," researchers can ask whether siblings' mentoring is more common in some families than others and whether it is related to culturally valued goals and outcomes (Weisner et al., 1988; Weisner, 2010).

Using parallel designs can lead to surprising and useful findings. In the following examples, scholars wanted to understand more than one cultural community without establishing one as the norm against which other communities would be measured. So they described culture-specific goals and values in each community, variation within groups, and similarities and differences across groups.

A team of Japanese and U.S. developmental psychologists used the parallel design to examine how Japanese, Japanese American, and European American adolescents develop their educational and career aspirations and identities as they encounter resources and challenges from families, schools, and peers (Gjerde, Cooper, Azuma, Kashiwagi, Kosawa, Shimizu, et al., 2000). Japan has had a persisting academic and career pipeline problem for female, working-class, immigrant, and ethnic minority youth (Sugimoto, 2010). For example, women have traditionally attended two-year junior colleges rather than four-year universities, with few women hired for the professional career tracks of Japanese corporations. The Japanese Equal

Employment Opportunity Law of 1985 mandates equal career opportunities for women, and rising numbers of women now attend universities with hopes of entering professional careers. Younger women have entered professional jobs in greater numbers than prior generations of women. Figure 2.1 captures this symbolic shift in women's roles in Japan. Still, barriers persist in Japanese women's career advancement and pay equity (Edwards & Pasquale, 2003; Toshiaki, 2010).

In the U.S., many Japanese American youth, like other children and grandchildren of immigrants, face challenges defining their identities in the face of conflicting expectations across the cultural worlds of their more traditional parents and those of their mainstream schools and peers. Multiple-heritage youth may have special difficulties in developing their ethnic identities. However, "interracial Japanese Americans ... may be more aware of their Japanese heritage because they have to struggle to affirm and come to terms with their dual racial background" (Mass, 1992, p. 266).

In a parallel design involving Japanese, Japanese American, and European American students, our research team adapted the Bridging Multiple Worlds focus group questions and survey. We began by conducting focus group interviews with students from the three cultural communities in Japan and the U.S.

These focus groups revealed the importance of gender in students' thoughts about the future in each cultural group. For example, in Yokohama, Japan, we asked Japanese junior high school students to write their responses to the same questions about challenges and resources that Cooper et al. (1995) had asked African American and Latino youth in California. The following were typical responses by Japanese

Figure 2.1 In a symbol of changing education and career opportunities for women in Japan, one woman wears a traditional kimono while another wears a business suit. © Catherine Cooper.

students to the question, "How is your gender a challenge or a resource for your future?"

> Within a boundary set by various situations around them, boys can do whatever they want. Boys can try many things that involve great risks.
>
> 15-year-old male

> Boys have to be strong enough to protect girls. Men have to have jobs.
>
> 16-year-old male

> People tend to view smart girls as unusual. Women are at a disadvantage in applying for jobs.
>
> 15-year-old female

> Women tend to get lower salaries than men even for the same kind of work. In the evenings or in foreign countries, girls have to go out in a group, not being alone, because of safety issues. This sometimes makes it difficult for each individual woman to have her own way.
>
> 15-year-old female

In a survey given in a later phase of this study, our team asked 145 Japanese, 53 Japanese American, and 80 European American college students to rate how much difficulty they expected because of their gender in attaining their educational goals, ranging from 1 = *not at all* to 4 = *very much* (Gjerde et al., 2000). As shown in Figure 2.2, young women in each cultural group expected significantly more difficulties than young men. In this study, the parallel design revealed important variations within cultural groups and surprising similarities across them.

The parallel design also revealed unique meanings and variations within cultural groups in how youth navigated challenges and resources across their cultural worlds. For example, in focus group interviews with Japanese American college students, Teranishi (1995) found that some students described their cultural worlds as strongly connected, and they felt strong and stable Japanese American identities across their worlds. They described growing up in communities with Japanese schools and in families who participated in traditional Japanese activities. As college students, they sought friendships through Japanese student organizations on their campuses. Some of their cultural worlds included Japanese friends, families, and church, while other worlds were "American." One student expressed anger that "people don't know the Japanese community exists." Others were frustrated by the lack of role models and information about their cultural heritage and reported not "feeling Japanese." Some Japanese American students anticipated challenges in future opportunities because of their ethnicity, but others felt the "model minority stereotype" of Asians as good students motivated them to work hard.

Besides these variations within cultural groups, we also found similarities across cultural groups. In all three groups, friends and student organizations were important resources for students' identity development. This finding also emerged in

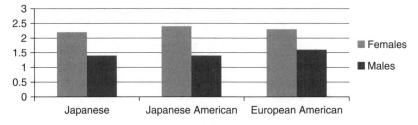

Figure 2.2 *Students' ratings (1 to 4) of anticipated difficulties because of their gender in attaining their educational goals.* In a study using the parallel design with Japanese, Japanese American, and European American college students, females in each cultural group anticipated greater difficulties in attaining their educational aspirations because of their gender than males (Gjerde et al., 2000).

a study of Japanese female university students, in which having friends and dating relationships predicted advances in identity development from their junior year to the end of their senior year (Sugimura, 2001). The role of peers in young women's identity development merits further study, particularly in light of changing gender roles in Japan (Kashiwagi, 2007).

A second example of the value of parallel designs for understanding community-specific meanings as well as similarities and differences across communities can be seen in a large study conducted in Minnesota. Included in a wider sample of high school students were a number of Hmong youth whose families were refugees from war in Laos. Although many cultural communities view early marriage as a sign of risk, more than half of the female Hmong students in this study married by their last year in high school. Most stayed in school, held educational goals similar to those of their unmarried peers, and also resembled their peers on measures of self-esteem, depression, academic ability, and future aspirations. These young mothers drew on their families and communities for help with child care (Hutchison & McNall, 1994).

In a report from the same study, Dunnigan, McNall, and Mortimer (1993) cautioned that translating terms about mental health between English and Hmong can be impossible. For example, these researchers found no direct equivalence between English words for emotions based on metaphors about the heart, such as *lighthearted* or *downhearted*. Hmong terms about emotions are based on different metaphors that involve the liver. Emotions felt in response to personal tragedies or troubles are called *nyuaj siab* (meaning *difficult liver*), and emotions felt in response to confusing experiences in the U.S. are called *ntxhov siab* (*obscured liver*). The researchers worked to paraphrase survey questions from English into Hmong, but for newly immigrated Hmong youth and their families, the team concluded that assessing mental health with U.S.-based surveys is inappropriate. This team later developed strategies for interpreters to use in bridging semantic differences with Hmong clients (Goh, Dunnigan, Schuchman, & Chin, 2004).

These examples show how parallel designs helped researchers combine the advantages of single-group and *emic* studies with those of multiple-group and *etic* designs. Parallel designs highlight the need to base diagnostic and evaluative criteria on meanings and experiences of participants and look for variation within groups as well as similarities and differences across them. This helps move beyond stereotypes, whether negative or positive. In new line of research, Bakken and Brown (2010) used the parallel design to study African American and Hmong adolescents' management of their parents' knowledge about their friends.

In working with parallel designs, one useful strategy is to link analyses based on variables with those based on cases (Mertens, 2010; Miles & Huberman, 1994; Roeser et al., 2008; Yin, 2008). A shared language allows the international scientific community to advance knowledge and frame better questions. The search continues for a shared scientific language for the analysis of cultures. For these reasons, researchers increasingly combine quantitative and case-based analyses in a *mixed-methods* approach. A student, family, school, community program, partnership, state, or nation can each be seen as a case. Although case studies cannot definitively resolve competing hypotheses, they can direct and inform variable-based analyses. Case studies often provide rich details, but by themselves cannot address how typical or representative they are compared to larger samples or populations. Throughout this book we will draw on new approaches for linking individual case studies and group-level quantitative analyses (Creswell & Clark, 2007; Teddlie & Tashakkori, 2008; Tufte, 1994; Weisner, 2005; Yoshikawa et al., 2008).

FROM "GIVING SCIENCE AWAY" TO CULTURAL RESEARCH PARTNERSHIPS

Whatever theories, designs, or measures are used, questions of ethics and mutual trust form the cornerstone of research with youth, families, and communities. These issues raise questions not always asked by researchers who are preoccupied with getting data: What is the relation between the research questions and the realities of participants' lives? What is the purpose of the study? Can participants anticipate any benefit from it? What are possible consequences of different outcomes of the research? What are participants' goals and fears? Does participating enhance or detract from these goals? There are many ways to coordinate the perspectives of different stakeholders in adolescents' lives in ways that enhance trust among them. (In the U.S., research conducted by universities and other institutions receiving federal funds must also pass formal review on their ethical merits.) The following examples illustrate this process in different cultural settings.

In a middle school on the Zuni pueblo in New Mexico, Roland Tharp, Lois Yamauchi, and their colleagues (Tharp & Yamauchi, 1994; Yamauchi, 1994; Yamauchi & Tharp, 1995) developed a research partnership with native and non-native teachers, students, parents, and administrators. Tharp and Yamauchi made videotapes during regular classes and held discussions with these partners about what factors contribute to an ideal classroom. This partnership helped members of the Zuni community, the largest of the Native American Pueblo tribes of the southwestern U.S., in restructuring the school. Their perspectives helped researchers understand how Zuni youth navigated across their family, peer, and school worlds (Yamauchi, 1994, p. 5).

Partners differed in their goals and concerns about participating in the study. Teachers were interested in learning from one another but anxious about other teachers evaluating them. The principal wanted to understand what was happening in the classroom and more about the study that Tharp and his team were conducting, perhaps because previous researchers had not kept their commitments to the school. Students appeared most interested in the excerpts where they and their friends appeared. Still, for both adults and youth, the researchers found that trying to "walk both [Zuni and mainstream] worlds" created tensions even in an ideal classroom:

> Being members of Zuni and mainstream worlds reflected the community struggle to maintain traditional identification as Native Americans, while still attempting to acculturate into dominant American life. In some circumstances it was not possible to do both at the same time. Some Zuni educators might resolve this by switching back and forth, like they do with their languages: English for school, Zuni for home—while others might seek more integration of the two cultures in the school setting (Tharp & Yamauchi, 1994, p. 2).

A second example of a cultural research partnership can be seen in a study of family relationships in an African American community in rural Georgia. Brody, Stoneman, Flor, McCrary, Hastings, and Conyer (1994) were concerned that typical measures were based on European American middle-class families. So these scholars held focus groups to consult with community leaders at their study site. The leaders rated the appropriateness of each possible measure and suggested changes in individual questions that they saw as unclear or irrelevant to their community. The leaders also helped university research staff select activities and topics for observing family communication and suggested ways to enhance families' comfort with researchers coming to their homes. For example, by advising researchers to choose topics that did not touch on financial matters, the leaders fostered the research and protected community members.

For some researchers, such university–community partnerships involve not only their desire to be sensitive, but also their willingness to solicit opinions of knowledgeable informants, including youth, from a community and allow these opinions to help guide the research. For other researchers, however, these partnerships are controversial because they violate scientists' obligations to be objective and independent.

NEXT STEPS

To describe and help explain the realities of culturally diverse youths' lives, a growing number of scholars call for going beyond demographic categories (Helms et al., 2005; Le, Ceballo, Chao, Hill, Murry, & Pinderhughes, 2008). Using parallel designs can counteract tendencies to interpret cultural differences as deficits, and building cultural research partnerships can help foster trust among stakeholders with a range of cultural experiences and different needs.

We now return to the three quotes from students that open this chapter to address the issues raised by each of their comments.

What if I'm both Black *and* Japanese?

Instead of asking students to "check one box" in reporting their ethnicity, we can ask them to describe their ethnicity or ethnicities in their own words. This allows mixed-heritage youth to describe themselves in valid terms. When possible, we can avoid pan-ethnic categories, like "Asian" and "Hispanic", and use more specific terms with local meaning. For example, scholars in a multi-site collaboration found that at their site in Providence, Rhode Island, the Asian students were largely Cambodian and the Hispanic students were mainly from the Dominican Republic and Puerto Rico. At the Oakland, California site, the Asian students were largely from Chinese families and the Hispanic students were mainly from Mexican families. And at the Los Angeles site, the Asian students were mainly Korean and the Hispanic students were mainly from Mexico, El Salvador, and Guatemala (Cooper, García Coll, Thorne, & Orellana, 2005).

What do I put under "mother" and "father" if I was raised by my grandmother and never knew my mother or father?

Like Fuligni (2007), we can ask students about the person "in the mother role" and "in the father role," rather than about "your mother" or "your father," to convey respect for the possible range of people who may serve in these roles.

In this survey, I found out [things] that I never even thought about before. I know more about myself and how family, friends, and teachers influence me.

Asking about household and family composition and roles provides insights to researchers and educators about the realities of adolescents' lives. More generally, engaging youth in gathering and interpreting data can contribute to their success in the academic pipeline. There are many possible explanations for this. For example, tabulating their resources and challenges may help students reflect on how to maximize the benefits of their resources and minimize the costs of their challenges. Examining their own pathways in the context of the educational requirements to attain their aspirations may motivate their academic efforts. Students who are active in examining these issues at a younger age may be more likely to serve as intergenerational college brokers as they grow older.

These three strategies can be difficult to use, but they reveal things we could never learn without them. The experiences of our research teams as well as those of others indicate that readers can adapt these strategies to the constraints and opportunities of many cultural settings. A key challenge lies in developing better ways to link culture-specific and more general perspectives. Equivalence across cultures, even with translations, back-translation, and related approaches, remains an ideal that is rarely attained in practice (see Erkut, 2010, for a comparison of these approaches). Taken together, developing alternatives to demographic stereotypes, deficit models, and mistrust can help us ask better questions to understand how access and retention in opportunities such as higher education can be enhanced.

PART TWO

Five Questions

3

AUTONOMY OR CONNECTIONS?
IDENTITIES AS INTERGENERATIONAL PROJECTS[a]

with
Harold D. Grotevant

This chapter takes a closer look at the first of the five interrelated issues of this book: what it means for youth to grow up. How we answer this question can shape our understanding of students' aspirations for pathways to college and beyond, as well as the resources and challenges they find as they navigate through school.

The traditional perspective on this issue—and an enduring one—is that achieving autonomy and independence from one's family is the most crucial sign of adolescents' growing maturity. One source of this view is the psychoanalytic concept of *separation-individuation* of Anna Freud (1958) and Peter Blos (1979), "in which adolescents physically and emotionally distance themselves from their parents (separation) and increasingly take responsibility for themselves without . . . relying on their parents" (Soenens et al., 2007, p. 633).

A growing body of evidence now challenges this traditional view. In a typical study, European American adolescents who scored higher on measures of emotional autonomy and felt emotionally detached from their parents reported more psychological problems and risky health behaviors than those youth who reported both autonomy and security with their parents (Allen, Hauser, Bell, & O'Connor, 1994; Beyers & Goossens, 2003). Such findings—not predicted by the traditional Freudian model—are motivating researchers to clarify the nature and desirability of autonomy and its links to family relationships within as well as across cultural groups (Lamborn & Steinberg, 1993; Steinberg & Silk, 2002; Zimmer-Gembeck & Collins, 2003).

Increasingly, scholars define adolescents' autonomy as multifaceted—reflecting their personal *agency,* especially their capacity for action and self-reliance, not just

---

[a] This chapter draws upon discussions of these issues by Cooper, Behrens, and Trinh (2009); Cooper, Baker, Polichar, and Welch (1993); and Grotevant and Cooper (1998).

feelings of emotional detachment and separation from their parents (Beyers, Goossens, Vansant, & Moors, 2003; Jackson & Goossens, 2006; Ryan & Lynch, 1989). In a sample of European American college students in Wisconsin, feeling both self-reliant and connected with parents predicted higher college grades and self-esteem, but feeling detached from parents predicted lower grades and self-esteem (Lamborn & Groh, 2009).

Such findings have prompted rethinking the Freudian paradigm. Culture has become an important element in our understanding of autonomy, and a different kind of paradigm is emerging. Rather than seeing autonomy as valued only in individualistic societies, some scholars have proposed that we consider *both* autonomy and relatedness as universal human qualities, with cultural variations in their expression and developmental timing (Fuligni, 2007; Kagitçibasi, 2007; Phinney, Kim-Jo, Osorio, & Vilhjalmsdottir, 2005; Rogoff, 2003). These scholars view identity development as an intergenerational project rather than a solitary journey. From this cultural perspective, we construct identities from our experiences as individuals, in relationships, and through institutional opportunities and constraints in education and in political, and economic conditions. In addition to cultural differences, striking parallels in this intergenerational project can be seen as adolescents take part in their coming-of-age ceremonies with the blessings of family and community members (Bjornsen, 2000). Figure 3.1 shows three examples of such ceremonies: a Mexican-descent girl's *quinceañera* on her 15th birthday in California, a Jewish *bar* and *bat mitzvah* ceremony among Ethiopian Israeli and British youth in Jerusalem, and an Apache Sunrise ceremony or *na'ii'ees* in New Mexico.

ERIKSON: IDENTITY AS A LIFESPAN AND INTERGENERATIONAL PROJECT

During the same years that Anna Freud and Peter Blos were defining adolescent maturity in terms of separation and detachment from their parents, Erik Erikson was crafting his influential theory of identity development that links autonomy and connections in cultural terms. In an example that is especially relevant to the academic pipeline problem, Erikson's accounts of how Dakota Sioux "young men and women of integrity and stamina" bridged their cultural worlds paved the way for recent studies with Native American college students. These studies reveal links among students' sense of bicultural efficacy, academic identities, and belief in the instrumental importance of school (Okagaki, Helling, & Bingham, 2009).

Erikson was especially intrigued by the powerful roles of culture, social class, and race in identity development through changing historical, political, and economic times. He based his astute reflections on his clinical and historical case studies, his collaborations with developmental psychologists on large longitudinal studies, and his work with anthropologists studying two Native American communities, the Yurok of Northern California and the Sioux of South Dakota.

Erikson was a pioneer in seeing how cultural communities shape identity development. In *Childhood and Society* (1950) and *Identity: Youth and Crisis* (1968),

Figure 3.1 *Cultural parallels and differences in coming-of-age ceremonies can be seen in a quinceañera in a Mexican immigrant family in California, a joint bar and bat mitzvah ceremony among Ethiopian Israeli and British youth in Jerusalem, and a White Mountain Apache Sunrise ceremony or na'ii'ees. in New Mexico. 3.1A © Catherine Cooper; photos 3.1.B and C are reprinted with permission of Douglas Guthrie and Rico Leffanta, respectively.*

he wrote about privileged youth in psychotherapy, Dakota Sioux youth on their vision quests, and African American youth in the struggles of the U.S. civil rights movement. In each of these cultural settings, Erikson saw identity development as reaching across the histories of individuals, families, cultural communities, and societies. For him and the many scholars who have built on his work, identity development reflects the breadth and depth of *exploration* and *commitment* across domains that are valued in cultural communities, such as schooling, work, and relationships with families and peers (Kroger, 2007; Marcia, 1994; Schwartz, 2001, 2002, 2008). Fortunately, scholars are now rediscovering many of his ideas about culture and identity that were overlooked for many years as scholars concentrated on searching for universal patterns of development.

Erikson's writings often convey a more poetic than scientific tone. They offer a wealth of insights about identity, although only some have been measured and formally studied. For example, in his account of the active and conscious process of "identity won in action" (1968, p. 300), each person seeks "a subjective sense of an invigorating sameness and continuity" that develops "in the core of the individual and yet also in the core of [one's] communal culture" (1968, pp. 19–20). Making sense of both conflicts and connections within ourselves, our relationships, and our cultural communities can foster what Erikson called "the wider identity" (1968). Erikson's clinical work with war veterans and with privileged youth revealed how those who struggle to integrate their past, present, and future can be vulnerable to depression and other problems, but he saw each person as having the potential for a growing sense of personal and historical continuity over his or her lifespan. Our challenge, in this book and beyond, is to understand the central role of this lifelong project of identity development for the academic pipeline problem.

Erikson's work has sparked progress on questions central to understanding the role of identity development as youth navigate their pathways through school. In this chapter, we draw from the research agenda proposed by the developmental psychologist Joachim Wohlwill (1973) to ask: What are the core domains of identity? How do identities emerge from childhood through adolescence and adulthood? What other developmental dimensions are related to identity? How do opportunities and constraints shape adolescents' identity development? What is the nature of individual variations in identity development?

Erikson saw identity and the aspirations that identity expresses as emerging across one's lifespan, rather than being completed during adolescence (1950; see also Arnett, 2003). For example, Erikson proposed that identity first emerges as infants experience themselves as distinctive persons, when they begin to recognize and trust their caregivers. Identity development continues as young children form a dual sense of what he called "the autonomy of free choice" in self-control (1950, p. 252) and connections with caregivers, and later as school-age children learn to evaluate their growing skills and achievements through the eyes of their families and cultural communities. Adolescents' cognitive growth allows them to consider future careers and relationships (Seginer, 2009), and middle adulthood is marked by the capacity to "give back" to the next generation. Older adults attain a mature sense of identity when they can see their lives as possessing personal and cultural coherence.

Families' Individuality and Connectedness in Identity Development

Research based on Erikson's work points to the central role of families in identity development. Rather than identity exploration being driven only by adolescents' desire for autonomy or independence from their parents, studies of youth and their families reveal the importance of both *individuality* and *connectedness* in their relationships. *Individuality*, which reflects the distinctiveness of the self, involves holding a point of view and expressing it in assertions, disclosures, and disagreements. *Connectedness*, which links the self to others, can be seen in expressing respect for and responsiveness to others' views. Patterns of individuality and connectedness are distinctive within each relationship, so an adolescent may have one close relationship that supports his or her expressions of individuality while others do not.

In a line of research that my colleague Harold Grotevant and I conducted with our students and colleagues on this issue, we did not define individuality and connectedness as mutually exclusive qualities like individualism and collectivism, or as opposite ends of one dimension such as independence–dependence. We considered, for example, that relationships could offer high levels of both individuality and connectedness, or low levels of one and high levels of the other. More specifically, we proposed that the interplay between individuality and connectedness matters for personal and relational development both in and beyond the family (Cooper, Grotevant, & Condon, 1983; Grotevant & Cooper, 1985, 1986, 1998).

Before we began our studies of these issues in the 1980s, much sociological research had focused more on social class or the family life cycle than on internal family dynamics or families' effects on adolescents. Although socialization models addressed parent–child relationships, most psychological researchers assumed that the main direction of influence led from parent to child. They measured general qualities such as warmth or restrictiveness based on parents' reports rather than on families' actual conversations. Major influences on our research extend from Erikson's pioneering work to Diana Baumrind's longitudinal studies of the interactive nature of parent–child relationships (1975, 1991).

Such insights about autonomy and connections from Erikson and Baumrind led our research team to focus on the roles of identity and relationships in the academic pipeline problem. Like Erikson, our team considered exploration and commitment in identity as a dynamic attunement among individuals, social relationships, and cultural contexts. Reformulating identity can occur throughout life because individuals, relationships, institutions, and communities all change—for better and for worse—and each can support or constrain such reformulations (Graafsma, Bosma, Grotevant, & deLevita, 1994). The following sections describe how we gathered and assessed evidence about the role of individuality and connectedness in adolescents' identity development, and how this changed our thinking about the way youth navigate the academic pipeline.

Measuring individuality and connectedness in family communication

Our team began studying the role of individuality and connectedness in family relationships in adolescents' identity development with secondary school students in the U.S.. The sample included 121 middle-class European American families living in Texas, each with a high school senior (average age 17.6 years).

We designed the Family Interaction Task (based on Watzlawick, 1966) so we could measure the dynamic interplay of individuality and connectedness in adolescents' family relationships. We asked both parents, the adolescent, and one sibling, if present, to talk together at their kitchen table in their home for 20 minutes to plan a two-week fictitious family vacation for which they had unlimited funds. The family's task was to decide and record where they would go and what they would do on each of the 14 days. We designed this task to provide many opportunities for the adolescents to contribute to their families' decisions. This format contrasts with tasks involving only one decision that are often used to study family conflict during adolescence. We audiotape recorded each family's conversation, transcribed and coded it, and tallied the frequency of 14 kinds of statements that reflect aspects of individuality and connectedness, as well as who was speaking and to whom they spoke (for details, see Grotevant & Cooper, 1985, 1986).

Measuring identity development

We assessed identity exploration in a home interview with each participating adolescent in six domains: occupation, religion, politics, friendships, dating, and gender roles (Grotevant & Cooper, 1981) and built on the interview developed by James Marcia (1966). An interviewer asked the following questions, among others, about the occupational identity domain:

What are you going to do after high school?
Are you planning to go to college? Do you know what you will major in?
What do you plan to do with it?
When did you come to decide on (career choice)?
What people or experiences have been major influences on your plans for the future?
What kinds of difficulties or problems do you see associated with your decision to _____?
If these things were to become difficult, what would you do then?

Trained coders rated these interviews for the extent of adolescents' identity exploration in the six domains. Because identity commitments during late high school are relatively transient, we considered identity exploration to be a more valid indicator of identity development than commitment at this age. For the studies with African American and Latino youth described in the next chapter, our research team adapted these questions to map how students draw upon their families, peers, schools, and other worlds in pursuing their goals and aspirations.

Individuality and connectedness in identity exploration

In general, adolescents who were rated as higher in identity exploration were encouraged by their families to express their own viewpoints in family communication. We controlled for variation in their verbal skills and the sociability of their personalities. Some gender differences emerged: sons who scored higher in identity exploration, compared to other boys, showed assertiveness and separateness that was especially supported by their fathers, whereas daughters scoring higher in identity exploration experienced more challenges from both parents. Perhaps sons needed only encouragement to support their assertiveness, while for daughters, parental challenges counteracted traditional gender role pressures to express connections but not assertions or disagreements (Cooper & Grotevant, 1987; see also Leaper & Ayres, 2007).

Overall, the family discussions of both females and males who scored higher in identity exploration were higher on both individuality and connectedness than the average for the sample (Grotevant & Cooper, 1985). These families negotiated by expressing different viewpoints, disagreeing, and arguing, as well as resolving their disagreements. In families of adolescents who scored lower in identity exploration, discussions more typically involved suggestions chained together without coordination and one family member (usually a parent) eliciting suggestions and imposing solutions unilaterally.

Two contrasting cases illustrate important patterns linking family communication and adolescent identity development (Cooper, Grotevant, Moore, & Condon, 1984). The first provides an example of high levels of both individuality and connectedness, and the second, low individuality and high connectedness. Our study of the family of a young woman we will call Carol shows how people in a relationship can contribute both individuality and connectedness. Her father's opening words set the tone:

> I think probably what we all ought to do is decide the things that we want to do, each one of us individually. And, then maybe we'll be able to reconcile from that point . . . . Let's go ahead and take a few minutes to decide where we'd like to go and what we would like to do. And maybe we'll be able to work everything everybody wants to do in these fourteen days. Okay?

All three family members were active and involved, and they showed humor, candor, spontaneity, and even vulnerability. Carol's mother observed, "I think we all have good imaginations."

During her identity interview, Carol said, "I have a say, but not a deciding vote in family decisions." A distinctive quality of her identity exploration was that she experienced her parents as providing room for her to explore beyond their own experiences. For example, in discussing the religious domain of her identity, Carol explained that both her parents felt that religion had been forced on them as children, so they decided not to force it on her. For this reason, she had been able to explore several religions with her friends as possible alternatives for herself.

In contrast, the family of a young woman we will call Janet expressed few disagreements, with self-assertions that largely coincided with the family's shared point of view and many expressions of connectedness. In their opening statements, this pattern was evident:

Mother: Where shall we go?
Father: Back to Spain.
Mother: Back to Spain.
Janet: Back to Spain.
Sister: Back to Spain.

Janet disagreed with her father only once during this discussion, and he never disagreed with her. However, she expressed connectedness to him 29 times, and he likewise showed connectedness to her 10 times.

In Janet's identity interview, her low rating on identity exploration may reflect her reluctance to explore issues outside such consensual family beliefs. Commenting on her career choice, Janet said, "I'm having a hard time deciding what to do. It would be easier if they would *tell* me what to do, but of course I don't want that." The family communication patterns that Janet observed and participated in resemble what family systems therapists call "enmeshed" patterns (Minuchin & Nichols, 1998), and they appeared to be inhibiting her identity exploration.

Replications and extensions to pipeline issues

The ethnic and socioeconomic homogeneity of our original sample in this line of research limited our ability to generalize the findings across cultural and social class groups. However, several U.S. and international research teams have reported replicating and extending our findings. Longitudinal studies conducted in the U.S. indicate that patterns of family individuality and connectedness during adolescence predict well-being and attachment in adulthood (Allen et al., 1994; Bell & Bell, 2005). Researchers in Europe also replicated these findings with students in college-prep tracks and with university students, particularly in the Netherlands and Germany (Beyers & Ryan, 2007; Bosma & Kunnen, 2001; Goossens, 2006; Kruse & Walper, 2008; Meeus, Iedema, Helsen, & Vollebergh, 1999). Reis and Buhl (2008) compiled studies in Germany and Sweden that replicated and refined the concepts of family individuality and connectedness in adolescence and emerging adulthood. In one study, parent–child attachment observed in German toddlers predicted their interactions on Grotevant and Cooper's Family Interaction Task 11 years later when they were adolescents (Becker-Stoll et al., 2008). As in all scientific research, these replications provide valuable evidence of the important role of family individuality and connectedness in adolescent identity development. We now turn to the question of how cultures matter in families' values and communication about identity.

THE ROLE OF CULTURE IN FAMILIES' VALUES AND COMMUNICATION ABOUT IDENTITY

Although many scholars, educators, and policymakers consider adolescents' autonomy, independence, and personal responsibility to be the key markers of their maturity, many cultural traditions accord a central role to *familism*—values and behaviors expressing mutual support, allegiance, and obligation in family life. In these cultural traditions, adolescents are expected to show support, respect, and reticence with family members, especially their fathers and elders (Azmitia, Cooper, & Brown, 2009; Baca Zinn, 1982; Fuligni, 2007). Familism has been defined as the aspect of collectivism that is expressed in close relationships as opposed to larger societal groups. Scholars are still working on how to measure and map relations among familism, individualism, and collectivism (Brewer & Chen, 2007; Matsumoto, 1999; Oyserman, Coon, & Kemmerlmeier, 2002; Tamis-LeMonda et al., 2007). However, they agree that cultural values play important roles in adolescents' communicating with family members about identity domains like school, careers, and family life (Fuligni, 2007; Phinney, Kim-Jo, et al., 2005). We will see in this chapter as well as Chapters 5 and 6 that these agreements are sparking progress on academic pipeline issues.

A crucial insight for understanding the academic pipeline problem is that in cultural traditions that emphasize familism, adolescents' achievements or failures bring pride or shame, respectively, to their families and communities rather than signifying their autonomy or independence from them. Familism has been considered an asset for immigrant and ethnic minority families, especially those with histories of immigration, poverty, and/or racism (Fuligni, 2007; Harrison, Wilson, Pine, Chan, & Buriel, 1990). The sense of obligation that immigrant youth feel to attend college to "give back" to their families and communities is an expression of familistic values (Phinney et al., 2005). In an ongoing line of research, our research team has probed how familistic values continue or change across generations in immigrant families, and how these values matter for adolescents' identity pathways through school to college and beyond.

We have examined familistic values and family communication of individuality and connectedness in a set of studies using the parallel design described in Chapter 2 (e.g., Cooper et al., 1993; Trinh, Tsai, & Cooper, 2007). We investigated meanings and variation *within* cultural groups by asking whether adolescents from immigrant families would endorse familistic values less strongly than their parents and grandparents. We looked *across* cultural groups to see whether adolescents from more recent immigrant groups would endorse familistic values more strongly than European American adolescents whose families had been in the U.S. for several generations. We predicted that immigrant youth would show more respect in communicating with their parents than European-descent youth by muting their expressions of individuality, particularly in asserting their ideas and disagreeing.

To understand individuality and connectedness when such familistic values of respect might make direct expressions of individuality rare, we decided to use a self-report survey rather than recording families' conversations. In two phases of this study—as we developed questions for the survey and as we analyzed the survey results—we held focus group interviews with college students from each participating cultural group to hear their reflections and understand more about their experiences (Stewart & Shamdasani, 1990). Shaping new research tools in line with what we knew about relevant cultural issues was useful in furthering our understanding of pipeline issues and continuing to unpackage culture, social class, immigration, and gender.

On the Family Perspectives Survey that we developed from these focus groups (Cooper et al., 1993), the college students in a culturally diverse Northern California sample (19.9 years old on average) described themselves with more than 30 different ethnic labels. Findings presented here involve those students who described themselves as of Mexican, Vietnamese, Filipino, Chinese, and European descent. Many were immigrants, including 27% of Mexican descent, 52% of Chinese descent, 50% of Filipino descent, 84% of Vietnamese descent, and 5% of European descent. The remaining students included about 10% multiple-heritage youth.

Familistic Values

Adolescents rated how much they, the people who were in mother and father roles in their lives, and their maternal and paternal grandparents endorsed a list of familistic values. This list, adapted from studies of familism and immigration, reflects how much families are seen as sources of support and obligation and as a reference group for decision making (Sabogal, Marin, Otero-Sabogal, Marin, & Perez-Stable, 1987).

For example, to the statement: "Older siblings should help directly support other family members economically," Vietnamese- and Chinese-descent students reported sharing their parents' strong endorsements, European American students reported sharing their parents' weak endorsements, and Filipino- and Mexican-descent students endorsed this value less than their parents. Students in all five cultural groups thought their parents held stronger expectations than they did to consider the family in making decisions. Students from all five groups strongly endorsed the statement: "Family members should make sacrifices to guarantee a good education for their children." However, compared to European American students, those of Mexican, Chinese, Vietnamese, and Filipino descent placed greater value on mutual support among siblings and turning to parents and other relatives in making important decisions.

Expressing Individuality and Connectedness

On this survey, we also asked students about expressing individuality and connectedness with their families and friends. Seven items assessed individuality (e.g., "I feel free to take a stand on something even if this person had a different opinion"), and seven assessed connectedness (e.g., "When we disagree, I really try to negotiate with this person to reach a compromise"); for details on this measure, see Lopez (2001). Students also rated how comfortable they felt discussing identity-related topics, like their education, careers, dating, sexuality, marriage, and cultural and ethnic heritage, across their different relationships.

On average, students in all five cultural groups reported that they expressed more individuality—such as personal opinions or disagreements—with their mothers, siblings, and friends than with their fathers. They also reported similar patterns in communication that was directed towards them. In each group, students reported more formal communication from their fathers and more open communication of individuality from their mothers, siblings, and friends. For example, students in all five groups rated the statements "this person communicates openly with me about their feelings" and "I discuss my problems with this person" as more true with their mothers, siblings, and friends than with their fathers. Students in all five groups, particularly Chinese-, Filipino-, and Vietnamese-descent students, also reported their fathers "make most of the decisions in our relationship," compared to other relationships.

Just as when we first developed the survey, we again held focus groups with students from each cultural group to hear their reflections about our results. We were especially eager to hear about what seemed to be contradictory findings: that students endorsed familistic values but did not necessarily follow these values in their actual communication. In lively discussions, immigrant students confirmed that they believed they *should* turn to older family members for advice on important decisions, but that communicating with parents, especially their fathers, was marked by respect, formality, and reticence. Students explained that they discussed safer topics such as school with their fathers, but withheld more sensitive facts, like having changed their college major from pre-medicine to humanities or social sciences (while knowing their parents wanted them to become doctors) or that they were exploring their sexual identity. Sometimes students also asked their mothers, aunts, or sisters to convey sensitive messages to their fathers. As discussed in Chapter 2, friends often played special roles for college students' identity exploration, both as "sounding boards" and as go-betweens with family members.

An example of the links among familistic values, family communication, and students' identity development can be heard in the focus group comments of a Filipina college student we will call Lourdes:

> I was with a single mother and I have one sister and it was really harsh .... We basically did whatever she said, to keep the family alive .... We went through a lot of rough times in our childhood .... But in terms of family values [my mother] would encourage family first. Since this is the family that is giving you support, you need to be loyal to it and respect authority .... I grew up with a lot of conflict with her, especially in my junior high and high school years. She wanted me to do really well in school, but she didn't understand that those extracurricular things you have to do to get into college mean taking you out of the home .... I think because she was so much on her own, she knew what it took

to survive and she wanted to make sure that I survived too . . . . There was a lot of pressure on us to make sure we do well. We are like representatives of this family.

Lourdes' insights provide an important window on how her identity development is unfolding as an intergenerational family project. In this process, the values and communication in her relationship with her mother reflect both continuity and change:

Right now my mom and I are really good friends and I think the reason is my awareness of her life . . . . She started listening to the things that I was agreeing with and I said, "a lot of the things that I do is because of the values that you taught me . . . loyalty and respect for people, to be caring and giving." So it's funny . . . I've kind of impacted her now.

In the focus groups, students commented that their informal conversations with friends involved the same topics as those addressed by our study. As Lourdes observed:

My friends and I have these same conversations about what are we going to do about our lives. That's why we are involved with student groups. They really function as a way to talk about what is on young Asian and Pacific Islanders' minds and our future . . . . I can talk to [my mother] about my career goals a little bit more now, but it definitely started with these people here [peers in focus group] because I don't think I could figure that out all by myself.

These findings vividly challenge definitions of adolescents' maturity that focus only on their autonomy from parents. When respect for immigrant parents makes relationships more formal, adolescents' siblings and peers may play especially important roles in their lives (Seginer, 1992; Seginer, Shoyer, Hossessi, & Tannous, 2007). As with the example of Lourdes and her mother, in some families, traditionally hierarchical patterns appear to be changing across generations toward more egalitarian patterns (Phinney et al., 2005).

A study by Hardway and Fuligni (2006) of adolescents' familistic values and communication with their families and peers supports and extends these findings. The researchers surveyed 15-year-olds of Chinese, Mexican, and European descent living in Southern California. The students rated how strongly they endorsed familistic values of family obligation and mutual assistance and reported their daily activities. Students' answers revealed variation within cultural groups, with stronger feelings of obligation and mutual assistance reported by youth from Chinese and Mexican immigrant families than second-generation families. Similarities across groups also emerged: European American students reported identification and closeness with their families at the same or even greater levels compared to Chinese- and Mexican-descent youth. Hardway and Fuligni concluded that "rather than being more or less connected to their families compared with one another, adolescents from Mexican, Chinese, and European backgrounds appear to differ more in the way in which their family connectedness is expressed" (2006, p. 1257).

OPPORTUNITIES AND CONSTRAINTS IN
IDENTITY DEVELOPMENT

A central assumption in the classic view of identity development is that it proceeds by exploration and choice among relatively unrestricted opportunities. This view may have been fostered by studies based on relatively privileged samples of middle- and upper-middle-class youth enrolled in college-preparatory academic tracks in the U.S. and Europe.

Scholars have criticized the failure by identity researchers to address constraints in adolescents' access to schooling and other opportunities related to social class, race, ethnicity, immigrant status, gender, and disabilities (Cooper et al., 1995; García Coll, Szalacha, & Palacios, 2005; Grotevant & Cooper, 1998; Kroger, 2007; Perez, Espinosa, Ramos, Coronado, & Cotes, 2009; Yoder, 2000). In an important exception, Kroger (1993a) traced the impact of shrinking opportunities on identity exploration in New Zealand between 1984 and 1990, a time of economic decline. Using Marcia's identity interview (1966, 1994), Kroger found that female college students reported less *identity exploration* in 1990 than in 1984, and fewer students reported high levels of exploration over this time. However, she also found that youth who were making identity commitments based on little exploration (*identity foreclosure*) had sometimes limited their own life options, and those who had engaged in extensive exploration while delaying commitment (*identity moratorium*) did so by expanding their options. When shrinking opportunities constrain identity exploration, understanding adolescents' agency and its limits is especially important.

Issues of opportunities and constraints in identity development can be particularly salient to ethnic and racial minority youth. Fordham and Ogbu (Fordham, 1988, Fordham & Ogbu, 1986) proposed that Black adolescents, like youth in other racial and ethnic minority groups with histories of restricted access to educational and occupational opportunities, may feel that success in such institutions requires them to develop a "raceless" persona that masks their true ethnic or racial identity. As Fordham and Ogbu wrote,

> Many of the successful students find themselves juggling their school and community personae in order to minimize the conflicts and anxieties generated by the need to interact with the various competing constituencies represented in the school context (1986, p. 80).

These conditions may lead some ethnic minority youth to define doing well in school as "acting White" (Fordham & Ogbu, 1986) or like a "Twinkie" (yellow cake with white filling), "Oreo cookie" (chocolate with white filling), coconut, or apple. These derogatory terms refer to looking Asian, African American, Latino, or Native American, respectively, while having a white identity.

These insults can stigmatize minority adolescents who are trying to explore their opportunities for school and work. But are such experiences and their costs inevitable? A study of low-income African American and Latino youth living in New York revealed that "cultural straddlers"—those students who could navigate across school and peer worlds while maintaining strong racial and ethnic identities—were also academically successful (Carter, 2005, 2006). They encountered less peer criticism when Black and Latino students participated in college-prep classes in proportion to their numbers in their school. This study points to the importance of mapping meaningful patterns among individual variations in identity development.

INDIVIDUAL VARIATIONS

Studying individual variations—including unusual cases—can reveal important features of adolescents' identity pathways. One study followed an exceptional group of European American and Mexican American high school girls, all from working-class families, as they forged academic identities and college pathways despite the many hardships that they and their families faced (Bettie, 2002). Compared to their working-class peers who did not plan to attend college, these exceptional girls were more active in extracurricular programs and sports. They understood how failing in school would limit their future opportunities. They had learned from their siblings' mistakes and drew support from middle-class peers as well as their parents and older siblings. Like the "cultural straddlers" observed by Carter (2005, 2006), these girls skillfully navigated both challenges and resources across their cultural worlds.

Striking individual variations in cultural identities have also emerged among siblings in immigrant families. When Pyke (2005) interviewed sibling pairs between 18 and 26 years old who were from Korean and Vietnamese immigrant families, she found that older siblings more often took on traditional cultural roles that upheld their parents' values and practices, including being respectful and obedient children and keeping their home language. Younger siblings, in contrast, more often valued cultural assimilation and professed ignorance, rejection, or indifference to maintaining their cultural identities.

NEXT STEPS AND IMPLICATIONS FOR
THE PIPELINE PROBLEM

This chapter considered the first of our five questions about cultures, identities, and pathways to college: how to define what it means to grow up. Researchers' interest in adolescents' autonomy continues, with growing evidence about the benefits of adolescents having a strong sense of agency and self-reliance, but also about the risks of emotional detachment. So this progress has clarified that healthy autonomy—seen in agency and individuality—is not the opposite of connectedness but co-occurs with it (Lamborn & Groh, 2009).

More broadly, scholars are reconsidering traditionally dichotomous views of societies as either individualist or collectivist, and their members, in turn, as valuing either autonomy or connectedness. Instead, taking up Beatrice Whiting's (1976) invitation to unpackage cultural categories, new studies map variation and change within societies in these values and practices (Chao & Aque, 2009; Chao & Kaeochinda, 2010). Researchers in many nations are also rethinking classic assumptions about autonomy and connections by studying their interplay with other cultural dimensions (Brown, Larson, & Saraswathi, 2002). For example, scholars are pursuing these questions in Italy (Ingoglia, Lo Coco, Inguglia, & Pace, 2006); Turkey (Kagitçibasi, 2005, 2007); Japan (Kashiwagi, 2007); Finland (Salmela-Aro, Aunola, & Nurmi, 2007); Israel (Seginer, 2008, 2009); the Middle East (Booth, 2002); and Taiwan (Lee, Beckert, & Goodrich, 2010).

As part of such work, scholars are finding that negotiating identities across generations can be especially complex when identities do not fit mainstream norms, when they are stigmatized, or when they do not emerge in a clear progression from exploration to commitment (Azmitia, Syed, & Radmacher, 2008; Solis, 2003; Thorne, 2004). For ethnic, religious, or sexual minority identities, or being adopted, disabled, or an undocumented immigrant, more research is needed to understand how youth navigate tensions between seeking a sense of personal coherence and confronting conflicts across their multiple identities and worlds (Perez et al., 2009). The cultural significance of this ability is reflected in its being given a name: *kejime* in Japanese (Bachnik, 1992) and *nepantla* in Aztec traditions (Burciaga, 2008).

Over the years, questions about the organization, continuity, and coherence among the domains of identity outlined by Erikson have been neglected (Grotevant & Cooper, 1998). Early research examined occupation, religion, and political ideology, reflecting Erikson's interests in these domains (1950). Studies in many cultural settings have shown that career identity is particularly important for young people (Alberts, Mbalo, & Ackerman, 2003). How it develops predicts overall patterning in identity development (Archer, 1994; Blustein, Devanis, & Kidney, 1989; Skorikov & Unritani, 2008; Skorikov & Vondracek, 1998). Career aspirations and identities also reflect adolescents' opportunities to explore alternatives and choices on which the ideals of many societies rest (Bellah, Madsen, Sullivan, Swidler, & Tipton, 1985). We need further research on how career identities and aspirations develop even when opportunities are constrained by economic, cultural, or other barriers.

Scholars are examining a growing number of identity domains, including relationships (Grotevant, Thorbecke, & Meyer, 1982; Kiang, Harter, & Whitesell, 2007); ethnicities (Phinney & Ong, 2007; Phinney & Rosenthal, 1992); and political and civic identities (Youniss & Yates, 1997). Evidence shows that adolescents engage in different degrees of exploration and commitment, as well as different patterns of communicating about them across domains (e.g., Taopoulos-Chan, Smetana, & Yau, 2009). In an important advance, social psychologists who study group identities such as ethnicity, race, gender, and sexuality have joined with developmental psychologists who study personal identity domains like career and schooling to consider intersections across group and personal domains (Archer, 1985; Azmitia et al., 2008; Phinney & Ong, 2007; Ruble et al., 2004). This work offers a promising way to look at identity issues along the academic pipeline, such as why it seems easier to be a "schoolgirl" than a "schoolboy."

Erikson wrote extensively about conflict as a central mechanism of identity development through the lifespan. Still, we have more to learn about how conflict and other challenges—whether internal, interpersonal, or institutional—function in identity development (Bosma & Kunnen, 2001; Orbe, 2008). We need to understand how adolescents and their families negotiate conflicts and connectedness in different identity domains. In one study, Cambodian immigrant college students reported dating without their parents' knowledge as a strategy for avoiding conflict with them (Su, 2008). In a recent study of Vietnamese immigrant college students, youth felt their parents saw their academic success as demonstrating good judgment and rewarded them with trust and respect that in turn reduced parent–adolescent conflict (Trinh & Cooper, 2009). For Canadian Aboriginal and Native American youth, activities that foster cultural continuities across generations, such as learning traditional languages, appear to serve as a protective factor against suicide (Chandler, 2006; Chandler, Lalonde, Sokol, & Hallen, 2003; LaFromboise et al., 2006; LaFromboise & Lewis, 2008). A wide range of people who are concerned about the academic pipeline problem would benefit from understanding more about how conflict functions in healthy identity development.

Finally, we need to understand the challenges and resources that youth encounter in school, work, and other settings that affect their identity development. The following chapters examine how youth build their pathways to college by navigating through both social and institutional worlds.

4

CAPITAL, ALIENATION, OR CHALLENGE?
WHAT MATTERS FOR PATHWAYS TO COLLEGE[a]

with
Robert G. Cooper, Margarita Azmitia, Gabriela Chavira, and Yvette Gullatt

In the previous chapter, we examined evidence that adolescents' growing maturity, including their college-going identities, can be energized by a sense of agency and connectedness in the service of their own dreams and those of their families. We now consider our second question: What factors lead youth along academic pathways toward or away from college and college-based careers? This chapter examines these pathways and the experiences that shape access to them.

MATH AND LANGUAGE PATHWAYS THROUGH SCHOOL

Beyond their aspirations for the future, students' academic skills, especially in mathematics and English, play a central role in their prospects for college and careers. In the U.S., passing Algebra 1 and, for English learners, being classified as eligible for regular English and math classes are crucial early milestones on the path to college. Scholars have mapped developmental progressions in mathematical and linguistic understanding and the remarkably wide range of settings, formal and informal, in which these skills can develop (Gutiérrez, 2008; Saxe & Gearhart, 1988; Tudge & Doucet, 2004; Vygotsky, 1978). But learning academic mathematics and language skills depends on having opportunities to acquire them. For example, it is difficult for students to learn calculus if it is not taught at their school, and mastering these academic skills may create challenges for immigrant youth whose families have not attended school in the U.S. (Bunch & Panayotova, 2008; Lager, 2006; Moschkovich, 2007).

---

[a] Parts of this chapter were adapted from Cooper, Cooper, Azmitia, Chavira, and Gullatt (2002).

What factors lead youth along different academic pathways? Across the U.S., working-class, immigrant, and ethnic minority students are more likely than middle-class students to attend schools that lack qualified teachers and a complete college-preparatory curriculum. They have parents who are less likely to have attended college themselves, and they are more likely to come from circumstances that require students to contribute economically to the family. Nonetheless, these youth are succeeding at higher rates in some settings than others (Education Trust, 2004; Engle & Lynch, 2009; Engle & O'Brien, 2007). We need to understand how this happens.

This chapter takes a closer look at the capital, alienation, and challenge models of the conditions through which youth build their pathways toward or away from college. Each model reaches across family generations. The *capital* model is based on the cultural reproduction of social class hierarchies across generations. This happens as college-educated parents, who have more resources compared to working-class parents, use them to help their children do well in school and go on to college and college-based careers (Bourdieu & Passeron, 1986; Coleman, 1988). Evidence of this process has been found all along the academic pipeline. In elementary schools, Lareau (1987) observed how European American middle- and working-class parents' contact with the schools and their knowledge of how to navigate the educational system predicted differences in their children's school achievement. A study of suburban middle schools revealed how college-educated parents helped their children get places in the college-prep mathematics track through their involvement in school affairs and their social networks with other parents (Useem, 1992). And in an urban high school, wealthy parents used their social networks to help their adolescents (and their adolescents' friends) get places in college-prep honors classes; in the same school, working-class and ethnic minority parents were not part of these networks, and few of their children got places in the honors classes (Yonezawa, Wells, & Serna, 2002). The capital model helps us to understand, as we described in Chapter 1, the growing global education gap between the rich and poor.

Pathways to alienation have been illuminated by Ogbu's (1991) descriptions of group differences in students' school engagement. He proposed that immigrant youth, as *voluntary minorities* who can compare the conditions they left with those in their new country, will be more optimistic about their chances for school success than *involuntary minorities* whose communities were incorporated by force (Fordham & Ogbu, 1986). Importantly, Ogbu also traced individual variations in how Black youth juggle school and community identities on their pathways through school (1989). Among these strategies, he described *assimilators* as adopting a "raceless" persona to succeed in school but lose their community ties, *regulars* as having the skills for moving between school and street cultures, and *encapsulated* youth as rejecting an academic identity because they see it as "acting White."

In response to Ogbu's proposal, scholars have mapped conditions in which immigrant, low-income, and ethnic minority students are more or less likely to develop a sense of alienation or one of belonging (see Flores-Gonzalez, 1999; Gibson, Bejínez, Hidalgo, & Rolón, 2004; Mehan, Villanueva, Hubbard, & Lintz,

1996). For example, Vigil (2004) observed how *multiple marginality* from families, schools, and school-engaged peers sent Latino, Asian American, and Black youth toward gang identities and illegal careers. In a pattern resembling Ogbu's *encapsulated* strategy, these youth lacked the social and academic support to navigate across their worlds (Phelan et al., 1998).

In contrast, the challenge model suggests that under some conditions, the hardships of poverty, racism, and immigration can motivate youth to succeed on behalf of their families and communities and even to prove gatekeepers wrong (Cooper, 1999). As discussed in Chapter 3, this proposal stems in part from Erikson's writings on how conflict, when coupled with support, can be a catalyst for identity development (1968). Support for the challenge model can be seen in findings that, despite many immigrant parents' modest formal schooling and unfamiliarity with U.S. schools (thus lacking conventionally defined social capital), their hopes and determination can motivate their children to succeed in school and college to repay parents for their sacrifices (Chao & Kaeochinda, 2010; Telzer & Fuligni, 2009).

Ongoing research about the capital, alienation, and challenge models is illuminating both the causes and remedies for the academic pipeline problem. Unfortunately, studies about each of these models have often appeared in isolation from work on the other two models. Many studies draw from one-time surveys that compare demographic groups, such as middle- and working-class parents or first- and second-generation immigrant students; these designs carry the drawbacks discussed in Chapter 2. Below, we consider what conditions send youth along different pathways, with particular attention to longitudinal studies of students' progressions in their academic skills and to understanding variation within demographic groups. We start with a study of how African American and Latino youth move along their math and language pathways to college and college-based careers.

AFRICAN AMERICAN AND LATINO YOUTH IN UNIVERSITY BRIDGING PROGRAMS

In the 1960s, many private and public universities in the U.S. launched pre-college "bridging programs" to enhance ethnic diversity among their students. However, few longitudinal studies have examined what factors contribute to successful pathways to college among participants in these programs (Gándara & Moreno, 2002; Tierney, Corwin, & Colyear, 2004). These programs typically attract high-performing students and expect their graduates to attend four-year universities. Such programs can be considered *highly selective,* compared to *moderately selective-*programs whose graduates more typically attend two-year community colleges. Public schools are in principle *inclusive* of students across skill levels, although high dropout rates, particularly among low-income and ethnic minority youth, challenge this ideal (Cooper, 2001; Orfield & Frankenberg, 2007; Rumberger & Lim, 2008).

To investigate how African American and Latino students build math and language pathways to the university, our research team developed a partnership with several pre-college bridging programs sponsored by the University of California, Berkeley (Cooper et al., 1995; Cooper et al., 2002). As discussed in Chapter 2, we started by interviewing founding and current leaders of several of these programs, including the Early Academic Outreach Program (EAOP); Mathematics, Engineering, Science Achievement (MESA); and the Partnership program, as well as university-level programs in engineering for Black and Latino students. We also held focus groups with African American and Latino students in these programs (Cooper et al., 1995). These students were eloquent in describing both challenges and resources across their many cultural worlds, as well as their "safe escapes" from the racism they experienced at school, in their neighborhoods, and on the university campus (see also Gibson et al., 2004). For these youth, building academic pathways to college and careers required vigilant navigating among these obstacles and resources from childhood on through the college years.

We drew on results from these focus groups to develop the Bridging Multiple Worlds Survey, which asks students' both open- and closed-ended questions about their parents' education, their family immigration histories, students' own career goals and identities, and the challenges and resources across their worlds (Cooper, Jackson, Azmitia, & Lopez, 1994, 2002). We also examined students' school transcripts and program records to trace their math and English pathways from middle through high school to university eligibility and college enrollment. Once again, our research team used the parallel design discussed in Chapter 2 to map similarities and differences in adolescents' experiences within and across cultural groups.

To compare evidence for the capital, alienation, and challenge models, we asked five questions: What were the immigration and educational histories of the students and their families who participated in these bridging programs? What were these students' math and English pathways through school to university eligibility and enrollment? Were these students exploring their career identities, or did they show signs of disengagement? What were students' challenges and resources on their pathways through school? Finally, what factors mattered across these dimensions in predicting their pathways to college enrollment?

The participating students included 120 self-identified African American and Latino students. When we first saw them, they ranged from 6th to 11th grades, most typically 10th grade, and averaged 15.2 years old. For 90% of the African American youth in the sample, their parents were born in the U.S. and had attended some college. Their mothers averaged 14.63 years of education and their fathers, 13.87 years. All of the African American students except one were born in the U.S. In contrast, 83% of the Latino youth in the sample had immigrant parents, primarily from Mexico; over 20% of the students were themselves immigrants. Their mothers averaged 12.18 years of education and their fathers, 11.01 years. Thus, the African American students were following their parents' pathways to college in the pattern of cultural reproduction predicted by the capital model, and the Latino youth were starting to exceed their parents' education in a pattern consistent with the challenge model.

Math and Language Pathways for University Eligibility

On average, these students were making good grades in college-prep math and English classes. Most (88.6%) had passed Algebra 1 by 9th grade. In math and English grades, respectively, the African American students' grade point averages (GPA) were 2.75 and 3.08, and the Latino students' were 3.05 and 3.24, with no significant differences between the groups. Students' math and English grades were highly correlated, rising and falling together from middle through high school.

We traced students' math and language pathways from their courses and grades over time. When we graphed each student's math pathways toward college, beginning with Algebra 1, five common patterns emerged that we called *high* (consistently strong), *slowly declining, rapidly declining, increasing,* and *back on track* (falling then rising). In this highly selective program, we were surprised to find that the majority of youth were on the slowly declining pathway in math. Students continued taking math classes only if they were doing well, and many stopped taking math classes altogether during high school. Importantly, students' grades in Algebra 1 were a strong and early predictor of their overall grades in college-prep classes ($r = 0.73$) and their later college eligibility ($r = 0.65$). Thus, pathways toward and away from the university diverged early, a finding with implications for practice and policy.

Through our partnerships with Dr. Gullatt and with these programs, we learned how the students we first surveyed at age 15 were doing at age 18. Consistent with the "immigrant paradox", immigrant Latino students were more likely to become eligible for university admission than Latino students born in the U.S. Students who were on high math and English pathways in high school were the most likely to enroll directly in four-year colleges and universities; students on other pathways were more likely to attend two-year community colleges. However, high school grades did not always predict where students went to college. Among those eligible to attend the University of California, some Latino students enrolled in California State Universities and community colleges, and some similarly eligible African American students chose private or out-of-state colleges and universities, including historically Black colleges and universities such as Spelman College, Morehouse College, and Howard University. Two-year community colleges, the least expensive option, might have appealed to students with financial challenges, even if they qualified for more prestigious institutions. Being close to family and friends at home was an important factor for many (Ceja, 2004; McDonough, 1997; Perna, 2000).

Exploring Career Identities or Disengaging?

We used the Extended Objective Measure of Ego Identity Status (EOMEIS-2; Bennion & Adams, 1986), a survey version of Marcia's identity interview (1966), to assess students' career identities. On this measure, youth who are actively exploring their career identities (called *identity moratorium*) tend to agree with statements like "I'm still trying to decide how capable I am as a person and what jobs will be right for me." Those who have made a commitment based on exploration (*identity achievement*) tend to agree that "It took me a while to figure it out, but now I really know what I want for a career." Youth with *diffused* identities report little exploration or commitment ("I haven't chosen the occupation I really want to go into. Right now, I'm just working at what is available until something better comes along"). Finally, youth with *foreclosed* identities have chosen a career without exploring alternatives ("I might have thought about a lot of different jobs, but there's never really been any question since my parents said what they wanted"). Given that these bridging programs focus on exploring opportunities for college and careers, we anticipated that students would be actively engaged in career exploration.

As shown in Table 4.1, most youth in our bridging program sample were indeed exploring their career identities in the identity moratorium pattern. In contrast, most Latino youth in a study conducted in a California high school reported identity diffusion, marked by low exploration and low commitment to their career identities (Lopez, 2001). This was especially true for those students taking remedial rather than college-prep math classes.

These strikingly different responses open new questions about how career identity pathways emerge. Do highly selective programs attract youth who are interested or already engaged in exploring their career opportunities? Do field trips and group discussions in these programs stimulate further career exploration? Are youth who are alienated or in identity diffusion more likely to be assigned to remedial classes, or do these classes engender alienation, or both? Finally, could these patterns also reflect the influence of dispirited teachers who have also been tracked into remedial classes (Kelly, 2006)?

Table 4.1 Youth from Highly Selective Program and School Samples in Four Identity Status Categories

	Identity Diffusion	Foreclosure	Moratorium	Identity Achievement
Highly selective program sample				
African American students	19%	0%	64%	17%
Latino students	12%	0%	62%	26%
School sample				
Latino students	57%	6%	28%	6%

Most African American and Latino students in a highly selective academic preparation program sample were exploring career identities in identity moratorium (Cooper et al., 2002). Most Latino high school students in a school-based sample reported identity diffusion, with little exploration (Lopez, 2001)

Challenges and Resources along Academic Pathways

In the bridging program study, we asked youth to write their responses to the following question, that was adapted from the identity interview described in Chapter 3 (Grotevant & Cooper, 1985):

> What people or experiences have been major influences on your plans for the future? Important people may be teachers, family members, friends, or other people. The experiences that have influenced you may be positive or negative, such as a field trip to a college or company or a friend getting into trouble. We would appreciate your telling us about your important experiences.

Students' responses illustrate how both resources and challenges across their worlds motivated their pathways to college:

> My mother and my friends have been a major influence on me. My mom . . . says prepare for the future because there aren't any more factory jobs out there . . . . I better get a college education or else my life will be very hard and I will regret not going to college. My friends don't care about school. Their life is all parties. I see their future . . . and I get scared because that could be me too. I get jealous at the fact that I can't have fun like them, but they notice how much I have stuck with school and are very proud of me. I'm just a sore thumb . . . . I'm stuck between choosing my future pathways in life.
>
> Latina high school student

> My mother has always taught me to appreciate and care for our environment as well as the people around me. She taught us how to recycle and how not to pollute our earth. In school, I always liked math and science (especially physics), so I joined MESA and eventually got involved with the U.C. Berkeley Partnership Program . . . . I attended the Pre College Academy where I took classes in Calculus, Engineering Applications, and Economics. Oddly enough, my Economics class helped me decide to pursue a career in environmental engineering. In my Econ class, I learned about the injustices of environmental racism and I knew that my call in life was to help put an end to these injustices by finding ways to eliminate hazardous wastes and clean up contaminated soil and groundwater.
>
> African American high school male

> Outreach programs and family have really been the major influences in my life; I have gone to programs since the sixth grade, so their faculty have helped me pull through. I have participated in [the pre-college program], where I have studied the components of engineering . . . and learned "fun" ways of solving problems. My family has always been right behind me, so I always knew that just about whatever I did someone would support me, even though they may have chosen something different. There have also been negative influences. People have implied and told me that I could never be a "Black" female engineer, so I decided I would prove them wrong and help my community.
>
> African American/Native American high school female

Major influences in my life and plans for my future are my mother and my best friend . . . . Most of the teachers I have had think I am not very smart and don't pay attention to me. My teachers pay attention to those who have good grades and are white.

African American high school male

My math teacher is racist and that make me feel less self-confident. My soccer coach is the same, causing me to wonder if I am worth anything. Going to MESA helped my self-confidence. So many people have told me I can't do it. MESA makes me feel as if I can.

Latino high school male

Some of these students focused on their resources, others were attuned to their obstacles, and still others followed program leaders' advice to view these challenges as "a good burden" and work to "prove the gatekeeper wrong." We need to know more about the impact of these different orientations as youth move along their pathways because challenges, such as racist episodes, occur through the college years and beyond (Syed, 2010a). For example, when can an experience of racism serve as a motivator, and when does it become a roadblock (Sellers, Copeland-Linder, Martin, & Lewis, 2006)? Understanding the development of qualities that help students build resilience through the years could be of great value to them and those who seek to support their success.

Overall, in response to our open-ended questions, students listed their mothers, fathers, and teachers most often as resources, with mothers providing more help than fathers, and fathers, more help than teachers. Parents, especially mothers, helped students with both instrumental and emotional support—with staying on track to college, schoolwork, planning for the future, and being a good person. Students most often listed teachers as helping them in math. This pattern aligns with research on students' social networks that mothers are typically *generalists* and teachers, *specialists* (Levitt, in press). However, students on high math pathways also listed teachers as helping them stay on track to college. Peers and teachers were students' greatest sources of difficulties. As predictors of pathways through school, parents' and teachers' help and siblings' challenges predicted students' grades, university eligibility, and admission to universities. Thus, youth on more successful academic pathways drew resources from more of their worlds while also navigating their challenges, and in some cases creating motivation from them.

ALIGNING FINDINGS WITH THE CAPITAL, ALIENATION, AND CHALLENGE MODELS

We now consider findings of this study in terms of the capital, alienation, and challenge models. As mentioned previously, the African American students were following their college-educated parents' pathways to college in the pattern of cultural reproduction predicted by the capital model, and the Latino youth were starting to exceed their parents' education in a pattern consistent with the challenge model. It is also notable that, consistent with the challenge model, for both African

American and Latino students, within each group, the fathers of students who were doing better in school had *less* education than fathers of lower-achieving students.

The African American and Latino youth in the bridging programs sampled in this study were achieving at high levels and actively exploring their career identities. Their academic and identity pathways contrast with those of their counterparts in studies with school-based samples. These findings reveal the importance of personal, family, and institutional resources in students' academic pathways to college (Stanton-Salazar, 2010).

Youth in these programs look different from the encapsulated youth described by Ogbu (1989) and other youth whose difficulties with families, schools, and peers can lead them to explore and adopt gang identities (Lopez, Wishard, Gallimore, & Rivera, 2006; Vigil, 2004). However, we saw signs of potential vulnerability in the program sample. First, it seemed easier to be a "schoolgirl" than a "schoolboy." More girls participated in program activities and persisted through school than boys. This pattern also appears in federal pre-college programs like Upward Bound (Myers & Schirm, 1999). On average, girls in our sample earned higher grades and moved along higher math pathways than boys. Gender disparities continue in college graduation rates within all ethnic groups (Bowen, Chingos, & McPherson, 2009; Saenz & Ponjuan, 2009). In addition to the gender gap, program leaders also worried that few working-class African American youth and non-immigrant Latino youth attended program activities.

Challenges among Working-class European American Youth

Ethnic minority youth are not alone in facing challenges on their pathways through school and using these challenges to help define their college and career identities. In a study at her former high school near Oakland, California, Jayme Barrett (2001) asked European American working-class youth in college-prep English classes to write about what experiences had influenced their plans for the future (Grotevant & Cooper, 1981), just as our team had done with youth in the bridging program study. The following responses were typical, and they reveal the powerful role that difficulties—here based on social class—can play in motivating identity development and pathways to college:

> I just look around at the town I live in and also because of my parents' help, I know I want a good education so I won't have to live like the other people in my town.
>
> European American working-class high school male

> The experiences that have influenced me are that my sister had a lot of problems when she was younger. She hardly went to school and she did drugs. I learned from her mistakes how to be successful. My parents also never went to college so I think it's important.
>
> European American working-class high school female

Responses in this study show that students who are dreaming of moving up from working-class family backgrounds do so in ways that are consistent with the challenge model. Beyond the compelling evidence that middle- and upper-income parents use their resources to maintain their families' social class standing, we also need better concepts of capital beyond parents' education and social networks to capture the assets of working-class youth and families that matter for their future pathways.

Identities Won in Action

As the processes identified by capital, alienation, and challenge models unfold, each model illuminates the actions that youth are (or are not) able to take in building their identities and academic pathways. In settings where youth develop engaged rather than alienated identities, evidence indicates that they can exercise their sense of agency. For example, in Gibson's studies in California of Punjabi Sikh (1988) and Mexican immigrant youth (1995; Gibson et al., 2004), successful students were optimistic about being able to build academic pathways while keeping their cultural identities, although they were mindful of the limited options of many of their peers. Similarly, in Walker's study (2006) of high-achieving African American youth and Latino youth (from the Dominican Republic, Puerto Rico, and Guatemala) in New York City, most of their families and teachers valued these students' school achievement, and youth could navigate between home and school and among their high- and low-achieving peers (like Ogbu's "regulars").

These settings—whether public school classes or bridging programs—provide high expectations, social and academic support, and a sense of belonging (Gibson & Hidalgo, 2009). As illustrated in Figure 4.1, supporting college-bound peer networks

Figure 4.1 Students work together at computers in a pre-college mathematics program. Courtesy of University of California, Santa Cruz, Educational Partnership Center.

helps create worlds where both academic and ethnic identities are valued (Datnow & Cooper, 1997; Flores-Gonzalez, 1999; Gibson & Hidalgo, 2009). We continue to strive to understand how, to paraphrase Erikson, both cultural and college identities can be won in action.

Math and Language Pathways to College in Research, Practice, and Policy

Growing understanding of academic pathways to college and careers advances (and is advanced by) educational practice and policy investments that address the academic pipeline problem. The set of academic pathways that our research team first identified while studying highly selective programs has evolved, based on studies of a broader range of programs, into those shown in Figure 4.2. This set of pathways also evolved from a research tool into one used for practice and policy.

This evolution began when I showed the diagram in Figure 4.2 to a group of civil rights lawyers during a presentation on the academic pipeline problem at the U.S. Office of Civil Rights in San Francisco. One lawyer walked up to the front of the room, put his finger on the *back-on-track* pathway, and announced to his colleagues, "This is *me*." His story of his own pathway sparked a lively discussion in the group about what factors help or prevent students from getting back on track. When I showed the same diagram to a group of middle school students in a pre-college program, one girl exclaimed to her peers, "So these are our math roads!" Experiences like these have shown us how adults and youth find personal meanings in stories and diagrams of pathways that can build their empathy and engagement in college-going partnerships. It has also shown us that a representation of one's situation can be a tool for change. Chapter 7 describes how these math pathways became part of a college and career identity curriculum in a pre-college program.

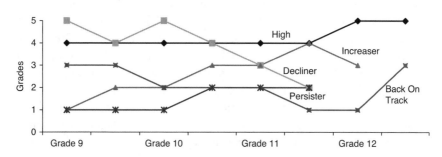

Figure 4.2 *Five typical pathways of math or language grades:* Studies of highly selective, moderately selective, and inclusive settings reveal five prototypic pathways: high, declining, increasing, "back on track," and persisting with low grades (Cooper, Domínguez, & Rosas, 2005). Each line on this graph shows one student's pathway. Reprinted with permission by Taylor & Francis.

Research about academic pathways has been used to effect changes in school practice and policy. Stephen Mello, a policy analyst at the Educational Partnership Center at the University of California, Santa Cruz, built on this set of academic pathways in guiding middle and high school students in getting on track to university eligibility by completing required classes, applying, and enrolling (Mello, 2005). In a further step, Yvette Gullatt and her team at the University of California Office of the President designed the Transcript Evaluation Service (TES; www.transcriptevaluationservice.com). TES offers clear charts of individual students' pathways—for students, families, and educators—of their progress completing the 15 classes required for eligibility for the University of California and California State Universities. School counselors across California have used TES to help youth stay on track or get back on track to college. Feedback from TES users has increased the number of college-prep classes offered at participating schools, thus guiding policy investments (Gullatt, personal communication). Chapter 6 describes how this cycle of research, practice, and policy about pathways to college is continuing.

CONCLUSIONS AND NEXT STEPS

Looking at students' academic pathways as well as the personal, social, and institutional conditions that shape them, is elucidating the academic pipeline problem. New evidence is revealing that capital, alienation, and challenge models each capture the realities of some students' lives and contribute importantly to the larger story.

New work has revealed both differences and similarities between voluntary and involuntary minorities and has illuminated the immigrant paradox that newcomers fare better than U.S.-born youth who have had opportunities to acquire cultural capital. For example, Gibson (1997) reviewed evidence for Ogbu's theory of alienation and school engagement from studies of immigrant youth in Israel, the Netherlands, Canada, France, and the U.S. She concluded that whether youth were voluntary or involuntary minorities did not fully explain variation in their school engagement and success. Similarly, Portes and Rumbaut (2006) expressed their own doubts, based on their longitudinal study of nine immigrant groups to the U.S. (Chinese, Cuban, Filipino, Haitian, Jamaican/West Indian, Laotian/Cambodian, Mexican, Nicaraguan, and Vietnamese), that the immigrant paradox—based on students' generation of immigration—explained variation within each immigrant group in their academic pathways. Instead, these scholars argue that individual, social, and institutional processes account for variations as significant as group differences. That is, these scholars urge us to move beyond the demographic category of generation of immigration to explain the processes that shape pathways.

Findings from two recent studies reveal the nature of these processes and align with those of the bridging program study discussed in this chapter. First, Portes and Fernández-Kelly (2008), reporting on a new wave of analyses in the longitudinal study described earlier by Portes and Rumbaut (2006), show how *meanings* of parents' educational and occupational histories, in concert with their reception in the U.S. and ethnic networks, propelled their children along upward, level, or downward pathways. In addition to statistical analyses, this report features longitudinal case studies showing how exceptions to downward pathways occurred when youth drew motivation from their families' lives of hardship and from the institutional resources of schools, pre-college programs, and community colleges.

Second, in a longitudinal study of immigrant students from Central America, China, Dominican Republic, Haiti, and Mexico, Suárez-Orozco, Rhodes, and Milburn (2009) found (as in our bridging program study) that the majority of students in their sample had moved along declining academic pathways. Examining variation within groups revealed that students on higher pathways actively drew for both social and instrumental support from multiple worlds. These studies reveal that while the capital, alienation, and challenge models seem to offer quite different perspectives, the evidence they yield is consistent.

Our understanding of adolescents' pathways has expanded from centering on the role of their families to greater appreciation of adolescents' agency in navigating among the challenges and resources across their multiple worlds. Students told us that thinking about our questions was itself a resource in this process.

Future research about capital, alienation, and challenge in students' academic pathways to college needs to continue to examine variation within immigrant, ethnic minority, social class, and other groups. For example, Lopez (2010) found that Latino high school students making higher grades in math, compared to lower-achieving students, had begun learning math at younger ages and done so with their families. The stronger students in this sample were more interested in math-related careers and, not surprisingly, more optimistic about their futures. These findings can inform policies and practice that build on the resources working-class families actually have (Gonzalez, Stoner, & Jovel, 2003; Yosso, 2005).

By comparing settings in which these three models each capture important mechanisms underlying youth pathways, this chapter has examined how youth in selective bridging programs and other high-performance learning communities navigate challenges and resources across their worlds to build academic pathways to college and careers. Further work is needed on what allows youth in more inclusive settings to draw resources from their worlds to help them succeed in school. When do obstacles shut students down and when do they motivate them?

As students move from childhood to young adulthood in the U.S., too many low-income, ethnic minority, and immigrant youth, especially boys, become underrepresented in college and college-based careers and overrepresented in juvenile and adult prison systems (Cass & Curry, 2007). Conventional views portray these youth as alienated and disengaged from school. Poignantly, interviews with youth reveal their familiarity with this stereotype, but also (and importantly) with its counter-narrative, in which minority youth succeed and keep their history (Nasir, Atukpawu,

O'Connor, Davis, Wischnia, & Tsang, 2009; Rodríguez, Jones, Pang, & Park, 2004). Understandably, there is much interest in how youth can build successful pathways to college without losing their ties to their families and cultural communities. We consider progress in understanding this issue by looking across a broad range of cultural communities in Chapter 5.

5

BROKERS AND GATEKEEPERS
HOW CAN YOUTH BRIDGE THEIR
CULTURAL WORLDS?[a]

with
Gabriela Chavira and Dolores D. Mena

This chapter examines how linkages work across the cultural worlds of adolescents' lives, such as their families, peers, and schools. When do cultural mismatches emerge across these worlds? When do youth navigate across their worlds while staying on the good path of life? Who serve as cultural brokers by helping youth link their worlds along their pathways? What do we know about cultural gatekeepers, especially those who block these linkages?

Whether adolescents' families, peers, schools, and communities are called *spheres of influence* (Epstein, 2001b); *activity settings* (Gallimore, Goldenberg, & Weisner, 1993; Rogoff, 2003; Tharp & Gallimore, 1988); *microsystems* (Bronfenbrenner, 1979); or *worlds* (Cooper, 1999; Phelan, Davidson, & Yu, 1991), scholars, educators, and policymakers are moving beyond binary thinking of only "two different worlds" that either match or compete with one another. Instead, they trace how all youth move—or attempt to move—within and across many social and institutional settings in their lives. In just one day, an adolescent girl may navigate across her worlds of home, school, sports, religious activities, and her online social network. Further, the constellations of these worlds evolve, as when part of a family immigrates, if parents divorce, or when high school friends leave home for college.

Early studies measured the "cross-pressures" across adolescents' worlds by asking questions such as "who helps you more, your parents or your friends?" (Brittain, 1963). More recent nationwide samples like the National Educational Longitudinal Study (NELS:88) and smaller studies ask youth about connections across worlds, such as what parents know about their children's friends; what teachers know about families' home learning activities; or how sports, religious, or enrichment programs

---

[a] This chapter is adapted from Cooper, Chavira, and Mena (2005), with permission of Taylor & Francis.

affect students' schoolwork and goals for college (Fredricks & Eccles, 2010; Gutman & McLoyd, 2000; Jarrett, 1995; Phelan et al., 1998).

Typically, studies conducted in the U.S. indicate that linkages across families, schools, peers, and communities are relatively weak in early childhood, become stronger in middle childhood, and then weaken again in adolescence, when many adults assume that growing autonomy will sustain adolescents' developmental pathways (Eccles & Midgley, 1989). Across ethnicity and gender groups, more successful students form links across their worlds, including ties with college-bound peers, whereas less successful students have weaker links in childhood that decline further in adolescence (Horn & Chen, 2002; Stanton-Salazar, 2004, 2010; Vigil, 2004). Healthy development is fostered when youth network or bridge across their worlds, and when adults and institutional agents who appreciate this can foster these links as cultural brokers. We now examine implications of such findings, including insights from what may appear to be competing theories, for work on the academic pipeline problem.

EPSTEIN'S THEORY OF OVERLAPPING SPHERES OF INFLUENCE

The Theory of Overlapping Spheres of Influence, developed by Joyce Epstein and her colleagues at the National Network of Partnership Schools, serves as a cornerstone of nationwide and international work on family–school relations and the standards for parent involvement of the National Parent Teacher Association in the U.S. (National PTA, 1997, 2009). This evolving theory traces how the spheres of families, schools, and communities interact in how they pursue their responsibilities and investments in children's learning (Epstein, 1990, 2001a, Epstein & Sanders, 2006). Epstein proposed six types of family–school–community involvement that work through the intersections across these spheres: 1) *parenting*—assisting families with parenting, child-rearing skills, and home conditions for learning; 2) *communicating* with families about school programs and student progress; 3) *volunteering* at school; 4) *learning at home* with homework and other activities; 5) *decision making* in school governance and advocacy; and 6) *collaborating* with community businesses and agencies to strengthen school programs, family practices, and student learning (Epstein & Sanders, 2006; Epstein et al., 2002; Hidalgo, Siu, & Epstein, 2003).

As children move from elementary school into middle and high school, Epstein and her colleagues have found that the spheres of home, school, and community may move farther apart, reflecting decreasing mutual involvement. For example, when Epstein and Dauber (1991) surveyed teachers of primarily African American and European American students in urban schools in Maryland, elementary teachers were more likely than middle school teachers to report using all six types of family involvement and also saw the parents of their students as more involved with their children.

Given these findings, it is especially important for opening the academic pipeline to understand that the nature of effective learning at home appears to change in adolescence. With data from the National Educational Longitudinal Study (NELS:88), Catsambis (2001) used Epstein's model as she traced adolescents' pathways from middle to high school. At the high school level, parents' conveying high expectations and consistent encouragement (Epstein's learning at home) and providing enhanced learning opportunities beyond the home were related to students' persistence and grades in college-prep classes. This pattern held across social class and ethnic groups.

SOCIOCULTURAL THEORIES

Studies from the perspective of sociocultural theories complement the views of Epstein and of Bronfenbrenner regarding linkages across contexts by focusing on families' community-specific practices as assets (Yamauchi, Lau-Smith, & Luning, 2008). As described in Chapter 2, scholars have built on Vygotsky's proposal (1978) that families in all cultural communities develop goals, values, and skills that allow them to seek meaningful lives (Harkness, Super, & Keever, 1992; Penuel & Wertsch, 1995; Rogoff, 2003; Tharp & Gallimore, 1988; Weisner, 2005, 2010). Children and adolescents learn by participating in *activity settings* such as household chores, classroom lessons, homework, sports, religious activities, and work, either in or outside the home (Coppens, Mejia Arauz, & Rogoff, 2010; Gallimore et al., 1993; Reese et al., 1995). With regard to the pipeline problem, this approach has illuminated how low-income families can have cultural capital that contributes to their children's pathways through school (Yosso, 2005).

Sociocultural researchers also map how *cultural mismatches* or discontinuities across families and schools in goals, values, activities, and ways of communicating can constrain students' pathways through school. Studies of such cultural mismatches between families and schools have been conducted with culturally diverse families across the U.S. For example, Peña (2000) conducted an ethnographic study of an urban elementary school in Texas with Latino immigrant parents, primarily from Mexico. Language differences constrained parents' participation, such as when the school held Parent-Teacher Organization meetings in English without providing Spanish translation (Chavkin, 1996; Delgado-Gaitan, 1990). Teachers assumed parents could not help because they could not read and write English, while families with modest levels of formal education did not tell their children's teachers that they were looking for ways to help their children succeed in school.

To address such family–school issues, educators and researchers who draw on sociocultural approaches view culturally diverse families as having expertise or cultural capital rather than lacking it. Their intention is to support linkages between home and school that foster children's learning. Such values and practices characterize each person with the potential for being both expert and novice, rather than school staff seeking to compensate for what they see as families' deficits.

Sociocultural approaches have served as the overarching framework for the Center for Research on Education, Diversity, and Excellence (CREDE; http://crede.berkeley.edu), a federally funded research and development program that focuses on improving the education of students challenged by language or cultural barriers, race, geographic location, or poverty. Among other activities, CREDE researchers have examined how teachers "connect teaching and curriculum to students' experiences and skills of home and community," one of five CREDE standards for culturally compatible teaching (for details, see Tharp, Estrada, Dalton, & Yamauchi, 2000).

My colleagues, students, and I have had the opportunity to bring together the work of nine of the 31 research projects in CREDE in which researchers have studied linkages among families, schools, peers, and community organizations. Located at sites in six states across the U.S., these studies have led to long-term partnerships in the following places:

- in Arizona, with Mexican immigrant, Native American, African American, and European American families (González, Andrade, Civil, & Moll, 2001)
- in Hawaii, with Native Hawaiian, Asian American, and European American families (Yamauchi, Billig, Meyer, & Hofschire, 2006; Yamauchi, Ceppi, & Lau-Smith, 1999; Yamauchi, Lau-Smith, & Luning, 2008)
- in four sites in California, with Chinese, Filipino, Vietnamese, Asian Indian, and Latino families (Chang, 1995); European American and Mexican immigrant families (Azmitia & Cooper, 2001; Azmitia et al., 2009); Mexican immigrant families (Durán, Durán, Perry-Romero, & Sanchez, 2001); and Latino, African American, Southeast Asian, and European American families (Gándara, Gutierrez, & O'Hara, 2001; Gándara, O'Hara, & Gutierrez, 2004)
- in Kentucky, with rural Appalachian families (McIntyre, Kyle, Hovda, & Stone, 1999)
- in New Mexico, with Zuni (Native American) families (Tharp et al., 1999)
- in Rhode Island, with Hmong, Laotian, Vietnamese, and Cambodian families (Collignon, Men, & Tan, 2001).

These researchers have traced overlapping age spans of students as they move through the academic pipeline from childhood to young adulthood. Together, they have asked how culturally diverse families, schools, and communities can connect in supporting students' pathways through the academic pipeline. How can we open the academic pipeline across cultures, regions, and social class? How can we sustain the aspirations and expectations of students, families, and teachers? How can we link culturally diverse families, schools, peers, and communities to support youth pathways through school? Finally, how can we sustain educational partnerships between schools and communities for long-term outcomes? The following sections address these questions. In considering each question, I draw on evidence from studies by CREDE researchers and related work.

OPENING THE ACADEMIC PIPELINE ACROSS CULTURAL COMMUNITIES, REGIONS, AND SOCIAL CLASS

Who stays in school from childhood to college? Who moves in and out of special education, gifted and talented, or advanced placement classes? Are programs able to attract and retain participants who are representative of their surrounding communities? Such questions help researchers, schools, and programs map inclusiveness along the academic pipeline across local, district, state, and national samples.

Demographic indicators of inclusiveness are used in reports to the U.S. Office of Civil Rights, who monitor compliance with the Civil Rights Act of 1964 by asking school districts to count their students in terms of a minimum of five racial and two ethnic categories. As of 1997, the racial categories include American Indian or Alaska Native, Asian, Black or African American, Native Hawaiian or other Pacific Islander, and White. The ethnic categories include "Hispanic or Latino" and "Not Hispanic or Latino." These demographic categories for race and ethnicity have the limitations that we discussed in Chapter 2. Consequently, researchers, educators, and policymakers use other demographic indicators, such as national origin, home languages, parents' education, and rural/urban location, and they have also developed indicators of key processes that shape students' pathways through school. These processes can be illustrated with studies conducted across a remarkable range of cultural communities.

New Mexico: Counting Elders' Voices at the Zuni Pueblo

In New Mexico, one partnership considered age, gender, and home language in collaborating with community members on behalf of Zuni students. The local situation mirrored national data on Native American communities, with school dropout and expulsion rates "alarmingly high" and "no parent involvement at all" (Tharp et al., 1999). Further challenges stemmed from bureaucratic and policy constraints, educators disrespecting Native Americans, teachers resisting outside influences, the community lacking confidence in their leaders, and students' resistance. To address these issues, the state Board of Education created the Zuni Public School District and asked it to develop a curriculum that was appropriate to its cultural needs and to state standards. Tharp and his team proposed that partners emulate Zuni leaders, who work with all stakeholders in the community to make decisions through patient consensus seeking, similar to the traditional Zuni process of *Yanse'lyona'* (Tharp et al., 1999).

The research partnership took this approach in surveying the community about what Zuni children should learn in school (Rivera et al., 2001). The partnership collaborated with the district, school board, and tribal council to survey adults, with elders surveyed in the Zuni language. Results indicated consensus across age and gender. For example, 84% agreed or strongly agreed that "Zuni schools must teach the history, beliefs, and the values of the community," and 93% agreed that "we want our children to go beyond a high school education, but educational success also includes maintaining our cultural values and traditions for the development of future leaders." Thus, including elders' voices linked the community, families, and school as resources for youth. Demographic data first prompted stakeholders' attention, and a more culturally responsive process followed.

Hawaii: Counting Native Hawaiian Language Speakers to Renew a Cultural Community

Papahana Kaiapuni, the Hawaiian language immersion program, developed from a grassroots movement of parents and community members seeking to revive the Hawaiian language. In their partnership, Yamauchi, Ceppi, and Lau-Smith (1999) found that all adults in the Hawaiian islands were once literate in the language, but it had become threatened with extinction following the U.S. overthrow of the Hawaiian monarchy in 1893 and the subsequent ban on the language from schools (Luning & Yamauchi, 2008). By 1984, it was estimated that only 30 native speakers under the age of 18 remained. Furthermore, compared to other state residents, Native Hawaiians were performing less well on traditional achievement tests and were overrepresented in special education and underrepresented in higher education (Yamauchi & Wilhelm, 2001).

As the first cohort of children in the Papahana Kaiapuni language immersion program moved through school, the program became a K–1, then K–6, and then a full K–12 program. All instruction was conducted in Hawaiian. Many parents and families began to learn Hawaiian with their children. As parents took their children to events where Hawaiian was spoken, home and school activities became more compatible. Interviews by Yamauchi et al. (1999) revealed multiple yet converging views of the program by families, teachers, students, and evaluators. Families saw teachers and the program as extended family, a strong value of many Hawaiians. Involvement among families in school was accompanied by their greater awareness of Hawaiian culture and history. Teachers saw their goal as transforming the school to be "more Hawaiian" through curriculum development and teaching "in a Hawaiian way." Some incorporated Hawaiian proverbs in their lessons by interviewing elders or *kūpuna*. Older siblings "are encouraged to look after their younger brothers and sisters and to teach them and supervise their work" (Yamauchi & Wilhelm, 2001, p. 90), so teachers incorporated this cultural goal by organizing multi-age groups for classroom activities.

Students saw the program as building positive attitudes toward the Hawaiian language and preserving Hawaiian language and culture. However, older youth and some parents worried about the lack of academic and extracurricular activities in the program compared to what they saw at schools conducted in English. From an evaluator's perspective, progress toward the partnership goal was marked by rising numbers of native Hawaiian speakers, increasing from 18 speakers of Hawaiian under the age of 30 to 2,000 children learning Hawaiian. By the end of kindergarten, Papahana Kaiapuni students who entered the program as English speakers were also speaking Hawaiian, with younger children doing so more frequently than older students outside of school (Yamauchi & Wilhelm, 2001). Papahana Kaiapuni students' English skills were comparable to those of peers enrolled in English classes in public schools.

Continuing studies with this program are assessing its benefits and costs. Having banned their language long ago, Hawaiian school leaders have now taken an exceptional step to restore the cultural practices of the Hawaiian indigenous community. This demonstration program, which has parallels in language revival programs in other indigenous communities, offers one site for learning how students' school and community worlds can be linked. This work also offers valuable lessons about how school–family linkages can foster academic and cultural identities.

Rhode Island: Mapping Who Got Out and Who Gets In for a Southeast Asian Community

In their partnership with community organizations and schools of Providence, Rhode Island, Francine Collignon and her colleagues (2001) worked to link four Southeast Asian immigrant communities—Cambodian, Laotian, Hmong, and Vietnamese—each with distinctive languages, cultural practices, and histories of war, to support students' school pathways. Their path to Providence began when the Cambodian, Hmong, and Laotian families fled first to Thailand, where they were placed in refugee camps. When their children ultimately entered school in Providence, school districts categorized them as Asian/Pacific Islanders. The partnership collected data from each Southeast Asian community to help educators understand students' distinctive needs and counter stereotypes of Asians as model minorities (Ngo & Lee, 2007).

The partnership traced three ways that these immigrant communities engaged with schools to address their issues. Drawing on the work of Paulo Freire (1970) on community empowerment, Collignon et al. (2001) described how the families and communities found their voices in schools when their representatives on the Southeast Asian Advisory Council met with the local school superintendent and other leaders. Second, to protect students during the summer months from street violence, support their school achievement, and preserve their cultural heritage, the Socio-Economic Development Center (SEDC) established an eight-week Summer Academy. Students who participated in the Academy for two or three years had higher rates of school persistence than comparable students in local schools. A third layer of this partnership involved building pathways into teaching careers. The need for Southeast Asian teachers was evident in Providence; in 1998, about 11% of students but only 0.04% of teachers were Southeast Asian. Federal funding supported a stream of Southeast Asian classroom aides as they became teachers in Providence schools. Once more, unpackaging demographic data led to insights and constructive actions on behalf of diverse communities.

ASPIRATIONS AND EXPECTATIONS FOR SCHOOL, CAREERS, AND THE GOOD PATH OF LIFE

What are families' educational and occupational aspirations and expectations for their children? What are students' own educational and career aspirations? In pursuing these aspirations, studies across ethnic and racial groups consistently report that students view their families as a greater resource than their peers, teachers, and others (Howley & Cowley, 2001; Otto, 2000; Peterson, Strivers, & Peters, 1986).

These findings contrast with pervasive views of low-income, immigrant, and ethnic minority parents as holding low aspirations and expectations for their children. Research evidence challenges the widespread "cultural deficit" view that has prompted intervention programs designed to raise these parents' aspirations (Valencia & Black, 2002). To the contrary, researchers have found that Latino, African American, and White parents hold high educational and occupational aspirations for their children to go to college (Henderson, 1997; Immerwahr, 2002; So, 1987; Voelkl, 1993), and that high proportions of low-income parents in all ethnic groups want their children to go to college and pursue college-based careers, thus avoiding the hardships that parents have endured (Cooper et al., 1994; Goldenberg, Gallimore, Reese, & Garnier, 2001; Henderson, 1997). Readers will have opportunities to listen for which view of families—as deficits or assets—guides practices and policies in their own communities and to bring research evidence to the attention of those who hold low expectations of families and their students.

California: Aspirations and Expectations of Low-Income Latinos and Families

Latino parents, primarily Mexican immigrants, have described their early adolescents as nearing the crossroads between the good moral path of life and the bad path. In Santa Cruz, California, Margarita Azmitia and I led a research team who conducted a longitudinal study with over 100 low-income Mexican immigrant and European American families that began as their children moved from elementary to middle school (e.g., Azmitia, Cooper, & Brown, 2009; Azmitia et al., 1996). Figure 5.1 provides a template that our team used to interview these parents about how they defined the good and bad paths of life and how their own children were faring as they navigated the path of life (Azmitia et al., 2005; Azmitia & Cooper, 2001; Cooper, Brown, Azmitia, & Chavira, 2005).

In this study, our team found that Mexican- and European-descent parents held similar moral goals and defined the good path as living a moral life, with academic work a part of this path (Cooper et al., 1994). The following examples illustrate how parents from both groups held high aspirations for their children to go to college and become doctors, lawyers, or teachers and thus escaping their lives of hardship.

> Anything ... as long as it isn't in the [strawberry] fields. ... When I was very young I started to pick strawberries and I wouldn't want him to do that.
>
> Mexican immigrant mother of 5th grade student

> We are people who are very poor, but we don't give them bad examples about anything. We behave well, hoping that they will learn to behave. If they see that we behave and are good persons, hopefully they will do the same.
>
> Mexican immigrant mother of 7th grade student

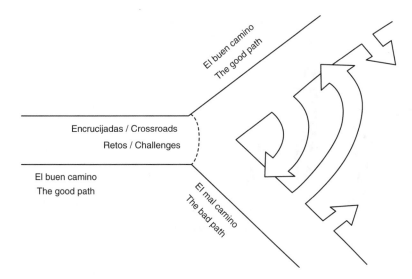

Figure 5.1 Diagram for the interview with parents about their views of the good and bad paths of life and their child's place on these pathways (Azmitia, Cooper, Rivera, Martinez, Lopez, Ittel, et al., 1994; Cooper et al., 2005). Reprinted with permission from Chicago University Press.

I would like her to complete high school and at least four years of college ... when I grew up a high school diploma was a real important thing. Now in this day and age a high school diploma doesn't mean beans. You've gotta have college.... The fact that I went back to school is a big help for her. [I] also take her going on some cleaning jobs with me [the mother cleaned houses for a living] and actually knowing how hard it is .... I told her the more education you get, the more money you get and the easier the job is.

European American mother of 5th grade student

As shown in Figures 5.2A, and 5.2B, respectively, Mexican immigrant mothers in this sample held jobs with modest levels of occupational prestige, but these same mothers held aspirations that their children would hold professional jobs. Many parents in this study, particularly immigrant parents, did not have the knowledge of U.S. schools and academic subjects to guide their children. These parents helped their children indirectly by making homework a priority over chores, using their lives of hardship to encourage their children to attend college, reminding them to think of their future, and encouraging them to stay in school.

Although researchers find that parents' aspirations and expectations predict their children's school performance (Fan & Chen, 2001), the influence of schools in students' pathways is also well documented. Teachers' beliefs can shape ethnic minority students' college aspirations, for better or worse (George & Aronson, 2003). In studies of schools that nurture a "college-going culture," McDonough and her colleagues (2004b, Jarsky, McDonough, & Núñez, 2009) have found that communicating clear college expectations by teachers, counselors, administrators, and staff—with mission statements, bulletin boards, and college centers—are key

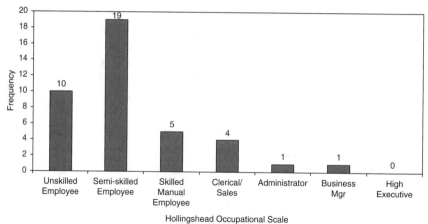

Figure 5.2A Mexican immigrant mothers' occupations.

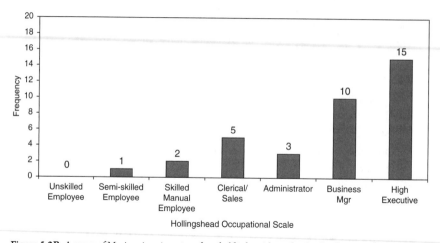

Figure 5.2B A group of Mexican immigrant mothers held jobs with modest levels of prestige (above); these same mothers held high career aspirations for their children (below) (Azmitia et al., 1996; Cooper et al., 1994).

factors in boosting college-going rates. Still, schools can also communicate ambivalence or low expectations about college pathways. Interviews and observations are especially valuable for identifying the intermingled hopes and fears of schools, families, and community members. Knowledge of these realities can help strengthen collaborations to support students' pathways.

BRIDGING WORLDS OF FAMILIES, PEERS, SCHOOLS, AND COMMUNITIES

As noted previously, researchers are moving beyond models of "two worlds" that either match or compete. Researchers now map both challenges (including gatekeepers) and resources (and their brokers) across many worlds. Challenges can be seen in structural barriers, such as when schools offer few college-prep classes, or when adults, even with positive intentions, constrain students' access to enrichment activities. Cultural brokering can be seen when a teacher values immigrant parents' use of sewing to teach geometry to their adolescents (Civil & Bernier, 2006), or when a religious leader supports students' college and cultural identities (Su, 2008).

Families as Resources and Challengess

In research, policy, and practice, the term "families" often refers only to parents. But research shows that besides parents, students' siblings and extended family are key factors in their developing and sustaining college goals and readiness (Caplan, Hall, Lubin, & Fleming, 1997). Parents and other family members can be cultural brokers when they build connections across school, community agencies, and other families to promote students' pathways to college and protect them from drugs, violence, and early pregnancy (Reese et al., 1995). Although students build more of their own connections in adolescence, many children of immigrants serve as language brokers for their families (Buriel, Perez, DeMent, Chavez, & Moran, 1998). Students translate for their immigrant families with schools, doctors, banks, and storekeepers (Dorner, Orellana, & Li-Grining, 2007; Orellana, 2009). One study of Mexican immigrant students found that language brokering could bring stress but also benefit their linguistic skills and valued family and community roles as advocates and tutors (Dorner, Orellana, & Jiménez, 2008). Another found that youth have brought their immigrant parents to meet with school counselors and teachers to learn about financial aid and other "college knowledge" (Cooper et al., 2008).

Beginning in childhood, families of higher-achieving students build links to school and community organizations. Gutman and McLoyd (2000) interviewed low-income African American parents of fifth and sixth graders in Michigan, comparing parents of 17 high and 17 low achievers from a larger study. Although parents in both groups encouraged educational activities at home and helped with homework, parents of high achievers used more specific strategies to help their children with homework and encourage academic success, whereas parents of low achievers focused on their children's non-academic behavior. More parents of high achievers reported being involved at school and initiating contact with teachers to ensure their children's school success, whereas parents of low achievers more often came to school in response to requests from the school about their children's poor work or misbehavior. Although parents in both groups involved their children in sports, the parents of high achievers connected their children to more art and music classes, religious activities such as choir and Bible study, and academic enrichment programs (see also Jarrett, 1995). This study provides a valuable window into how parents serve as brokers for their children's successful school pathways, and how specific proactive strategies—not just general involvement—matter. In Chapter 6 we will see how these insights are being implemented in programs that empower parents to advocate for students' opportunities for college-prep classes.

Peers as Resources and Challenges

Peers can constitute distinctive networks of emotional and instrumental support. The names used by students to label familiar cliques—jocks, nerds, burnouts, slackers, and independents—point to the future pathways of their members (Eckert, 1995). For youth and adults, students' peers are salient and controversial. Peers may offer emotional and practical resources for doing homework, staying in school, and going to college. Horn and Chen (2002) found with the nationally representative NELS:88 data set that high school youth whose friends had plans for college, independent of other factors, were six times more likely to go to on college than those without such peer networks. Peers may also serve as cultural brokers by helping students move across ethnic group lines, especially when school staff and families do so as well (Hamm, 1994). Challenges can arise when youth struggle to keep friends who do not have college dreams, and when these friends accuse them of being "school boys" or "school girls" or "acting White."

California: Comparing peers as challenges and resources for urban and rural youth

A partnership in Davis, California, traced peer influences for Latino, African American, European American, and Asian American youth from 9th grade to graduation from high school (Gándara, Gutierrez, William-White, & O'Hara, 2001; Gándara et al., 2004). The study began with more than 500 students in two schools, one urban and one rural. Peer pressure to engage in risky behavior is thought to peak early in high school and then wane. However, at 9th grade, the percent of youth reporting peer pressure for risky behavior was higher for Latinos than for other students, and it declined much less for males (from 35% in 9th grade to 20% in 12th grade) than for females (from 22% to 5%). Even so, isolation from supportive peers was a challenge for Latinas. For example, many urban Latinas in the sample wanted to be known as good students but felt their friends did not support their academic aspirations. Not surprisingly, these young women seldom discussed school or future plans with their friends. Latino males, especially rural youth, reported continuing pressure toward risky behavior. Many reported that they did not care how well they did in school and were unsure of their plans after high school. These findings add up to a troubling picture of isolation and potential alienation for too many Latino youth, compared to national studies showing that successful students build lasting networks or "convoys" of peer resources for school achievement and pathways to college (Antonucci et al., 2009; Horn & Chen, 2002; Levitt, 2005, in press). Schools and community organizations could do more to nourish college-bound peer networks.

Schools as Resources and Challenges

Teachers and counselors—from any ethnic background—can act as cultural and institutional brokers, helping to link students' worlds along their pathways when they help youth succeed in school and achieve their dreams (McDonough, 2004a). Teachers and counselors can also act as gatekeepers when they misjudge students' eligibility for vocational and remedial classes and college-prep programs, discourage them from taking classes for university admission, or steer them into vocational tracks solely on the basis of their ethnicity, race, or social class (Erickson & Shultz, 1982).

Arizona: Bridging from school to families' funds of knowledge

A partnership in Tucson, Arizona, involves teachers connecting families' own expertise or "funds of knowledge" in mathematics to school math, thus building teachers' professional development and student learning. In essence, these teachers are recognizing and using parents' cultural capital. Gonzales and her team worked in study groups with elementary and middle school teachers of Latino, Native American, African American, and European American students (González & Moll, 2002). Teachers visited their students' families at their homes to learn from them, build mutual respect and trust, and uncover the "mathematics in everyday life settings." Teachers asked families how they came to live in Tucson, thus eliciting their histories, work activities, and goals and values. Teachers then designed school activities to reflect what they had learned from the families. For example, in a dinner activity for "family math night", teachers used family recipes to develop multistep problems. Home visits also led to class units on gardening and architecture, such as a "build your dream house" unit (Ayers, Foseca, Andrade, & Civil, 2001).

Kentucky: Teachers learning from families in Appalachia

A partnership in Kentucky also built on the "funds of knowledge" approach with elementary schools serving low-income African American and European American urban and rural children (McIntyre et al., 1999). Similar barriers as those experienced in the Arizona partnership (González & Moll, 2002) were present in Kentucky, where educators had previously assumed that schools' middle-class values and skills should be delivered in one-way communications from schools to families. In contrast, McIntyre and her team predicted that respectful teacher–family connections would boost children's attendance, motivation, test scores, and achievement, so they listened to families, implemented what they learned in classrooms, and measured the impact of these new practices on children's math and language pathways.

The researchers followed a sample of children through the primary grades with family interviews, classroom observations, and teacher interviews as well as standardized tests in reading and math. At the beginning of each school year, teams made home visits to build trust and respect and to interview parents about their beliefs, practices, and goals. The researchers asked about parents' goals for their children's academic progress and parents' knowledge of their children's interests, abilities, and academic weaknesses (McIntyre & Kyle, 2001).

These parents wanted their children to stay close to home in their rural community and to be happy; they placed only a modest focus on financial success. Teachers brought the parents into their classrooms to share their knowledge, such as in agriculture. In addition, teachers were rated on their use of the CREDE standards for culturally compatible teaching. In a study of 56 children in this school, McIntyre and her team traced their math and language pathways from fall to spring with standardized test scores. The teachers' goal was for the children to gain more than one grade level for each year in school. Overall, 86% did so in math. The research team categorized students' academic pathways into categories that resemble those presented in Chapter 4: *Maintainers'* scores began and remained high, *Leapers'* scores began in the low-to-average range but increased more rapidly than "a year for a year," *Stuck kids'* scores remained low, and *Regressors'* scores declined. In math, but not in reading, teachers of Leapers scored the highest on implementing CREDE standards. This study of low-income European American families shows the value of longitudinal studies of culturally compatible teaching and learning. It also cautions us to listen for variation and cultural mismatches between schools' and families' definitions of successful pathways, a topic to which we return in Chapter 7.

Communities as Resources and Challenges

Community programs and organizations can serve as cultural bridges when they help students gain educational experiences and acquire bicultural skills for success in school and work. Those who share a common language can pass on how to retain community traditions while succeeding in school and college. Some benefits of community programs appear to be mediated through improving parents' relationships with their adolescents. In one study, 959 youth from age 10 to 16 in Big Brothers/Big Sisters programs were randomly assigned to treatment or control groups (Rhodes, Grossman, & Resch, 2000). Mentoring youth in the treatment group led to declines in their unexcused absences from school and gains in their sense of school competence, although not to better grades. Rather than directly influencing outcomes, mentoring appeared to strengthen students' ties with their parents, which in turn predicted improved outcomes. This finding suggests that institutional bridges and cultural brokering may work by augmenting the resources that youth already have within their worlds but are not fully utilizing.

We are just beginning to learn about the contributions and challenges of different kinds of community organizations, including religious organizations. Haight's pioneering ethnographic study of African American children in church reveals how beliefs, practices, and brokering in religious settings can support children's educational pathways (2002). Likewise, Su (2008) found that Buddhist monks served as both cultural and college brokers for Cambodian immigrant youth. In many communities, religious organizations offer intergenerational activities and "culture

Figure 5.3 Religious activities can be important cultural worlds for identity pathways. In Providence, Rhode Island, children dressed as angels walk in a Holy Ghost parade in the Portuguese immigrant community. Reprinted from García Coll et al. (2005), with permission from Taylor & Francis and from Cynthia García Coll.

camps" with weekend and summer programs to help children and adolescents in coordinating their cultural and academic identity pathways (see Figure 5.3). Little has been documented about how these programs work and what qualities distinguish more and less effective activities, although general principles have been developed for effective community organizations serving youth (Eccles & Gootman, 2004).

For individual students, resources and challenges for bridging their worlds of families, peers, schools, and communities may wax and wane along their pathways to adulthood. For some, particularly in rural and conflict-torn areas, such resources are rare (Quijada, 2005). In such communities, schools and community organizations may confront profound obstacles in working to shape curriculum around realities of poverty, violence, and disease.

California: A community program linking family traditions and children's futures with computers

In an after-school program in Santa Barbara, California, a university–community partnership focuses on developing computer-based literacy and empowerment among low-income Latino parents and their children (Durán et al., 2001). Rather than only receiving services, parents have also gained influence in program decision making and activities. Parents made significant gains in their knowledge of computers and writing skills, while both parents and children developed expertise in desktop publishing, making Web pages, and transforming memories reflecting their family and cultural values and histories into written products that were available electronically. At the organizational level, a short-term project became an ongoing community organization. And as university students worked with families and community members, children saw their parents being valued by program staff. It has been more of a challenge to trace the program's impact on students' school language and literacy and to extend benefits to more families. Still, this partnership became part of the nationwide Kellogg ENLACE (Engaging Latino Communities for Education) network of Hispanic-serving university partnerships and broader efforts through the University of California, Santa Barbara to open pathways to college that are described in Chapter 6.

NEXT STEPS

One of the most important findings about linkages across students' cultural worlds is that families are a key factor in students' developing and sustaining their educational and career aspirations from childhood to young adulthood. Although this might be expected among college-educated parents, new research shows that low-income, minority, and immigrant families often inspire and help their children set and maintain these aspirations. So the common view that ethnic minority and low-income parents have low educational goals for their children is a myth. Still, parents who have not attended college in the U.S. may not know the specific steps required for their children to realize these dreams.

So our task is to sustain families' high hopes, not to implant them for the first time in their minds. Schools and community organizations can convey information about achievement tests and grades as well as "college knowledge" about applications, placement tests, and financial aid (Lopez, 2000; Tornatzky, Cutler, & Lee, 2002; Zarate & Meyer, 2007), while treating low-income, ethnic minority, and immigrant families as assets rather than as deficient (Yosso, 2005). As we learn more about how to do this, we also have much to learn about who can serve as cultural and college brokers.

Theories about linkages across students' worlds along the academic pipeline continue to evolve. Epstein has developed her Theory of Overlapping Spheres from focusing on families, schools, and communities as separate spheres to building partnerships and synergies among them (Epstein & Sanders., 2006). This shift has influenced the National PTA to move from "parent/family involvement" in schools (1997) to "family-school partnerships" (2009). Sociocultural researchers have compared teaching based on linking home and school learning with traditional teaching methods (Gutierrez, 2008; Tharp et al., 2002). Sociocultural researchers are also extending their analyses of home-school-community linkages from preschool through the academic pipeline into the college and post-graduate years (Yamauchi, personal communication).

Students' success is often measured in terms of their academic achievements, whether in school grades, standardized test scores, high school graduation, completing college-prep courses, or college enrollment and graduation. We need to understand how students, families, and community members may define their own aspirations for youth in ways that extend beyond school success. Further work is needed to trace more than one dimension of the "good path of life," including cultural, linguistic, and religious identities that keep community traditions alive and give meaning to students' school and career choices.

More delicate and complex issues may emerge when families do understand what it takes to achieve in school or attend college but do not choose that pathway for their children. For example, among low-income families in Appalachia, McIntyre and her team found that some parents held modest career expectations for their children and ranked their living near the extended family as a higher priority than leaving for college (Kyle, McIntyre, Miller, & Moore, 2006). Such attitudes may be difficult for educators and researchers to understand because these goals do not match the "American dream" of upward mobility and achievement. The key to this complex issue is to listen to families and offer choices while respecting what they value and choose. Cultural mismatches continue as to who should define the "good path," a topic to which we return in Chapter 7.

The evidence presented in this chapter holds important implications for teachers' and counselors' preparation and their ongoing professional development. As educators learn how families can enrich the school curriculum, both attitudes and behaviors matter. We need to learn more about how powerfully adults' expectations—high or low—affect students' pathways, and how to move outside of schools to listen to families (Shartrand et al., 1997; Weiss et al., 2010; Zarate & Meyer, 2007). In contrast to viewing immigrant families as endorsing collectivist values that conflict with the individualism of schools, studies show these families' goals and values often match those of schools. Rethinking the commonly described dichotomy between individualism and collectivism can help researchers and educators identify how youth find resources for school and career pathways by building connections across their worlds (Greenfield, 2010; Raeff, 2010).

Many schools and programs acknowledge that families influence students' pathways through school, but sustaining programs that bridge students' worlds remains a challenge (Tierney, Corwin, & Colyear, 2004). The next chapter takes a closer look at how families, peers, schools, and community members can become part of these bridging programs and partnerships. On a promising note, continuing demographic changes and concern for the effectiveness of education in the global context are sparking new coalitions to strengthen diversity along the academic pipeline. A consensus that neither schools nor families nor programs alone can solve the academic pipeline problem has led state and federal agencies, the private sector, and community organizations to form alliances with families, schools, and universities (Cohn, Dowell, Kim, Lindahl, Maldonado, & Seal, 2004). Public agencies and private foundations are forging alliances among research centers, families, schools, community organizations, and universities. These alliances are the focus of the next chapter.

6

FROM FRAGILE BRIDGES TO ALLIANCES
OPENING INSTITUTIONAL OPPORTUNITIES[a]

Despite widely held ideals that youth should be able to advance through school based on their merits and freely explore and choose their future careers, it is clear that many adolescents face institutional obstacles and restricted options for school and work. This chapter examines recent work designed to overcome these obstacles and build institutional bridges along their pathways through school. In principle, such bridges can connect students' families, schools, mentors, and peers along the path to college and help open the academic pipeline. In reality, these bridges may be very fragile, so finding ways to strengthen them is crucial.

CONNECTING WORLDS ALONG PATHWAYS TO COLLEGE

Programs for students who are the first in their families to go to college have strengthened ethnic, racial, and socioeconomic diversity in higher education and college-based professions in the U.S. Similar programs have begun in countries such as the Netherlands, some in collaboration with U.S. partners (Tupan-Wenno, 2009). In the U.S., these programs were first called *outreach programs*, but this name passed out of favor when many who were served by the programs protested that the word "outreach" was condescending. They are now more often called *college-prep*, *pre-college*, or *bridging* programs. Examples include the high school and community college Puente Project (*puente* means "bridge" in Spanish), AVID (Advancement Via Individual Determination), EAOP (Early Academic Outreach Program), MESA (Mathematics, Engineering, Science Achievement), Upward Bound, I Have a Dream,

---

[a] Parts of this chapter were adapted from Cooper (2002), with permission of Taylor & Francis; the chapter also draws on discussions of these issues from Cooper and Mehan (2006).

and GEAR UP (Gaining Early Awareness and Readiness for Undergraduate Programs) (Alvarez & Mehan, 2006; Gándara & Moreno, 2002; Hayward, Brandes, Kirst, & Mazzeo, 1997; Mehan, Hubbard, Villanueva, & Lintz, 1996).

As we discussed in Chapter 4, these programs differ on many dimensions, including the academic skill level required for students' admission and how programs define successful pathways. Some, like EAOP and MESA, can be considered *highly selective* programs, whose graduates typically attend four-year universities. Graduates of *moderately selective* programs, like the Puente Project, typically attend either universities or two-year community colleges, from which they may transfer to four-year institutions (Cooper, 2001). U.S. public schools are—in principle—*inclusive,* offering equal access to college-prep classes, although they do not always do so in practice. One inclusive pre-college program is GEAR UP, which links entire schools in partnerships with universities, community organizations, families, and students. (In contrast, *preventive* programs seek to reduce youth pregnancy, drug use, and gang violence. These programs rarely build pathways to college, although some guide youth toward "second chance" pathways through community colleges and technical training.) Researchers, policymakers, and practitioners are working to analyze the impact of these bridging programs (Gándara & Bial, 2001; Mehan, 2007; Perna & Swail, 2001; Tierney, Corwin, & Colyear, 2004).

The Puente Project, first introduced in California in 1981, provides a useful example of how a long-standing program offers cultural and institutional bridges across students' multiple worlds on their pathways to college and from community college to four-year universities. This program is designed to increase the numbers of Chicano/Latino and other underserved students who become eligible for the University of California and ultimately enroll in four-year colleges and universities. The Puente High School Program admits students from a range of skill levels, with a selective approach that requires participants to enroll in 9th grade college-prep English classes, where the core program activities take place. The Puente Community College Program supports community college students transferring to four-year universities. Puente leaders' openness to collaborations with researchers will give us the unusual opportunity, in this chapter, to learn about these bridges from case studies of Puente students.

The Puente Project's long-term goal is for youth to earn college degrees and "return to their communities as mentors and leaders of future generations" (www. puente.net)—a goal that many youth call "looking up and giving back." Puente's co-designers, Felix Galaviz, a community college counselor, and Patricia McGrath, a community college English teacher, designed five core elements in the high school program to achieve these goals: high school *teachers* providing intensive college-prep English classes in Latino literature in 9th and 10th grades, bicultural school *counselors* guiding students through high school toward college, Latino community professionals acting as *mentors, families* supporting students' pathways to college, and *peer networks* among Puente students supporting one another's college pathways (Duffy, 2005; Gándara & Bial, 2001; Gándara & Moreno, 2002).

In a four-year study of the Puente High School Program, Gándara (2002) compared 1,000 Puente students and 1,000 non-Puente students from 18 high schools, as well as 75 matched pairs of Puente and non-Puente students. Compared to non-Puente students, Puente students held more positive attitudes toward school, stronger preparation for college, and higher aspirations to attend college. Puente students reported going to four-year colleges at nearly double the rate of non-Puente students with the same high school grades and test scores.

Puente students' skills ranged across four levels of achievement and motivation. Based on its requiring applicants to take Algebra 1 in 9th grade while also including a range of academic skill levels, Puente can be considered a selective program. The *highest achievers* began high school with average grades of 3.5 (on a scale from 0 to 4) and aspired to attend four-year colleges and universities. Even so, most showed significant declines in both grades and college aspirations over their high school years. The *moderately high achievers* began high school with average grades of 3.0 but graduated with an average of 2.8, so their college plans focused on state universities or private four-year colleges rather than the more competitive University of California campuses. The *lower-achieving* students began high school with less well-developed skills and modest goals. Their grades averaged 2.5 and dropped to 2.0, but they graduated from high school with plans to attend two-year community colleges and transfer to four-year colleges or universities. Finally, the *lowest-achieving* students began high school with an average of 1.7, but all still wanted to go to college.

The Puente Project elements are designed as social and institutional bridges to link students' worlds along their pathways to college. They can be illustrated with case studies of four high school Puente students who were followed from the time they entered the program in 9th grade through their high school graduation and beyond. I adapted these cases (Cooper, 2002) from material developed by Gándara (n.d.), who intensively studied a sample of 27 students with similar demographic backgrounds: most of their parents were Mexican immigrants with modest levels of formal education, and their families spoke Spanish or both Spanish and English at home. These cases illustrate how individual bridges may function—or falter— on the pathway to college for students who represent a range of academic skill levels.

Families' Involvement: Promoting "the Good Path" to College and Careers

Family involvement is one of the most widely discussed and touted of the bridges in pre-college programs, although the nature and intensity of activities with families vary greatly across these programs (Chrispeels & Gonzalez, 2006; Tierney, 2002; Tierney et al., 2004). Still, students' obligations to their families can be both a resource and challenge. The following case of a moderately high achiever shows how she drew inspiration from her family. She also drew on Puente for academic skills and "college knowledge" and for help coordinating family responsibilities with her new life at college so she could sustain her dream, and that of her father and sister, for her college education.

> When Raquel immigrated to the U.S. with her family, she was in 4th grade. Her parents lacked a formal education and came to this country so their children could get one. Her sister earned her teaching credential and supported Raquel's schooling. Raquel began high school with average grades of 2.6, wanting to go to college but also needing to acquire more English skills. Her grades dropped to 2.1, but she still hoped to go to the University of California. Raquel did not spend time with other Puente students, although her friends said they wanted to go to college. She took geometry in summer school to raise her grades and get back on track to take calculus. When she graduated from high school, she chose to attend the local state university. She still worried about studying at home amidst the pull of her family responsibilities, so her Puente counselor helped her set a study schedule at the library. At the time of her most recent interview, Raquel was doing well and pursuing a degree in business administration. Raquel gave Puente credit for helping her with writing, teaching her about the importance of her GPA, and giving her information about college. She named her father as the person she admired most because he worked so hard to give his family a better life, and she felt a debt for his sacrifices.

Raquel's case shows how a program can offer students bridges as they navigate resources and challenges along their pathway to college. Raquel's family provided crucial emotional and inspirational resources but also challenges, while the program provided both college knowledge and ways to coordinate family and school responsibilities so she could maintain her important family ties and go to college.

Teachers, Counselors, and Schools: Both Enrichment and Bridging

Culturally enriched teaching in English classes is a central part of Puente's mission to make school a relevant and safe place for students to develop their cultural and college identities (Cazden, 2002; Gibson & Hidalgo, 2009; Pradl, 2002). In the following case, a high-achieving student drew inspiration and brokering along his pathway to college from Puente teachers and from counselors, whose help was needed beyond his high school years.

> Andrés finished 9th grade with all As and dreamed of a career in law enforcement and joining the FBI. He lived with his mother and stepfather and helped his mother deliver newspapers early each morning. Although Andrés spoke positively about his biological father, tensions eroded their relationship. Andrés supported his Puente friends by tutoring them and encouraging them to take Advanced Placement and Honors classes. He too took college-prep classes and graduated with a 3.7 average and 1120 SAT score. His counselor and teachers helped him apply to a nearby prestigious four-year college, but his concerns about money and helping his family led him to join the Marine Corps Reserves

to help pay for college. He attended community college, joined its Puente program, and maintained a 3.5 average, with plans to graduate from the local state university.

Some policymakers argue that high-achieving students like Andrés do not need programs to make it to college, and programs should invest in more vulnerable or "at-risk" students. These critics call selecting high-achieving students for pre-college programs "creaming," like skimming cream from the top of milk. The critics say that such students will succeed without special help. However, these students' personal lives, responsibilities, and financial challenges can make their pathways to college uncertain. Especially when students' families are unfamiliar with the educational system, but also when family life brings ongoing challenges, the continuing support from teachers and counselors in programs like Puente appears to provide students with a crucial bridge from high school into college (Gándara & Bial, 2001; Gándara & Contreras, 2009).

Community Mentors: A View of the Future

Community mentors, from a diverse range of ethnic backgrounds, can act as cultural and college brokers when they help students gain educational experiences and bicultural skills for success in school (Cooper, Denner, & Lopez, 1999). In her study of Puente community mentors, Mejorado (2000) found that these mentors helped by accepting how youth defined their own success, providing tutoring, teaching time management and how to choose friends, talking about the future, and going with youth on field trips. Mentors provided both support and challenges when students' grades slipped. Mejorado found that students with stronger relations with their mentors made higher English and math grades and were more likely to become eligible for university admission. Still, the Puente mentoring component appears, like family involvement activities, to be one of the more fragile bridges in the program: it is a persistent challenge to implement and sustain mentor relationships (Gándara, 2002). Carlos's story shows that mentors can inspire even the most vulnerable students and provide them with college knowledge as well.

> Carlos, one of Puente's lower-achieving students as he entered high school, credited his mentor in the program for his caring about college and learning how to prepare for a future career. Carlos was determined to do better than his brothers. He started high school with low grades—a 1.5 GPA in 9th grade—and improved to 3.5, although he slipped to 2.9 as he began cutting classes. He chose friends outside of the Puente program who pressured him to cut school. After a fight at school, he was asked to leave the program, but Carlos ultimately graduated from another high school.

Carlos' story illustrates that effective mentors can spark a sense of purpose for students to stay in school, whether or not they continue to college. We will benefit from further studies about why some mentoring relationships succeed and others falter at different points along students' pathways (e.g., Chemers, Syed, Goza, Zurbriggen, Bearman, Crosby, et al., 2010). And we also have more to learn from longitudinal studies into young adulthood about vulnerable youth like Carlos. Among the possible directions his pathway may take, Carlos has the prospects for a "second chance" pathway by returning to school, a pattern we examine more closely in Chapter 7.

Peers: Crucial Resources and Continuing Challenges

Peers can make school and pre-college programs appealing. Along the academic pipeline, peers can provide emotional and practical support for going to college, but youth may also find it difficult to maintain ties to neighborhood friends who do not understand their college dreams and accuse them of being pretentious and disloyal (Azmitia & Cooper, 2001; Cooper et al., 1995). The following case illustrates that peers may enhance Puente's effectiveness, but they can also create challenges for students trying to navigate pathways to college.

> Ofelia, one of the higher-achieving students, credited her Puente peer study group and her boyfriend with her academic comeback. Ofelia came to the U.S. when she was seven. She began high school with a 3.8 GPA and hoped to become a doctor, lawyer, or corporate executive. To help pay for college, she wanted to join the military or go to the Naval Academy. Her parents separated when she was young, and she spent most of her childhood with foster families. Her mother had an elementary education and found it difficult to maintain a stable home and work life. When her mother was imprisoned on drug-related charges, Ofelia had to augment the family's income and lived with her older brother and later with her boyfriend's family. Taking on several jobs to help support herself took a toll on her health and grades, which fluctuated from a high of 3.7 to failing all her courses. She took night classes and went to summer school to make up the failed courses and raise her grades. She often studied with Puente friends. She graduated with a 2.4 average and 900 SAT score, and enrolled in a state university with financial aid. Although Puente staff encouraged her to stay, she eventually returned home, where she and her boyfriend enrolled in the local community college.

Ofelia's story illustrates how peers are often the most controversial of students' worlds. As detailed in Chapter 5, peers can be both powerful resources and daunting challenges, as readers will note in many of the students' comments throughout this book.

Taken together, these four cases direct our attention to the shifting and sometimes daunting challenges youth face across their worlds as they forge their college and career identities. The rich details of these students' lives, gathered in personal interviews, reveal nuances that would be missed by standardized survey questions with multiple-choice answer formats. Programs like Puente can expand the resources youth draw from each world and help them balance expectations across worlds. However, even after graduating from high school, many Puente students worried about school and continuing issues with their families and peers, so they needed sustained academic and emotional support. These four cases also point to future vulnerabilities, with many students leaving for college still tentative about their decisions and feeling homesick and isolated. Through their college years, students continue to benefit from support, whether emotional, instrumental, or both (Engstrom & Tinto, 2008; Kuh, Kinzie, Buckley, Bridges, & Hayek, 2006).

Programs, students and families, researchers, administrators, legislators, and education writers can all be partners in keeping academic pipelines open. Unfortunately, programs have proliferated with few studies of who participates over time, what activities help which students, and how programs develop as organizations. Ironically, many program activities are underused, an important issue for future research (Gándara & Bial, 2001; Gándara & Contreras, 2009).

In their analysis of pre-college programs across the U.S., Gándara and Bial (2001) found that programs like Puente recruit individual students and their families, screen applicants with various selection criteria, and group students into classes. (These practices are typical of highly and moderately selective programs.) What program evaluators call *dosage* effects indicate that spending more time in these programs is linked to greater benefits. Inevitably, most serve some students and miss others, and their impact fades when their services end. Gándara and Bial (2001) conclude that modest gains in grades and test scores indicate that many programs start too late—most in high school—and do not operate sufficiently long or intensively.

Our goal in looking at these cases is to consider how students' cultural worlds can be resources but also present challenges, and how the institutional bridges that support these worlds can be surprisingly fragile. So we need to learn about how to strengthen these fragile bridges and their connections to one another along the path to college. Students' relations with caring and knowledgeable adults appear crucial, but research on mentoring programs has just begun to answer basic questions (Larson, Pearce, Sullivan, & Jarrett, 2007). The same is true for the role of supportive friends and peer group "convoys" as students navigate their pathways to college (Antonucci, Birditt, Akiyama, Bengston, Gans, et al., 2009; Horn & Chen, 2002; Levitt, in press). We also need greater understanding of students' cultural and family traditions in their college-going identities as new cohorts of students become more culturally diverse (Tierney et al., 2004). Finally, the impact of financial pressures, seen in the stories of Puente students Andrés and Ofelia, indicates that financial aid counseling—if not scholarships—could be a bridge that is even more crucial in difficult economic times, although most programs, including Puente, cannot provide scholarships.

Taken separately, individual bridges along the path to college can have an impact, and evidence is growing for the effectiveness of bridging programs (University of California Office of the President, 2010). However, the next section shows how erratic funding policies make such bridges fragile and proposes a new strategy for strengthening bridges and their interconnections.

INTEGRATING BRIDGES INTO P–20 ALLIANCES

Closing the education gap has been a rising priority on policy agendas across the U.S. (Achieve, Inc., 2009a, 2009b; Business-Higher Education Forum, 2001, 2004, 2005; University of California Board of Regents, 2003, 2005). Achieve, Inc. (www. achieve.org), the American Diploma Project (www.americandiplomaproject.org), and the Education Trust (www.edtrust.org), among others, are national organizations dedicated to opening the academic pipeline. In California, for example, the University of California Board of Regents adopted its *Policy Affirming Engagement in the Preschool through Postsecondary Education System as Fundamental to the University of California Mission as a Land Grant Institution*:

> As a land grant institution with a mission of teaching, research, and public service, the University of California is committed to excellence and equity in education for all of California's students to secure the social well-being and economic prosperity of the individual and the state. The University affirms that a fundamental part of its mission is to engage in efforts to promote the academic achievement and success of all students, including students who, because they are educationally disadvantaged and underrepresented, therefore need additional assistance. . . . It is essential that the University work in collaboration with public and private sector organizations that share these responsibilities; in particular California schools, community colleges, universities, community organizations, and students' families (University of California Board of Regents, 2005, p. 1).

This policy is consistent with a growing national consensus that more inclusive and seamless educational systems are key to our civic and economic future (Venezia, 2004). *P–20 alliances*, spanning from preschool through professional or graduate school, have developed partnerships to improve services and extend innovations to underserved communities beyond their initial service regions. P–20 alliances in university systems involve extensive cross-campus coordination, communication, and research.

Erratic funding can threaten effective pre-college programs and the alliances among them. One example can be seen in the dramatic rise and fall of state funding for educational partnerships in California. In 1996, the level of funding was $15,354,000. By 2000, a plan to open access to the University of California in light of Proposition 209, a policy that banned affirmative action, raised funding to $101,805,000. A statewide financial crisis then triggered a series of funding cuts—to $34,992,000 in 2002 and $29,594,000 in 2010 (University of California Office of the President, 2010). The impact of this rise and fall could be seen first in the expansion and then reduction of program services statewide. However, perhaps in response to shrinking resources, there has been a growth in alliances among programs to augment effectiveness.

Developmental Approaches to Educational Equity and Access

As demographic and political changes across the U.S. have sparked concerns about equity in access to higher education, the U.S. Office for Civil Rights (2004) decided that new policies and practices were needed to expand from *admissions* approaches of competitive universities—that focus on the point of admission to the university— to *developmental* approaches that start early to prepare all students for college, workforce, and civic participation. This shift evolved from policy debates about affirmative action and the role of race and ethnicity in university admissions, as well as from evidence from studies such as those presented in this book. In line with the shift to developmental approaches, the University of California redefined its goal to increase diversity in its campus enrollments with the broader goal of opening the academic pipeline more generally (2003).

The goal of P–20 alliances to include all students in their educational activities distinguishes them from selective programs. These alliances seek to engage the full range of student populations, achievement levels, and family circumstances in their regions and to enhance cooperation and coordination among programs with similar goals—such as AVID, GEAR UP, and EAOP. In contrast, most individual programs, of necessity, can serve only some students in their regions, so they choose students based on criteria such as having passed Algebra 1 by 9th grade, English proficiency, or families pledging to participate in program activities (Gándara et al., 1998; Mehan, Villanueva, Hubbard, & Lintz, 1996; Myers & Schirm, 1999).

Often called P–20 or K–16 alliances, these collaborations extend from preschool through graduate and professional schools into adult work and community roles. Their leaders aspire to link local, state, and national educational systems by working with business partners, public agencies, community organizations, private foundations, academic preparation programs, and students' families. Their goals are to improve students' learning and college opportunities, thereby enhancing their civic and economic well-being and those of their wider communities (Gomez, Bissell, Danziger, & Casselman, 1990; Houck, Cohn, & Cohn, 2004; Moran, Cooper, Goza, & López, 2009).

For example, alliances in California collaborate with national groups such as the GEAR UP program of the U.S. Department of Education, the Education Trust K–16 Councils, Collaborating for Educational Reform Initiative (Bodilly, Chun, Ikemoto, & Stockly, 2001), ENLACE, the National Council of Community and Education Partnerships (NCCEP), the Pathways to College Network, the National Network of Partnership Schools (Epstein, 2001a, 2001b), and the American Bar Association's P–20 Consortium.

P–20 alliances in California have attracted funding from federal and state agencies and private foundations and individuals. Funding agencies value three common features of these alliances: their improving student learning with strategies that reflect distinctive regional issues; working as partners rather than with one-way outreach in local schools and community organizations; and the contributions of college faculty in attracting funding and teaching service learning classes that support the K–12, undergraduate, and graduate students.

In California, these alliances now involve the 10 University of California campuses, the 23 California State Universities, and other public and private colleges and universities. In many cases, alliances collaborate with the Alliance of Regional Collaboration to Heighten Educational Success (ARCHES) and the California Academic Partnership Program (CAPP) of the California State University System.

Readers can investigate alliances in their own regions or other regions that use approaches compatible with their own. Many alliances maintain Web sites with materials that can be adapted to other settings. For example, in one rural county, the California Academic Partnership Program has supported college tours, an "SAT bus" (transporting youth to take their college entrance exams), and the writing and distributing of *Tasha Goes to University*, an illustrated story of how a Yurok Native American girl applies for and attends a university without losing her family ties and place singing in her tribe's ceremonial dances (Kurtz, 2009). The sequel, *Tasha Comes Home* (Kurtz, 2010), recounts Tasha's return to her tribe to teach high school classes in the Yurok language, by drawing on the practices of the Hawaiian language revival described in Chapter 5. Such narrative materials can be assets for cultural bridges to college in many settings.

BUILDING A COMMON LANGUAGE

Like advances in technology and medicine, improving P–20 educational systems can usefully draw on evidence across scientific fields. Just as physical scientists view water as both individual molecules and continuous wave systems, social scientists study the flow of culturally diverse students through school systems by tracing changes in both individual students and educational systems. Aligning concepts and models across fields holds the promise of building a common language to unify and advance progress in research, educational practice, and policy investments. Cross-disciplinary work is proving valuable for mapping how the intersections of personal, social, institutional, and cultural factors can support student pathways. As in all scientific research, conclusions about effective approaches are based on systematic observation, testing predictions over time, controlled experiments, and comparing a range of field settings—from rural counties to urban neighborhoods—across culturally diverse communities and regions.

To advance a common language for progress on the academic pipeline problem, Jeannie Oakes, then director of the University of California All-Campus Consortium on Diversity (UC ACCORD), worked with a team of scholars from education, sociology, anthropology, and psychology to align evidence across these fields. From this synthesis, Oakes (2003) proposed seven critical conditions for equity in access to college:

1) safe and adequate facilities
2) a college-going school culture
3) a rigorous academic curriculum
4) qualified teachers
5) academic and social supports from adults and peers

6) opportunities for youth to develop a multicultural college-going identity
7) family–school–neighborhood connections.

Of course, alliance leaders must adapt these services based on evolving and locally defined goals, assets, and constraints. Still, when my colleagues and I surveyed P–20 alliance leaders across the 10 UC campuses, we found that each regional alliance targeted more than one of these conditions across multiple segments of their educational systems (Cooper, Mehan, & Halimah, 2006). The matrix in Table 6.1 shows that almost all 10 of the campus alliances offered academic and social support to middle and high school students, and many supported students' multicultural college-going identities and teachers' professional development in middle and high school. Two were building family—neighborhood—school connections of preschoolers as they move to elementary school. This matrix became a useful road map to coordinate local realities in each region with a shared model across regions.

The following sections describe how P–20 alliances can draw on complementary scholarly approaches to organize, deliver, and evaluate services that embody the common language and principles for fostering access to higher education

Table 6.1 Number of UC campuses (of 10) Reporting Activities to Support Each of Seven College-Going Conditions (Oakes, 2003)

7 Conditions for Equity and Diversity in College Access	PreK	Elementary	Middle School	High School	Community College and University	Graduate and Prof. School
Safe and Adequate School Facilities	1	1	3	3	1	1
College-Going School Culture	2	4	8	9	6	2
Rigorous Academic Curriculum	3	5	9	8	4	2
Qualified Teachers	3	7	9	8	5	4
Intensive Academic and Social Supports	1	3	9	8	5	
Opportunities for Multi-Cultural College-Going Identity		5	9	8	4	3
Family-Neighborhood-School Connections	2	6	9	9	5	

P–20 partnerships link research, policy, and practice with a common framework. Leaders at the 10 University of California campuses aligned their services along the academic pipeline with seven conditions for increasing access to college. Most offer academic and social support in middle and high school; two start college-going activities at preschool/kindergarten.

proposed by Oakes (2003) and her team. Alliances may start from distinctive scholarly viewpoints, but many show evidence of effectiveness in opening the academic
pipeline.

Bridging Institutions with a College-Going Culture

Sociologists describe schools that disrupt cultural reproduction by sending more
low-income students to college as building a *college-going culture* (Alvarez & Mehan,
2006; McClafferty, McDonough, & Núñez, 2002; McDonough, 2004a; Mehan,
2007; Mehan et al., 1996). Drawing on Bourdieu's writings about social and cultural
capital (1986), Patricia McDonough and her colleagues at UCLA analyzed how
schools enhance their college-going cultures by providing: "college talk," clear
expectations that all students will have the choice of going to college, information
and resources about college-going, comprehensive counseling, college-prep testing
and curriculum, faculty and family involvement, college partnerships, and better
alignment across the educational system (McClafferty et al., 2002, p. 6).

Alliances at UC Berkeley and UC San Diego have adapted McDonough's
model of college-going culture in designing college-preparatory schools. At UC San
Diego, sociologist Bud Mehan, director of the Center for Research on Educational
Equity, Assessment, and Teaching Excellence (CREATE), played a central role in
designing the Preuss School on the campus (Alvarez & Mehan, 2006). This middle
and high school serves primarily African American and Latino youth from low-
income families whose parents did not graduate from a four-year college. Students
are chosen by a lottery among eligible applicants. Preuss staff foster a college-going
culture through college-prep classes, intensive academic and social supports (including a longer school day and school year), advisory classes, college visits, tutors from
UC San Diego, links between middle and high school, and continuing interaction
with Preuss graduates.

Preuss students are building college-going identities (Khalil, Morales, & Mehan,
2006): in one survey, over 90% of 8th, 11th, and 12th grade students agreed that, "I
am confident that I will continue on to university studies when I graduate from
Preuss." More than 80% of the first three graduating classes enrolled in highly competitive colleges and universities.

From students' perspectives, their teachers, school peers, and Preuss alumni are
resources for their pathways to college. Still, navigating across their cultural worlds
can be difficult: most Preuss students (66.7%) reported feeling that their friends at
Preuss understood their lives at school, but most (65.3%) also felt that their neighborhood peers did not (Khalil et al., 2006). Despite evidence of success for many
Preuss students, CREATE researchers are cautious:

> Before we gleefully conclude that the hierarchy of access is being dismantled, we must
> witness more sustained efforts—those that are institutionalized, survive through time,
> and are instantiated in many different locations (Khalil et al., 2006, p. 51).

CREATE leaders are working with local businesses, schools, government agencies, nonprofit organizations, churches, and parent groups to help other schools adapt practices from the Preuss School to their local realities (Mehan, 2007). Locating the Preuss School on a university campus conveys the expectation that students are college material. Such a setting cannot be a solution for all communities but offers a "field station" for learning about the conditions under which youth can succeed.

Bridging Cultures: Connecting Families, Communities, Schools, and Universities

As discussed throughout this book, when schools see low-income, immigrant, and ethnic minority families as resources for students' school success rather than only in terms of risk factors or cultural mismatches, schools can engage families as cultural partners. Oakes calls this building *family–neighborhood–school connections* (2003) and Tierney, a *culture-sensitive* approach (2004). One example of this approach is the Parent Institute for Quality Education (PIQE), supported by all 23 campuses of the California State University System. PIQE helps immigrant parents learn about the U.S. education system and how to help their children with homework. PIQE has taught its 9-week curriculum in 16 different languages (www.piqe.org). In a related approach, the Parent-School Partnership (PSP) curriculum of the Mexican American Legal Defense Fund (www.maldef.org/psp), parents attend workshops designed to build confidence and skills in advocating for their children at school and supporting their children's pathways to college.

As part of its P–20 alliance with UC Santa Barbara, the Santa Ana Partnership based at Santa Ana College offers the *Padres Promotores de la Educación* (Parent Education Promoters Program). It mentors Latino parent leaders, who visit more than 1,000 homes annually and hold informal discussion groups, or *pláticas*, with parents in laundromats and other community settings. The eight-lesson bilingual curriculum, *Padre à padre (Parent to parent): Lessons to guide the path toward higher education* (Santa Ana Partnership, 2006; www.sac.edu/community/partnerships/sapartnership/) compares educational systems in the U.S. and Latin America and explains high school graduation requirements, college options, and financial aid. Surveys of parents who completed the program revealed their growing confidence in "discussing their child's educational progress with teachers, counselors, and school administrators" and "knowing how to help their child participate in public school and prepare for college" (Tanakeyowma, 2008). However, assessing effects of the program on children's high school graduation and college attendance has not yet been done (Lundquist, Martinez, & Harrizon, 2008; Tanakeyowma & Castellanos, 2009).

Work is underway to develop common measures of the nature and benefit of the services that P–20 alliances offer to open the academic pipeline. For example, the California GEAR UP program developed a School Self Assessment Rubric (California GEAR UP, 2009) that offers a self rating scales for six of the seven college-going conditions proposed by Oakes (2003). As shown in the example in

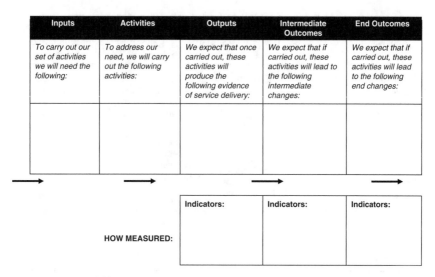

Inputs	Activities	Outputs	Intermediate Outcomes	End Outcomes
To carry out our set of activities we will need the following:	To address our need, we will carry out the following activities:	We expect that once carried out, these activities will produce the following evidence of service delivery:	We expect that if carried out, these activities will lead to the following intermediate changes:	We expect that if carried out, these activities will lead to the following end changes:

HOW MEASURED: | Indicators: | Indicators: | Indicators: |

Figure 6.1 *Logic model for P–20 partnerships:* The University of California Office of the President developed this logic model template for reporting to the California legislature about how P–20 partnerships and program activities align with student learning outcomes (adapted from Halimah, 2005).

Figure 6.1, alliances across the U.S. are using logic models to build a common language in partnerships (see Coffman, 1999 for guidelines on logic models with family/school/community partners).

Bridging Generations: Connecting Pathways of Youth, College Students, and Adults

Recent longitudinal studies show that youth who stay on track or get back on track to college and careers tap resources in themselves and across their cultural worlds. And they do so not in spite of their parents' and grandparents' poverty and modest formal education but because of their challenges and with their support. Alliances that bridge across generations can support youth on their identity pathways to college by building intergenerational connections, not only in families but also among students of different ages. In the framework proposed by Oakes (2003), these offer opportunities for multicultural college-going identities.

For example, the UC Santa Cruz Educational Partnership Center (EPC) developed a P–20 alliance that connects partner programs from childhood to college and careers, as shown in Figure 6.2 (Moran, Cooper, Goza, & López, 2009). As part of its federally funded GEAR UP programs, the EPC developed a bilingual college awareness curriculum and evaluation tools to enhance the college knowledge of students, families, and middle school teachers. The goal is to sustain children and families' aspirations and build math and language pathways to college (Moran et al., 2005). In intergenerational teams, undergraduate and graduate

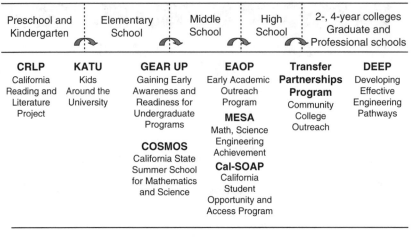

Preschool and Kindergarten	Elementary School	Middle School	High School	2-, 4-year colleges Graduate and Professional schools

CRLP	**KATU**	**GEAR UP**	**EAOP**	**Transfer**	**DEEP**
California Reading and Literature Project	Kids Around the University	Gaining Early Awareness and Readiness for Undergraduate Programs	Early Academic Outreach Program	**Partnerships Program** Community College Outreach	Developing Effective Engineering Pathways
		COSMOS California State Summer School for Mathematics and Science	**MESA** Math, Science Engineering Achievement **Cal-SOAP** California Student Opportunity and Access Program		

UCSC Educational Partnership Center

Figure 6.2 *Aligning programs along the academic pipeline in a P–20 alliance:* One P–20 alliance, the Educational Partnership Center at the University of California, Santa Cruz, aligns its partner programs from childhood to college and careers. Key strands focus on pathways to algebra and STEM careers (science, technology, engineering, and mathematics).

students serve as tutors, research assistants, and in other leadership roles that build their own career pathways. The "20" of P–20 can be seen as these graduate students complete master's and doctoral degrees and move into leadership roles, including the professoriate (Burciaga, 2008).

The EPC has also forged intergenerational bridges through cross-age peer mentoring that creates long-term networks of support for pathways to college. For example, the Youth Leadership Program creates student networks that start in 8th grade and continue through college. Students plan the annual Youth Leadership Conference, which brings 8th graders to a weekend camp at the university to provide college-prep information and link them with older peer mentors, who guide them on a college-going pathway through high school. Many mentors stay involved after they go on to college by arranging visits to their campus for high school students. Some students have participated in the program for eight years, bringing younger siblings into the program and returning each year for the conference and building the support network.

In the work of the EPC, gains can be seen in math and language arts grades and in rising rates of university eligibility, applications, admissions, and enrollment, as well as transfers from community colleges to four-year universities. Figure 6.3 shows the rising numbers of students from UCSC partner high schools attending UC compared to the state average. These are especially notable because students in UCSC partner high schools are more likely to be the first in their families to attend college.

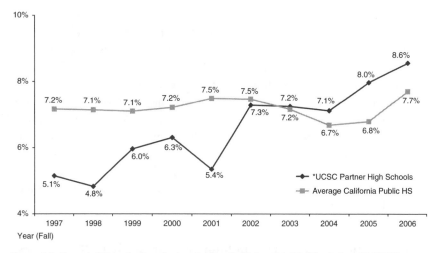

Figure 6.3 *Percent of high school graduates attending the University of California from 13 UCSC partner high schools compared to state average.* In its 13 partner high schools, the Educational Partnership Center at the University of California, Santa Cruz, mapped rising numbers of students attending UC compared to state averages. (Data courtesy of the UCSC Educational Partnership Center).

NEXT STEPS FOR RESEARCH, POLICY, AND PRACTICE

P–20 alliances to open the academic pipeline have been established in at least 38 states across the U.S. (Kirst & Venezia, 2004; Núñez & Oliva, 2009). To some extent, their goals and activities reflect the educational systems and political discourse of each state.

Why should states, universities, private foundations, public agencies, community organizations, and educators invest in these alliances? Our civic and economic future depends on an educated workforce and population. Monitoring students' progress through school to careers can foster accountability and improvement for state, private, and federal investments. The next steps for P–20 alliances involve building a common language to align their activities, indicators of student learning, and organizational effectiveness.

From Benchmarks to Levers of Change

P–20 alliances across the U.S. are investing in ongoing coordination, defining common goals, and aligning outcome measures (Bodilly et al., 2004; Núñez & Oliva, 2009). Growing numbers of alliances are developing student-level longitudinal data systems that link P–12 to postsecondary systems (Education Trust-West, 2010; Ewell, Schild, & Paulson, 2003). These include Maryland, Texas, North Carolina, Tennessee, and Florida, with Florida having the most fully developed system. One alliance links data from the college-prep activities in which students participated to their academic outcomes (Compton Unified School District, 2004.)

These data systems require consistent definitions and secure, unique student identifiers to link databases across the segments of the academic pipeline. Linking these databases—even incrementally—and obtaining resources to maintain and analyze them are crucial next steps (Vernez, Krop, Vuollo, & Hansen, 2008).

Although advocates of longitudinal data systems see them as essential for gauging cause–effect relations, partnerships need more than demographic and student learning data to close the education gap. Drawing on research expertise is crucial for moving beyond these benchmarks to analyzing how the actions of educators, families, and students become the mechanisms of improvement. In our experience, combining "narratives and numbers" through longitudinal case studies and quantitative analyses is an engaging strategy for these partnerships both to monitor their work and communicate about it to others.

Shifting Sands of Policy and Building Investments in P–20 Alliances

Sustaining P–20 alliances for long-term outcomes can be daunting, especially with tightening budgets and ongoing political debates around diversity and educational opportunities. Critics of this approach, including those in private and public policy roles, have pointed to the slow pace of progress, competition for scarce funding, and difficulties reaching across bureaucratic divides along the academic pipeline (Dean & Levine, 2008; Winograd, 2007).

Still, a remarkable number of alliances have proven resilient, and investments are growing in many states in both established and new alliances, despite erratic funding levels in some states. California's Alliance for Regional Collaboration to Heighten Educational Success (ARCHES) has invested in new regional collaborations across California by drawing on expertise from more seasoned ones (Siri, 2005). Partnerships increasingly support students being able to prepare for the university and technical careers through the same courses, instead of being tracked into either college-prep or vocational classes. Educators are adapting classes in the health professions, digital media, public safety, agriculture, and engineering so the same courses count for both college and career preparation (Mehan, 2007).

The U.S. National Governors' Association, including 30 of its 50 member states, has also been working to align accountability across federal laws that affect different segments of the academic pipeline. These laws include the preschool Head Start program, No Child Left Behind (NCLB) Act, Individuals with Disabilities Act, Carl Perkins Vocational-Technical Act, Higher Education Act, and Workforce Investment Act. Proponents expect that such alignment will enhance standards-based reforms and leverage federal funds, while eliminating duplication and inconsistencies. As the P–20 strategy moves forward, advances in policy accountability, scientific work, and educational practices can strengthen one another.

The emerging findings presented in this chapter document the growing effectiveness of a range of approaches to opening institutional opportunities for higher education. Continued efforts will be important to align these still-fragile bridges into a systemic whole that is available to all students—thereby transforming the academic pipeline. Defining and creating successful pathways for all students are the themes of the next chapter. We will also take a closer look at the Bridging Multiple Worlds model, which is designed to bring the analysis of the resources and challenges from students' cultural worlds into a single framework.

7

SOLEDAD'S DREAM

HOW IMMIGRANT YOUTH AND A PARTNERSHIP BUILD PATHWAYS TO COLLEGE[a]

with
Elizabeth Domínguez and Soledad Rosas

The last of the five major questions addressed in this book asks: How do communities define success for their youth and themselves in cultural terms? This question will lead us to consider when multicultural communities see their ideal as cultural homogeneity and thus view diversity as a deficit or threat to overcome, or when multicultural communities seek ways to build more than one successful pathway for all of their youth.

We begin by looking at the pathway of one young woman, Soledad Rosas[b], and a partnership between a community program and university researchers. Soledad participated in this program from 6th grade through high school and has continued as a partner through college and beyond.

Soledad was born in central Mexico and came to California as a young child with her family. Both of her parents went to elementary school (*primaria*) in rural Mexico. When they immigrated to a rural California community, her father painted houses and her mother stayed at home to care for her[c] as they dreamed of college and professional careers for their children. We begin to hear Soledad's story at age 11, when she wrote an application essay in Spanish for a community college bridging program about her ideal job, her resources, and her obstacles:

> I would like to write stories that will teach children many things, like becoming interested in reading. I want to help my community by finding economic resources so that the

---

[a] Parts of this chapter are adapted from Cooper, Domínguez, and Rosas (2005), with permission of Taylor & Francis.

[b] Soledad's real name is used at her request, but all other students' names are fictitious.

[c] As Soledad remembers, "Mother stayed home for most of the time until I was in the university. This was a great help and key for my overall success in school."

children don't leave their studies and other things.... My obstacles are that I have cerebral palsy. Another obstacle is the English language.

At age 13, as a participant in the program's Summer Institute, Soledad wrote in English:

I want to be a writer and a DJ at a radio station. I have decided to go to [the University of California at] Berkeley. I want to go to Berkeley because it has a program for disabled people and I have problems like that. The college is close but not too close.... My challenges are my disability, working to pay for college, and having problems in college.... My resources are my teachers, college, books, and DJs of other radio stations.

At age 15, Soledad read five of her poems, in English and Spanish, on her first radio appearance and encouraged her listeners to become writers themselves (See Figure 7.1). By age 16, she had started her own weekly show on a university public radio station, entitled *Teen Power/Poder de Juventud*, that featured an eclectic blend of Latino music, soccer score announcements, guest interviews, and call-in participation from her listening audience. At 19, Soledad continued her show while completing her first year at the local community college. She co-taught a summer class for youth on radio broadcasting, in which she taught younger students. After transferring to a four-year university, she majored in broadcast journalism and completed

Figure 7.1A Soledad Rosas at age 15 reads her poems on her first radio broadcast, with the guidance of graduate student Cathy Angelillo. © Catherine Cooper.

Figure 7.1B At age 19, Soledad hosts her own radio show, Teen Power/*Poder de Juventud*. © Catherine Cooper; both photos reprinted with permission by Taylor & Francis.

an internship at a radio station. Now a college graduate, she is planning her own radio show and hopes to have it sponsored by a commercial radio station.

Like Soledad and her family, generations of immigrant families have come to the U.S. and other countries with dreams of a better life for their children. Although some immigrants come as war refugees trying to save their lives (García-Coll, Szalacha, & Palacios, 2005), many also come with dreams of education for their sons and daughters (Azmitia et al., 1996; Cooper et al., 2005; Rumbaut, 2000; Suárez-Orozco et al., 2008). As Soledad explained, her dream "to help my community by finding economic resources so children don't leave their studies" grew from her mother's stories of Mexico, where she left school to help support her family.

In the U.S., Mexican-heritage students and families are of special interest on issues of culture, identity, and pathways to college. Although they have been the largest immigrant group and the largest group among Latinos in the 1990 and 2000 U.S. census counts (Immigration and Naturalization Service, 2002), Mexican-descent youth are dramatically underrepresented in higher education. Still, we must be cautious in generalizing our findings to other immigrant communities and to Mexican immigrants in other receiving countries.

HOW DO MULTICULTURAL COMMUNITIES DEFINE SUCCESS FOR THEIR YOUTH AND FOR THEMSELVES?

To address the question of what is success, this chapter continues examining the role of capital, alienation, and challenge models. We also consider how one challenge model, the Bridging Multiple Worlds model, helps to illuminate students' experiences navigating their pathways and how communities define success for their youth. As shown in Figure 7.2, the model targets five dimensions:

1) *family demographics*—national origin, ethnicities, home languages, and parents' education and occupations—that reflect access to education among students moving along their pathways to college compared to those who leave school
2) *youth aspirations and identity pathways to college and careers*
3) *math and language academic pathways through school*
4) *challenges and resources* across the worlds of families, peers, schools, and communities
5) *cultural research partnerships* between universities and communities that can boost the resources youth draw from each world as they build pathways to college and adulthood.

A PROGRAM AND A PARTNERSHIP

We have conducted the studies highlighted in this chapter in a cultural research partnership with a community college bridging program, the Cabrillo Advancement Program (CAP), which serves about 500 children and youth at any one time. The program has awarded $1000 scholarships (recently increased to $2000), donated

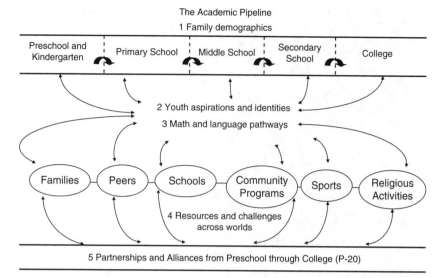

Figure 7.2 The Bridging Multiple Worlds Theory models how youth develop their identities as they navigate pathways from childhood through school (Cooper, 2003). This theory traces five dimensions over time to ask how ethnically diverse youth build their pathways to college and careers without giving up their ties to their families and cultural communities.

by local businesses and individuals, to 6th graders from low-income families. The students can use their scholarships when they enroll in Cabrillo Community College. A yearly cycle of activities helps students stay on track from 6th grade to their high school graduation and college enrollment. Academic, college, and career guidance take place in an annual week-long Summer Institute as well as in Saturday Academies that take place each fall and spring, in addition to year-round tutoring at students' schools, individual meetings with the program director, and family activities. Robert Swenson, president of the community college when CAP began, was inspired to create CAP in 1991 by Eugene Lang's "I Have a Dream" Program in New York City (for a program evaluation of the latter, see Kahne & Bailey, 1999). Figure 7.3 shows students exploring their career identities at the CAP program's Summer Institute.

Elizabeth Domínguez, the program director, created a cultural research partnership with our university research team in 1994 to learn how CAP works and help it improve. The partnership is ongoing and includes regular meetings to identify questions and integrate data collection and analysis with program activities. Program staff and youth participate in data collection, analysis, and interpretation, and university students help with program planning, activities, and communicating with donors (Denner et al., 1999). Partners have asked questions such as: Who participates and who is missing? Who comes to specific program activities, such as tutoring? Do students' grades rise and fall or are they stable? How do peers influence pathways to college and careers? How useful do program alumni find the program activities?

Figure 7.3 In a CAP Summer Institute, students learned about careers in the health professions, public safety, agriculture, and in engineering and technology. Here, students learn how to detect fingerprints in a class about careers in public safety. Photo courtesy of Elizabeth Domínguez.

A key event for the partnership is the annual Summer Institute. Beginning in 1996, students have written about their college and career goals, charted their math and English pathways, and described their challenges and resources in building their pathways through school. Youth have also reflected on the partnership findings, contributed their ideas for improving the Summer Institute, and described how the program has affected their lives. The partnership created a longitudinal database for students' program records, application essays, school grades, and Summer Institute writings.

One of our longitudinal studies with the program has focused on 116 students (76 females and 40 males) who entered the program at age 11 or 12 (in 6th or 7th grades). The students live in two adjacent communities in one California county, 34% in a small city with a majority European American population in "north county" and 66% in a slightly smaller, predominantly Spanish-speaking community in "south county." The community college is located midway between the two communities.

The partnership has drawn on census data; the perspectives of students, parents, teachers, and program staff; and observations by university graduate students and faculty. To tap students' views, we adapted the Bridging Multiple Worlds Survey originally developed for high school youth (described in Chapters 2 and 4) into a bilingual activity format called *It's All About Choices/Se Trata De Todas Las Decisiones: Activities to Build Identity Pathways to College and Careers* (Domínguez, Cooper, Chavira, Mena, Lopez, Dunbar, et al., 2001). These activities, with embedded measures, have become a regular part of Summer Institute classes.

Group Patterns over Time

Enriching the benefits of demographic data:
Who came? Who was missing?

Over the years, the partnership has explored ways to increase the benefits of demographic data for the program. We gathered demographic data when we asked students, "Who is in your family?" "Where were your parents born?" "How far did they go in school?" "What are their jobs?" We also tracked age and gender patterns in who came and who was missing from program activities, and we showed students the evidence that fewer boys than girls and fewer high school than middle school students attended the Summer Institute, a pattern that mirrors the national academic pipeline problem.

Students who participated in the program were primarily Latino, and of these, almost all of Mexican descent. Their parents' formal education, usually in rural Mexico, was typically less than high school and for many, stopped at elementary school (*primaria*). Parents worked picking strawberries, mushrooms, or lettuce, on cannery and factory assembly lines, and cleaning houses and hotels.

In selecting students for the program, a panel of teachers at each participating school and the director met to review applications from students whose families were considered low-income by their eligibility for federal free and reduced-price school meals. When we surveyed teachers participating in this selection process, we found that some placed greater weight on students' academic records; others, on students' family challenges (Denner, Cooper, Dunbar, & Lopez, 2005).

When students entered the program, their math and English grades were comparable to those of a school-based sample from the same communities (Azmitia & Cooper, 2001; Azmitia et al., 2009; Azmitia et al., 1996). However, more girls than boys applied for the program and were selected. This gender imbalance increased from elementary through high school as greater numbers of girls than boys persisted on their pathways to college. The state and national imbalances in college enrollment discussed in Chapter 4 show the same pattern (Edgert & Taylor, 1996).

Students' aspirations and identity pathways to college and careers

The partnership assessed *students' career goals* from their program application essays ("describe your ideal career goal") and Summer Institute pre- and post-session surveys ("name the career you would like to have when you finish school") as they continued through the school. In their application essays, students described their dreams of college-based careers—becoming doctors, lawyers, nurses, and teachers as well as secretaries, police officers, firefighters, and mechanics. These goals contrast sharply with their parents' modest levels of formal education and lives of physical labor. As in other studies reviewed in this book, hardships in parents' lives play a central role in CAP students' college and career aspirations and identities.

In addition to students' aspirations, as part of the Summer Institute activities, we have also measured students' *college and career knowledge* (e.g., "How many years after high school would you need to attend school to attain your career goal?" "Match the degree to the school that offers it") (Chavira, Mikolyski, Cooper, Domínguez, & Mena, 2003; López, Gonzalez, Domínguez, Cooper, & Cooper, 2010).

Students' math and language pathways diverged early, but some got back on track

We coded students' math and English classes and grades from their school transcripts from 6th grade through high school, based on our prior studies of academic pathways, as *high, declining, increasing, back on track* (declining then increasing), and *low* (Cooper et al., 2002). The year in school that students passed Algebra 1 with a grade of C or higher was used as an indicator of their being on track to a four-year university.

We coded records of 106 students for whom we had transcripts from 6th grade through high school (Azmitia & Cooper, 2001; Chavira et al., 2003). By 9th grade, 40 (38%) had taken and passed Algebra 1, a key step to eligibility for four-year colleges and universities. In general, the earlier students took Algebra 1, the more likely they were to pass it. These figures compared favorably to the local high school, where 30.4% of 9th grade students had passed Algebra 1. Students' math pathways diverged early: those who passed Algebra 1 by 9th grade had made higher grades in 6th grade than students who failed this class or took remedial classes.

In some ways, these students' math pathways resembled those in the highly selective programs described in Chapter 4: consistently *high* (15%), *declining* (18%), *increasing* (5%), often shown by immigrant students learning English, *back on track* by declining and then increasing (8%), and those persisting at *low* levels (8%). We also saw pathways that we had not seen earlier; we called *struggling* (8%)—increasing and then decreasing in the opposite pattern to *back on track*—and *rollercoaster* (38%). Over time, some students moved back on track after challenging personal events, and others moved up from remedial math to Algebra 1, sometimes retaking it before more advanced classes. The distribution of students along these pathways resemble that in the school-based sample of Dominican, Portuguese, and Cambodian immigrant students in Providence, RI, described by García Coll and her colleagues (2005) but differed from the highly selective bridging program sample discussed in Chapter 4, which included more youth on the high pathway that led directly to four-year universities.

Shifting challenges and resources across students' worlds

As 11-year-olds writing their application essays, students described challenges to attaining their college and career dreams, such as their families needing them to work, peers pressuring them to take drugs, and being immigrant minorities ("people that don't like us people [who are] brown"). Students saw resources in their families, friends, teachers, counselors, coaches, and outreach program staff; in their own qualities ("never giving up and studying a lot"); and in scholarships and loans.

As part of the Summer Institute *It's All About Choices* activities, students complete a "career pyramid" by describing their goals and their challenges and resources in attaining them. In one typical year, students listed their families as resources more often than as challenges (70% vs. 10%), but named peers as challenges and resources at similar rates (30% vs. 40%). Students' challenges from peers included "boyfriends," "girlfriends," "peer pressure," "temptation of friends dropping out," "friends as bad examples," "gangs," "bad friends," and "enemies." Many also listed "drugs," "sex," "having babies," or "pregnancies." As resources, students wrote "friends," "boyfriends," "bigger students," "girlfriends," and "leave your boyfriend if he takes too much time" (the last item appears to be a resource and a bit of advice). These vivid descriptions give us a sense of why the program director sees building a network of college-bound peers as one of the program's most important components.

We have learned about specific processes involved in students' resources and challenges by asking them, "Who helps you?" and "Who causes you difficulties?" across a range of topics. As students continued in the program, they increasingly saw parents (especially their mothers) as resources in thinking about the future, staying in school, and staying on track to college. They saw peers as helping them more with schoolwork and math. These findings offer an important contrast with reports from school-based samples that parents and teachers provide less support for students as they move from elementary to middle school and that peers often undermine students' school engagement (Azmitia & Cooper, 2001; Azmitia et al., 2009; Eccles et al., 1993).

One study invited CAP youth to write short paragraphs about the people who help them the most in different areas. Students described how they drew emotional and instrumental help from across their worlds of families, peers, schools, and the CAP program. It is striking how often these students named their immigrant parents—many having completed only elementary school—as resources. Indeed, for thinking about going to college, the majority of students (61%) named their parents as their resource, and many (30%) named the program (Holt, 2003). Students described how their parents helped them by providing advice about what to do and also by using their own lives as examples of what *not* to do, just as the Mexican immigrant parents reported telling their own children in the school-based studies described in Chapter 5 (Azmitia et al., 1996).

> My mom helps me think about going to college because she [says] that if I don't go to college I wouldn't have a good future. Also, because she doesn't want me working on the fields [picking crops, as the mother did]. She makes me understand that a good education is good for me. Also that I could study whatever I wanted to be in the future.
>
> Latina middle school student

> My mom loved to go to school, but had to quit school to start working at the age of 12. Her mom didn't let her do her homework and she really liked to do homework. Instead she had to do chores. She's always telling me about how good it is for me. She tells me that I need to seize the time that I have to go to college and not drop out of school.
>
> Latino middle school student

My parents told me to go to college because if I wanted to get a house I had to get a good job. Going to college helps you get a career instead of being a gangster, drug dealer or other things that cause you to get in trouble with the cops even though you get good money in a dangerous way.

Latino middle school student

Students in this sample reported that teachers (34%), siblings (34%), parents (29%), and peers (15%) were resources in helping them with math, and 20% named themselves as their key resource in math. What is striking here is the range of worlds from which students were drawing resources for support in math.

No one helps me but my math teacher. Sometimes I ask my mom but she doesn't know that kind of math.

Latina middle school student

The reason my family helps me the most is by telling me to do my homework and telling me that if I keep trying I would be someone in my life. It doesn't mean that just because my mom does not know anything about the work that I do she can't help me. . . . She helps me a lot.

Latina middle school student

The person who helps me out the most when it comes to math is one of my friends. She goes through the math problem step by step as clearly as she can. Most of the time I understand how to do it but I still have trouble a lot of the time. For example, the day before a quiz I always get extra help from her.

Latina middle school student

This bridging program appears to help students to access resources from their worlds of families, teachers, and peers. This finding parallels reports that the Big Sisters/Big Brothers program benefited youth by boosting the impact of their mothers' contributions (Rhodes, Grossman, & Resch, 2000). Still, for some students, the program's contribution was direct and distinctive:

If it wasn't for CAP I probably would never have thought about going to college.

Latino middle school student

The cultural research partnership: Defining success as "more than one path"

The director, scholarship donors, and community college executives defined students' success broadly to include what they called "more than one path": graduating from high school; attending college—whether community colleges, technical schools, or universities; or entering military service. In the early years of the program, about half of the students enrolled in community college and about 5% in four-year universities after graduating from high school. Just under half finished

Table 7.1 Math Pathways Though School: Six Longitudinal Case Studies

	Year passed Algebra 1	Math Pathway	Follow-up at age 18
Luis	9th	high	directly to university
Monica	9th	high	community college and then technical school
Soledad	10th	increasing	community college and plans for university
Jana	10th	back on track	community college then to university
Raul	9th	declining	high school graduation
Mike	unknown	low	high school graduation and community college

This chart shows, for six prototypic students, their grade level when they passed Algebra 1, their math pathways, and their schooling at age 18. Reprinted with permission from Taylor & Francis.

high school but did not attend college immediately, and some enrolled later. Five years later, a new pattern emerged. About one-fourth enrolled in community college, one-fourth went directly to four-year universities, and one-half finished high school. This indicates growing effectiveness of the program. Table 7.1 shows the range of pathways that the program supported.

A Closer Look with Longitudinal Case Studies

Three longitudinal case studies of students in this bridging program, followed from childhood to young adulthood, show the interplay of students' family demographic backgrounds, their college and career aspirations and identities, math pathways, challenges and resources across worlds, and pathways at age 18. These cases show how group-level findings occur in individual lives. They also reveal distinctive constellations of challenges and resources that make the meaning of each student's pathway through school unique. This set of cases offers a useful perspective on the capital, alienation, and challenge models.

Luis: A high math pathway to the university

A son of immigrants from Mexico, Luis was born in the U.S. His parents owned a small catering business. As a child, he hoped to become an engineer. His family—parents, brothers, and cousins—and his program tutor encouraged him and helped him stay on track to college. "My mom didn't know about college, and she wanted to learn what I was feeling, and about the qualifications." He built peer networks by making friends from different schools, and even hung out with students from his rival high school. Luis was one of the most engaged students in the bridging program: his attendance was very high, as he participated in almost every activity—in his words, "every time they had them"—from 6th to 12th grade. He did not attend the program's after-school tutoring very often because he worked, although he said he needed help with math. He explained that he went to most program events because "I wanted to know about college. . . . I knew I wanted to go to college, and I was looking for a school. [The program director] knew all my family, and the information was helpful. . . . I wanted to look at other schools besides the local community college and she would take me." Luis passed Algebra 1 in 9th grade, moving along the high pathway in math and in English, took honors classes, and graduated from high school eligible for the university. He now attends a four-year university and majors in engineering.

Monica: A high math pathway and the challenge of early parenthood

Monica and her parents were born in Mexico. At age 11, when she applied for the program, her career dream was to become a surgeon. Monica and her sisters were very involved with the program, and Monica participated in all program activities. She actively built bridges across her multiple worlds—when she became a cheerleader at school, she invited the program director to a football game. And when she became a teen mother, she did not lose sight of her college dream. The director visited Monica when she came home from the hospital with her baby, and her first words to the director were, "Don't worry, I'm going to graduate from high school." She did graduate on time with her class. Monica drew support for staying on track to college from her parents and sisters, her baby's father, the teen mothers' program at her high school (which provided child care), as well as the pre-college program. Monica was on the high pathway in math, taking and passing Algebra 1 in 9th grade. She enrolled in the local community college and claimed her scholarship. After two semesters she transferred to a technical college, where she earned a Medical Assistant certificate. She worked for a time as a Medical Assistant in a local clinic, then returned to the community college, earned her degree in their nursing program, and now works as a nurse.

Mike: A low math pathway of alienation, persistence, and disengagement

Mike's story includes economic hardship, being homeless and separated from his family, stealing bicycles with gang-affiliated peers, and being chosen for the college outreach program in 6th grade. His participation in the program was limited by his moving in and out of school because of his spending time in the juvenile justice system for stealing bicycles. When another student in the program told the director that Mike was back in high school, this allowed her to contact him at the end of his junior year. Mike said that being in jail made him appreciate life and appreciate that the program remembered him. He thanked the director "for not giving up hope in me." Mike was on the low persisting pathway in math and graduated from high school without having passed Algebra 1. He enrolled in the local community college and claimed his scholarship from the program, but since then the program director has not heard from him.

These case studies show more and less successful pathways from childhood to college. Luis's story provides an example of a child of immigrants with high math grades and aspirations for becoming an engineer who built ties across his worlds of family, peers, school, and community programs along his pathway to college and career. His story shows how a student can play an active role in creating social and cultural capital for college and career mobility. The case of Monica shows how a high math pathway and a dream of becoming a surgeon can be challenged by early parenthood but also supported by a student's family, the baby's father, school, and both pre-college and teen mother programs. Monica sustained her high math pathway and built her identity pathway to college and her college-based career. Finally, Mike's story shows the limits of resiliency. He faced many challenges from family and peers and found help from a friend and the program director, but his ongoing difficulties appeared to undermine his long-term pathway, at least for the time being.

These three cases reveal the impact of challenges and resources in students' identity pathways, as predicted by the challenge model and the Bridging Multiple Worlds theory. They also exemplify the processes described by social capital and alienation models. These case studies were not designed to test rival hypotheses or determine which theory best fits the data. Following Yin's (2008) *pattern matching approach*, we are developing case-based analysis templates for our new studies to help align and compare social capital, alienation, and challenge models. The templates consider the fit of each student's constellation of resources, challenges, and pathways to each model. This approach complements statistical analyses within and across cultural communities (see Mayer, 2007 for an application of this approach).

We can learn a great deal from these identity narratives. Although it is common to hear "success stories" about bridging program graduates, the CAP director has also followed the pathways of more vulnerable youth in her program. The longitudinal case studies have revealed more than one successful pathway and, sometimes, the opportunity for a second chance.

NEXT STEPS FOR MULTICULTURAL COMMUNITIES

Aligning Models of Capital, Alienation, and Challenge

The long-term evidence presented in this chapter adds to other longitudinal studies with Mexican immigrant families that show these parents often hold high hopes of their children moving up from parents' lives picking crops, working on factory assembly lines, or cleaning houses and hotels, to technical or professional careers (Azmitia et al., 1996). In essence, these parents and youth are seeking to beat the odds that social class hierarchies will be reproduced from generation to generation. They are trying to enact the "American dream."

Evidence from this research partnership suggests that families, schools, peers, and community programs provide students with bridges to community colleges and universities. Moreover, they can support both college-bound and remedial students who might otherwise become pessimistic, disengaged, and alienated as they move through school (Fordham & Ogbu, 1986; Gibson et al., 2004; Matute-Bianchi, 1991). Programs that begin before adolescence may be especially important for keeping students engaged in school and continuing through the academic pipeline.

We need better maps of the shifting constellations of resources and challenges in students' lives with their families, peers, schools, and community programs as they navigate their pathways. Linking longitudinal case studies to variable-based analyses revealed that life histories exemplify patterns predicted and illuminated by different theories. Designing and viewing case studies through more than one theoretical lens can be useful for scholars and educators.

Requests from many partners—families, principals, teachers, counselors, program leaders, university researchers, and students—prompted us to develop a set of tools available at www.bridgingworlds.org. Written in English and Spanish, these include questions in survey and interview formats and the activity format in *It's All About Choices/Se Trata De Todas Las Decisiones,* as well as templates for analysis, graphing, and presentations that link longitudinal case studies with statistical analyses. More details appear in Appendix 1.

Linking Generations by "Looking Up and Giving Back"

Partnerships like the one described in this chapter are joining the broader P–20 alliances described in Chapter 6 to keep academic pipelines open. A major commitment of the partnership, and many alliances, is mentoring ethnically diverse community college and university students (undergraduates, graduate students, and postdoctoral fellows) to become researcher–practitioners and to enhance their mentoring skills and educational leadership. These experiences enrich their roles as frontline program staff and as students. These experiences also build leadership, as youth and young adults "look up" to their dreams of college and careers and "give back" to their families and cultural communities.

Each fall, university students in this partnership have presented graphs of key data and summaries of key findings from that year's Summer Institute to youth in the program and asked them to write about their reflections on these findings, while the students also learn math skills in graphing and data analysis. For example, students have contributed their insights about why so many more girls than boys participate in the program activities and their suggestions for how to engage more boys, such as by improving the food and hosting speakers about careers interesting to boys like public safety and forensics (see Figure 7.3). In this way, youth have participated to help improve their program.

Finally, program director Elizabeth Domínguez describes an example of looking up and giving back in her own life:

My parents immigrated from Mexico to Los Angeles in search of a better life for their children. They made sure we did our homework and maintained frequent contact with the school, and nine of their thirteen children completed college. Most of my peers dropped out before they reached high school. Their parents also came to the U.S. to give their children a better life, with dreams for their children to obtain a college degree. But like many non-educated immigrant parents, they did not feel comfortable helping their children with school because they did not understand the system. My parents had a *comadre* [godmother] who took them under her wing, explained how U.S. schools function, and reassured them their participation was demanded for us to be successful (Domínguez, 1995, cited in Cooper, Denner, & Lopez, 1999).

GENERALIZING FINDINGS: HOW TYPICAL?

When students entered this pre-college program, they resembled a school-based sample studied in the same community in families' immigration histories, parents' education and occupation, and school grades (Azmitia et al., 1996). In contrast with the highly selective pre-college programs described in Chapters 4 and 6 that require students to have passed Algebra 1 by 9th grade, such as the Early Academic Outreach Program, AVID, and the Puente Project, this moderately selective community college program did not draw only academic stars. Youth at all skill levels attended. The only variable on which participants were not representative of their broader community was gender. Greater numbers of girls applied to the program, were accepted, and attended, in a pattern typical for pre-college programs (Gándara et al., 1998). However, the cultural world created by the program was unusual. Longitudinal evidence of students' changing aspirations, academic pathways, and peer and family resources indicates that the program helped students to become unusual. Settings that create resources for children of farmworkers to go to college are exceptions to the typical patterns of cultural reproduction and alienation, so it is important to understand conditions where such exceptions take place.

This study of children of immigrants in a pre-college bridging program resembles samples in other studies whose goal is to inform science, policy, and practice. This study used a non-experimental design, and did not, for ethical reasons, randomly assign those who did and did not receive program benefits. The design did not allow testing causal hypotheses or controlling for self-selection, but it did map how children of low-income Mexican immigrants built pathways across their worlds of families, peers, schools, and communities to college.

Just as youth struggled to navigate their worlds along their pathways through school, the program has struggled for funding and space. As a private–public partnership, the program encountered financial challenges that constrained resources, but it also attracted donors who expanded the number of students served and doubled the scholarship each student received. Such private generosity can be a crucial asset for sustaining university–community engagement on behalf of diverse youth. At the time of this writing, the program continues, with financial resiliency from its private endowment but with cuts in funding from state sources. Our university–community partnership has launched a follow-up study with CAP alumni. Alumni have served as tutors in the program and as inspirational speakers at program events.

A new alumni component of the program is being designed, at their request, to open up more opportunities for "giving back."

Conclusions

We have used evidence from this community college bridging program and partnership to consider the fifth core question of this book: how multicultural communities define success for their youth. For these children of immigrants, success means attaining their own and their families' dreams of their going on to college and college-based work. For the program, success means sustaining program activities, improving effectiveness with program analysis, and advancing knowledge. The educational leaders at the community college continue to wrestle with questions about the best size for the program, the ideal investment per student for the program to survive through tough economic times, and the best indicators of student learning for program evaluation and the community college accreditation. Regional alliances, policymakers, and public and private investors also track indicators of success in terms of the program's sustainability, leveraging of funding, and scaling up its benefits to more students. For example, to promote college-going identities, several local middle schools now require all students in their English classes to write the program's application essay as a regular class assignment.

This chapter shows how quantitative patterns in group-level data and unique stories of individual lives are each valuable in understanding the roots and remedies of the pipeline problem. The partnership has provided a case study (Cooper, Domínguez, Azmitia, Holt, Mena, & Chavira, 2010) for a casebook for new teachers about using multiple theoretical lenses in partnerships with ethnically diverse families and communities (Weiss et al., 2010).

How should we define success for youth and communities in multicultural societies? We hope this case study of a program and partnership stimulates readers to ask what we want for all of our children. Beyond worldwide goals for successful development through schooling, industrialized countries define higher education as a crucial phase of this path, even though vocational and college-preparation classes often form separate tracks that diverge in childhood (Hamilton, 1994). In some communities, educators and policymakers have begun to open multiple pathways to college and careers so that students prepare for both with the same classes (Mehan, 2007).

PART THREE

Looking Ahead

8

IMPLICATIONS AND FUTURE DIRECTIONS

with
Robert G. Cooper

It is not necessary for you to complete the work [of perfecting the world], but neither are you free to desist from it.
Rabbi Tarphon, an early Judaic leader who lived between 70 and 132 of the Common Era
Pirke Avot (The Sayings of the Fathers)

This final chapter considers progress in work on the academic pipeline problem in terms of the five core questions that have shaped this book, the new Bridging Multiple Worlds model, and advancing productive cycles of research, practice, and policy. Following the words of Rabbi Tarphon, we recognize that we will never finish working on the academic pipeline problem. This may be especially difficult to admit for someone of our generation, who came of age during the U.S. Civil Rights Movement, when many thought that if we could keep our "eyes on the prize," social justice would come in our lifetime. Progress has been made in achieving civil rights, but there is much more to be done. So, too, for the inevitably incomplete work on the academic pipeline problem, including this book, we can measure gains, limits, and losses, and also foresee challenges and resources for the path ahead.

We must first acknowledge that, despite almost universal governmental endorsement of the ideals of equal access to education, inequities have actually grown over the past 10 years in many nations in the rates of college enrollment and completion. In the U.S., significant gaps persist between different ethnic and income groups (Engle & Lynch, 2009), and similar gaps are evident in China, South Africa, Brazil, India, and many European nations (Carjuzaa, Fenimore-Smith, Fuller, Howe, Kugler, et al., 2008; Gupta, 2006; Lloyd & Hewett, 2009; UNICEF, 2002; Zhiyong, 2007). Nonetheless, it is worth taking stock of the progress we have made, if not yet in global practice, at least in our understanding of this complex issue.

WHAT HAVE WE LEARNED ABOUT THE FIVE CORE QUESTIONS?

Researchers have made striking progress on each of the five questions that shape this book. New evidence is advancing scientific understanding as well as promoting more effective practice and social policies, although economic realities have often constrained widespread applications. In some cases, what once looked like irreconcilable views are now converging or are being integrated into more comprehensive models. Like research on complex health issues that also requires interdisciplinary perspectives, it is heartening to see collaborations emerging across the social sciences on these five questions about the academic pipeline problem.

Autonomy or Connections? Defining Identities in Cultural Contexts

From examining the first question, we have learned that supporting the development of both autonomy and relatedness leads to better developmental outcomes (Lamborn & Groh, 2009). Despite some gender and cultural differences in how autonomy and connections are expressed, both are key to students' abilities to navigate their pathways. Understanding cultural differences and similarities in expressing both autonomy and connections can help create "safe spaces" where youth can build their sense of identity and belonging. Particularly for future schooling and careers, focusing on adolescents' sense of identity and agency rather than only on their autonomy has practical benefits (Destin & Oyserman, 2010).

Evidence for the continuing importance of family support well into early adulthood (as seen especially in the "boomerang generation" of college graduates in the U.S. returning home to live with their parents) is opening new questions about how autonomy and connections matter in fostering pathways beyond college to careers (Aquilino, 2006; Arnett, 2004; Mitchell, 2005). Researchers have begun to examine how students chose their college majors with an eye toward giving back to their communities, and how other students mentor siblings and cousins along their own college pathways (Azmitia et al., 2008; Syed, 2010b). We need studies that trace the fading and the persistence over generations of the values of mutual support and obligation that have motivated youth to go to college on behalf of their families and communities (Fuligni, 2007; Sabogal et al., 1987).

Capital, Alienation, or Challenge?

Capital, alienation, and challenge models each help to explain both successes and failures in students' navigating the academic pipeline. Traditional capital models are useful for understanding the academic success of students from middle- and upper-income families. These models, however, are also useful for understanding the success of other students by focusing attention on the capital they may possess. Alienation models are most useful in understanding the development of immigrant, working class, and ethnic minority students who do not have other capital to foster their sense of belonging and academic success. Finally, challenge models are useful in providing a framework for understanding the success of students who do not have substantial amounts of traditional social capital.

Because this book focuses on educational equity and improving the chances for academic success of students who may leave the academic pipeline disproportionately, those who succeed by interpreting their challenges as a source of motivation are particularly crucial for us to understand. Much of the research we have reviewed has helped to do this. The key roles played by supportive parents and, to a lesser degree, siblings, peers, and teachers, stand out in the research we have reviewed. Pre-college bridging programs and other learning communities are important for teaching students how to transform their challenges into motivation to succeed rather than becoming alienated.

We need to learn more about capital, alienation, and challenge pathways. Can youth change their pathways? When can alienated youth find ways to obtain social capital? How do youth access resources from mentors who have already navigated these pathways? When do challenges lead to alienation or spark resiliency?

Brokers and Gatekeepers: How Youth Navigate Across Their Cultural Worlds

Are competing worlds and cultural mismatches inevitable? When can youth navigate across their worlds while staying on the good path of life—or get back on track—toward their aspirations? The classic viewpoint on this question endures today in the drama of "two different worlds," seen in book titles such as *Between Two Worlds: How Young Latinos Come of Age in America* (Taylor, 2009) or *Between Two Worlds: Escape from Tyranny—Growing up in the Shadow of Saddam* (Salbi, 2005). Researchers take this "two different worlds" approach in examining the *cultural mismatch* hypothesis, that families of immigrant, low-income, and ethnic minority students in the U.S. will endorse collectivist values and practices that conflict with the individualistic values and practices of American schools (Rothstein-Fisch, Turnbull, & Romero, 2009). This dichotomy underlies the negative stereotype that Mexican immigrant students and families do not value education because of their "third-world values" (Valencia & Black, 2002).

Evidence about cultural mismatches across adolescents' worlds reveals that conventional wisdom about these issues is frequently inaccurate. Three important findings have recently emerged on this question. First, as discussed in Chapter 5, immigrant families' goals and values often match those of U.S. educators in aspiring for their children to move up to college and college-based careers (Auerbach, 2006; Cooper et al., 1994). Second, teachers who see their students' cultural values as more similar to those enacted by schools also rate their students' academic skills more positively than teachers who see families and schools as holding more discrepant values (Sirin, Rice, & Mir, 2009). Such differing perceptions may launch students onto diverging pathways through school (Stipek et al., 2005). And third, cultural mismatches may not always be problematic. In one study, Chinese immigrant parents gave their children structured math lessons at home with materials from China and Taiwan, but did not volunteer at school like European American parents. The Chinese parents also did not follow the school's advice to avoid structured teaching at home, but their children developed more positive attitudes toward school and made better grades compared to their European American peers (Huntsinger & Jose, 2009).

Despite these positive findings, there will always be cultural differences that some will interpret as deficits, and children and adolescents will be called upon to navigate among competing demands, norms, and values. We have reviewed evidence that some youth are able to navigate among cultural worlds with contradictory expectations. Furthermore, students skilled in "cultural straddling" are more likely to succeed academically (Carter, 2005). Everyone meets differing norms and expectations across their worlds, but immigrant, ethnic minority, and working-class youth who leave the academic pipeline too early may have more challenges in this regard. To pursue our goal of equity in educational opportunity, we need to understand more about how to foster students' capacities for moving among their worlds and how to design worlds that offer youth a greater sense of agency and belonging.

The studies we have reviewed show that when students' academic ambitions, families, and cultural traditions are treated as assets by teachers and others, they serve as capital and foster success. When they are treated as problems, risks, or liabilities, they may function as challenges that motivate success but they may also lead to alienation. Thus, whether capital or challenge models best explain a particular student's success may depends on the particular sociocultural context in which that student lives.

We have more to learn about the resources and challenges involved in navigating across worlds. What can adults and youth do at different points along the pathways to college? What kinds and combinations of practical and emotional support typify students moving along different pathways? What do youth need as they grow up in different cultural communities? How can institutions change to maximize the benefits of the assets students bring?

Fragile Bridges and Alliances:
Opening Institutional Opportunities

The fourth question concerns the obstacles that limit adolescents' opportunities to explore their identities and pathways to college and effective ways to open institutional opportunities along the academic pipeline. Researchers may assume that opportunities are available if they ask youth about exploration and commitments in their identity development but not about their obstacles (Yoder, 2000). Institutional bridges—many of them fragile and often hidden—include families' involvement, schools' academic instruction and counseling, supportive peer networks, and community mentors who can serve as cultural brokers.

We can also see progress in opening institutional opportunities for college pathways in states like California, Arkansas, and Texas, where school district leaders have taken the bold step of making the college-preparatory curriculum the standard for all students, so that all high school graduates will be eligible for college. The district leaders did this by enhancing teachers' professional development, increasing instructional time, eliminating remedial classes, and increasing academic and social supports (Oakes, 2003; Tierney, Bailey, Constantine, Finkelstein, & Hurd, 2009; Warner, 2005).

At least two major institutional challenges lie ahead. One is to assess systemically how institutional bridges are working together. P–20 alliances appear to be a promising strategy for linking these bridges, but researchers and policy analysts are still working to develop tools for assessing the impact of P–20 alliances on students' learning and college pathways with longitudinal student-level data (Vernez et al., 2008). Much can be learned from successes and even noble failures that result from thoughtfully planned innovations.

A second challenge is that few academic institutions have enough economic support to ensure that academic success in primary and secondary schools can lead to a college education. In the U.S., it is ironic that just as state legislatures are uniting to align high school graduation requirements with college readiness (Deyé, 2009), economic constraints are forcing many of them to cut funding to state universities. This means dramatically fewer seats for the growing numbers of college-eligible youth. As Linda Murray, former superintendent of the San José Unified School District in California, warned, "The challenge now is to make college a reality for everyone who is ready" (Leadership Conference on Civil Rights, 2009, p. 1).

What Is Success in Multicultural Societies?

The fifth question asks how we define success for youth and communities in multicultural societies. Do communities see themselves as culturally homogeneous and thus consider cultural diversity in youth and families as deficits? Or do communities see themselves as multicultural and work to open more than one pathway for youth? What are the costs and benefits of homogenous vs. differentiated concepts of success? What is the role of cultural diversity in success? In what settings are our concepts of success related to diversity?

Fostering opportunities for success for all members of diverse multicultural societies is a major challenge that many nations have begun to address. Of course, there is no single answer to the question, "What is success?" Classic answers to this question rest on universal definitions of access to and achievement in schooling and work. For many, going to college has become synonymous with success. The work reviewed in this book demonstrates that we need to view pathways to success more broadly. For example, we need to learn how community colleges can be more effective in offering second chances for working-class students while preventing the cooling of their aspirations to transfer to four-year universities (Frye, 2002; Rendón, Jalomo, & García, 1994; Taylor, 2009). Second chance pathways may be especially important for immigrant youth from rural areas who arrive in new countries with little schooling.

Among nations working on the pipeline problem, policymakers define diversity in different ways that, in turn, influence their judgment of the success of their educational systems. For example, the Organization for Economic Co-operation and Development (OECD), a consortium of 30 nations, compared members' strategies for increasing equity in higher education (Santiago, Tremblay, Basri, & Arnal, 2008). These countries define success as entering higher education and completing baccalaureate degrees but vary in how they define diversity, for historical and political reasons (Clancy & Goastellec, 2007). Some target race, ethnicity, and social class (Australia, Mexico, New Zealand, and the U.S.). Others target social class but consider ethnicity to be a private matter (Japan, Czech Republic, Portugal, and Spain). Still others target gender, disabilities, or isolated rural residence.

Given the state of global efforts to foster educational equity, this diversity of approaches is an asset. We need to develop techniques to support the success of all children and adolescents, so if one region develops effective ways to redress gender inequities and others develop ways to redress inequities based on class, ethnicity, disability, or place, each will be contributing useful knowledge that can guide programs to better serve all students. An accessible clearinghouse for pipeline-related research could be useful, especially for those who may hesitate to enter this international conversation but whose contributions would advance it.

Findings from Research Using the Bridging Multiple Worlds Theory

Based on findings so far, the Bridging Multiple Worlds Theory holds promise for work on the academic pipeline problem by focusing on a multilevel set of dimensions that yield useful knowledge about how youth can build pathways to college. For example, looking at the interplay of parents' education, occupation, and immigration experiences (indicators of family demographics) *and* their aspirations for their children reveals how low-income families pursue their goal for youth to "move up" to a better life. In one study, Mexican immigrant parents, who had less than a high school education and worked picking strawberries and cleaning hotels, dreamed that their children would find careers as doctors, lawyers, and other professionals as part of staying on the good moral path of life (Azmitia et al., 1996, 2009; Cooper et al., 1994). These findings show important links between families' immigration, education, and occupations and their cultural and college aspirations for their children.

The work with academic pathways has been especially adaptable across research, practice, and policy. In three longitudinal studies of African American, European American, and Latino youth, we traced math and language pathways from each student's grades and classes over time (Azmitia et al., 2009; Cooper et al., 2002; Cooper et al., 2005). Across these three samples, the proportions of youth on *high, declining, increasing, back on track,* and *low* pathways reflected whether students were taking part in highly selective, moderately selective, or inclusive programs. Even in highly selective programs, many youth moved along high pathways to four-year universities, but many also slipped onto declining pathways. Our new work examines the "second chance" pathways of youth who leave school because of early parenthood, prison, military service, or needing to work to support their families and then returned to their studies. Taken together, these findings and the graphing templates that have been developed from them have attracted the interest of practitioners and policymakers as well as researchers.

When we asked youth who helped them stay on track to college, they expressed one of our most important findings: their parents were central to their staying on track to college and even during the college years, not in spite of parents' modest education but because of it (Cooper et al., 2008). Families could also cause difficulties, such as when parents kept daughters home from science camp to protect their virtue or when older siblings lacked the academic skills or "college knowledge" to help them. Still, successful students found emotional and instrumental resources by reaching across their worlds. As young adults, they named parents and peers as top resources, as well as teachers, counselors, the program director, and tutors.

Beyond individual actions and social networks, we have learned how cultural research partnerships along the academic pipeline can boost the resources that youth draw upon across their worlds. Evidence of the impact of these partnerships has stimulated state and federal agencies to work with private foundations and community organizations, including religious groups. Leaders increasingly connect and align programs across educational segments, thus advancing beyond the typical practice of targeting one point along the pipeline, such as kindergarten or moving from high school to college.

Parallels and Variations across Nations

Building on their partnerships on behalf of immigrant youth, the United Nations Alliance of Civilizations convened a group of scholars, community leaders, and elected officials from 11 European nations in Vienna in 2009 to consider how to support the integration of Muslim immigrant youth in Europe. The conveners asked me to address how work with the Bridging Multiple Worlds Theory could help identify strategies relevant to Muslim immigrant youth (Cooper, 2009). This request made sense since the influx of Muslim immigrants into Europe parallels in some ways the flow of Mexicans to the U.S. Both groups have experienced discrimination in housing, education, health care, and employment. Conference participants found three findings to be especially relevant. First, immigrant youth and families share dreams that dispel myths about their low aspirations to succeed, and they retain a desire to preserve their cultural traditions (Ross-Seriff, Tirmazi, & Walsh, 2007). Second, many youth who go to college give back by encouraging and guiding siblings, friends, relatives, and other youth, thus becoming cultural and college brokers (Crul, 2002). And third, participants noted that one major difference between the U.S. and Europe is students' access to college bridging programs. Unfortunately, programs and partnerships to encourage young Muslims and other immigrant youth to go to college are rare in Europe, although pioneering efforts have begun (De Bresser, 2009). As many nations struggle with their own academic pipeline problems, multinational partnerships like the European Access Network (www.ean-edu.org) and The Integration of the European Second Generation (TIES) Project are proving valuable (www.tiesproject.eu; Crul & Schneider, 2009).

Although the Bridging Multiple Worlds Theory has been useful in focusing attention on specific effects at different levels of analysis, its key contribution is in providing a framework for integrating results from these differing levels of analysis. Such integration is necessary to guide the development of a system to foster student success so that its pieces work together synergistically. For example, knowing that parents and families are key resources in supporting student success throughout the pipeline needs to be considered in designing programs to augment traditional K–12 education into the college years. Understanding the demographics of attrition from the pipeline identifies key groups for whom supplemental programs may be necessary. The Bridging Multiple Worlds model does not specify an optimal system, but it provides the framework for measuring effective configurations of components and thus the evolution of more effective systemic approaches.

ADVANCING CYCLES OF RESEARCH, PRACTICE, AND POLICY

Bridging across the research, practice, and policy sectors can be daunting (Shonkoff, 2002). Lewig, Arney, and Scott (2006) found that barriers emerged from different timetables between the scholars working to produce results and the practitioners who needed them; from using different languages in communicating about findings; and from competing political, economic, and organizational priorities. Researchers often seek to "give science away" through "translational" writing for practitioners and the public. Another useful strategy is to build collaborative ties that advance each phase of the cycle in an ongoing way. So in addition to translating and transmitting research findings, partners can also collaborate in doing the research (Denner et al., 1999).

For researchers, evolving models of capital, alienation, and challenge offer complementary approaches for understanding the multiple levels of the academic pipeline problem. Aligning institutional and personal levels is important so we can understand youth and families as social actors and thus potential assets, not simply as outcomes who are deficient or incomplete in their assimilation. Effective partnerships among researchers, practitioners, and policymakers use demographic data but also move beyond national origin, socioeconomic status, and gender to map levers of change. We now need to build clearer interdisciplinary alignment of models, concepts, and measures to track cultural parallels and variations across communities.

For practitioners working on the pipeline problem, intergenerational bridges provide settings for college students to serve as cultural brokers who can help build or strengthen ties between youth and elders. Research has shown how successful

youth bridge values and practices across their cultural worlds. Materials about pathways to college in families' home languages can help bridge across generations
for cultural, college, and career identities. As shown in Figure 8.1, immigrant college
students can serve as cultural brokers by providing materials about college in English
and the language of their country of origin. Such findings point to the importance of
providing linguistically diverse materials to open pathways to college. Such practical
changes may rest on two paradigm shifts: considering immigrant families as resources
and partners in building students' pathways to college and transcending discomfort
in communicating across the range of languages spoken by families. These materials
can be assets for both issues.

In policy investments, private foundations and private–public partnerships
are key players in work on the pipeline problem because of their autonomy and nim-
bleness (Cooper, 2008). They help advance research and practice as well as guide
further investments. Foundations can inspire and support learning communities to
consider sensitive issues such as undocumented youth and fragile innovations. An
ongoing challenge is to support the transition of successful activities and programs
from foundation funding to sustainable institutionalized sources.

Finally, international research on the adaptation of immigrant youth can offer
valuable guidance for public and private investments by mapping similarities and
differences across nations in policies and their consequences (Berry et al., 2006;
Berry & Sabatier, 2010). Foundation groups like the European Foundation Network

Figure 8.1 "Ask us about college." Cambodian immigrant college students serve as cultural brokers at
the Cambodian New Year celebration at their Buddhist temple by providing materials about college in
English and in Khmer. © Catherine Cooper.

are addressing issues of discrimination and equal opportunity in the integration of immigrant youth into the educational and ultimately the occupational and civic systems of their receiving countries. Given global economic challenges, our next steps for research, practice, and policy involve sustainability over the lean years ahead. Strengthening ties both within cultural communities and across them—what Putnam (2000) calls *bonding* and *bridging* capital—will be crucial assets.

PROMISING STRATEGIES: TOWARD A COMMON LANGUAGE

A promising strategy for building a common language on the academic pipeline problem is to compare and align core concepts and measures across different models. These include meaningful indicators of family demographics of the youth trying to move through school, personal and social identities, math and language skills, challenges and resources in bridging across cultural worlds, and institutional partnerships. For example, our growing understanding of how youth bridge their worlds draws on concepts of social capital and institutional agents (Putnam, 2000; Stanton-Salazar, 2010); alienation and belonging (Gibson & Hidalgo, 2009); and language brokering (Orellana, 2009). Such progress is beginning to unify research on the academic pipeline problem across the social sciences and points to links with policy and practice. Still, a major limitation in this work and this book lies in the gaps that remain across disciplinary frameworks, many of which have not been aligned before, and across research, practice, and policies. We hope the next steps will be made easier by this book.

A second useful strategy for forging a common language lies in developing and distributing shared tools for these collaborations. For example, regional, state, national, and international partners are using longitudinal databases that include data in quantitative and narrative formats (Achieve, Inc., 2009b; Data Quality Campaign, 2009; Vernez et al., 2008).

Such tools help bring together researchers, policymakers, and educators to make better investments by choosing the most effective activities for youth pathways to college. In the Appendices that follow this chapter, we offer a compilation of such tools that align with many current models. These tools help partners ask their own questions and connect their work across regions, states, and nations.

Clearly, we do not have all the answers yet, but we are making progress. As with other complex social and scientific problems, scientists, practitioners, and policymakers are taking incremental approaches. The problem of expanding access to higher education for greater numbers and a greater diversity of young people challenges us to look carefully at the lenses we use to view this problem.

Learning communities are bridging generations by engaging youth, young adults, and adults as researchers. Worldwide, ethnic minority, low-income, and immigrant youth are beginning to transform academic pipelines as they move through college and graduate school into the professoriate as scholars with lifelong experiences with these issues (Cooper & Burciaga, 2011; Cooper & Verma, 2009). They are bridging disciplines, and they are bridging nations by linking local and systemic practices across cultural communities.

The work reviewed in this book has contributed to opening more just worlds. In the long term, the success of the book depends not on scholars alone. It is what readers from many different sectors do with this book that will matter the most.

When we think about how far we still need to go to realize our aspirations for equity, it can be daunting. But when we consider how far we have come, it is encouraging. We are most optimistic when we think of the aspirations and actions of youth, families, and communities; the commitment of those who work with them; and the ongoing progress of researchers to understand and illuminate their pathways.

APPENDIX 1

Tools for Advancing Research, Practice, and Policy

with

Dolores D. Mena, Gabriela Chavira, Dawn Mikolyski,
Moin Syed, and David Cooper

As the evidence in this book has shown, in many nations, despite widespread belief in equal access to education and the resulting high hopes of students and families, too many working class, ethnic minority, and immigrant youth leave their pathways through school and do not make it to college and college-based work. This is especially likely when their parents have not attended college, schools lack qualified teachers and counselors, and support programs target only small segments of the academic pipeline, often in isolation from other programs. The more we understand why and how students stay on or slip off their pathways to college and careers, the more effectively we can support them.

Appendix 1 and 2 take a more technical look at the academic pipeline problem. Here we align concepts and measures to help build a common language among researchers, educators, and policymakers. We hope this common language will be useful for researchers asking what conditions support ethnic minority, working class, and immigrant youth as they build pathways to college; for educators asking how to engage and support these students and their families more effectively; and for public and private funding agencies in their efforts to enhance their investments in this work. We also hope that these tools offer readers new ways to ask their own questions.

This Appendix provides sample questions, coding formats, and research findings for five dimensions of partnerships and pathways to college and careers based on the Bridging Multiple Worlds model (Cooper, 2003). As shown in Chapter 7, the model traces five interrelated dimensions that are particularly relevant to the academic pipeline problem:

1) *Family demographic variables* along the academic pipeline reflect students' access to educational opportunities—e.g., families' national origins, ethnicities, home languages, and parents' education and occupation
2) *youth aspirations and identity pathways to college and careers*
3) *math and language academic pathways through school*
4) *resources and challenges across the cultural worlds of families, peers, schools, community programs, sports, and religious activities*

5) *cultural research partnerships* that reach across nations, ethnicities, social class, and gender to open pathways through school. These partnerships, extending from preschool through graduate school, can also connect children, families, schools, community programs, and university staff as researchers.

To advance progress on the academic pipeline problem with common tools for scientists, policymakers, and educators as well as youth and families in multicultural societies, these dimensions can be aligned with related models, each of which continues to evolve. These include theories of social capital and college-going cultures (Gonzalez et al., 2003; Jarsky, McDonough, & Nunez, 2009), community cultural wealth (Burciaga, 2008; Yosso, 2005), sociocultural theories (Moran et al., 2009; Rogoff, 2003; Tharp et al., 2000; Weisner, 2010); future orientation (Seginer, 2009); academic self-efficacy (Chemers et al., 2009); overlapping spheres (Epstein et al., 2009; Yamauchi et al., 2008); possible selves (Oyserman et al., 2006); academic resiliency (Perez et al., 2009); and ecological and dynamic systems (Lerner & Steinberg, 2009; Weiss et al., 2010), among others.

We collected many of the tools in this Appendix and developed others from years of working with youth, families, teachers, counselors, program staff, school superintendents, researchers, and policymakers across a range of cultural communities. In addition, sample consent forms for students and families, focus group interview and survey measures in English and Spanish, and activities for schools and programs, such as *It's All About Choices/Se Trata De Todas Las Decisiones* are available free, all with prototypes in English and Spanish, at www.bridgingworlds.org. Family guides to college in English and Spanish are available on request from bmwa@ucsc.edu.

FIVE DIMENSIONS: SAMPLE QUESTIONS, CODING, AND RESEARCH FINDINGS

Demographics Along the Academic Pipeline

Researchers, educators, and policymakers often ask how typical are the students and families participating in a school, program, or study compared to their broader communities or to other regions, states, and nations in terms of their national origin, home languages, ethnicities, gender, or parents' education, occupation, or income. The U.S. Office of Education requires all schools receiving federal funds to report achievement by demographic subgroups. As discussed in Chapters 2 and 5, demographic measures are useful for describing and monitoring equity (and inequity) in access to educational opportunities through the academic pipeline, but explaining causes of and remedies to attrition through the academic pipeline rests on assessing individual, social, and institutional processes.

National Origin

Sample Questions	Closed-ended: *Please check the country where you and your family members were born.*
	Open-ended: *Where were you born? Where were your family members born?*
Sample Coding	A current list of nations is available from the United Nations (www.un.org).
Sample Findings	Researchers and educators can map variation and similarities within and across groups of students by country of origin. In one study, described in Chapter 3, Chinese, Mexican, Filipino, and Vietnamese American college students, who were mostly immigrants, valued consulting with their families about important educational decisions more than non-immigrant students. Students in all groups, including European American, felt more comfortable talking with their mothers than fathers about personal topics (Cooper et al., 1993).

Home Languages

Sample Questions	Closed-ended: *Please check the languages spoken in your home.*
	Open-ended: *What language(s) is/are spoken in your home? What is your first language? Do you speak a language other than English? If yes, specify the language.*
Sample Coding	Based on the Home Language Survey required by U.S. law, some states, such as California, report the languages spoken by English learners in each school (www.cde.ca.gov); see Appendix 2. Other states report the number of English learners.
Sample Findings	Departments of Education in six states (Arizona, California, Hawaii, Kentucky, New Mexico, and Rhode Island) reported that families of students in these states speak 150 different languages (Trinh, Tsai, & Cooper, 2007). The California Department of Education found that the most common home languages in the state were English, Spanish, Vietnamese, and Hmong, and it distributes materials about college in these languages (www.cde.ca.gov). Our research team helped to produce materials in Khmer (Cambodian) that are available at www.cde.ca.gov and www.bridgingworlds.org. We gathered materials on pathways to college in the following languages: Chinese (Mandarin), Chuukese, French, Hawaiian, Hmong, Ilocano, Japanese, Korean, Laotian, Marshallese, Portuguese, Russian, Samoan, Spanish, Tagalog, Tongan, Vietnamese, and Visayan (Trinh et al., 2007). These materials are available at no cost at www.bridgingworlds.org/language/index.html.

Ethnicities

Sample Questions	Closed-ended: *Please check one box.*
	Open-ended: *What is your ethnicity or ethnicities?*
Sample Coding	The U.S. Office of Education uses five racial categories (White, Asian, Native American, Hispanic, Black) and two ethnic categories (Hispanic and non-Hispanic) to monitor access to education. Other coding systems include more racial–ethnic and multi-ethnic identities.
Sample Findings	In one study described in Chapter 4, researchers asked 120 California high school students, "What is your ethnicity or ethnicities?" Youth reported 38 different ethnic identities, including 20 multi-ethnic identities, such as Black/Ethiopian, American/Filipino, Black/Chinese, Black/European American/Italian, Chicano/Native American, Colombian/Italian, Creole/Native American, Filipino/Pakistani, Mexican/Japanese, Mexican/Polish, and Peruvian/Japanese (Cooper et al., 2002).

Parents' Education

Sample Questions	Closed-ended: *Please check the highest level of education your mother has completed.*
	Open-ended: *What is the highest grade your mother has completed?*
Sample Coding	Responses can be coded by the number of years of schooling (0–20); by level, such as no schooling, elementary school, middle or junior high, high school, some college, bachelor's degree, or post-graduate; or completed college vs. less than college education. Identifying students as the first generation in their family to attend college has been based on both parents completing less than a bachelor's degree (GEAR UP, 2005) or less than high school (California Department of Education, 2005).
Sample Findings	Schools compare students' achievement by their parents' education to monitor education gaps (www.cde.ca.gov). To monitor inclusiveness in students' persisting through school, U.S. educators often track the percent of yearly student retention from a baseline year and grade level by demographic subgroup. Under federal law, public elementary, middle, and high schools report achievement scores by socioeconomic disadvantage (either students whose parents both have not received a high school diploma or those who participate in federal free or reduced-price meal programs); English learners; race; ethnicity; and students with disabilities.

Parents' Occupations

Sample Questions	Closed-ended: *Please check your mother's job or occupation.* Open-ended: *What is your mother's job or occupation?*
Sample Coding	Occupations can be coded by rank, based on education and responsibilities, ranging from 1 = professionals and higher executives to 7 = unskilled employees and manual laborers (Hollingshead & Redlich, 1958). International codes can be used (e.g., International Standard Code of Occupations www.ilo.org/public/english/bureau/stat/isco/index.htm).
Sample Findings	In a study described in Chapter 3, Vietnamese immigrant college students reported that their parents had worked as professionals in Vietnam but took lower-skilled jobs in the U.S. because their credentials were not accepted. Many parents expected their sons and daughters to attain professional careers (Cooper, 1999; Cooper et al., 1993).

Aspirations, Expectations, and Identity Pathways to College and Careers

Aspirations represent hopes or ideal choices, *expectations* reflect more realistic or accessible options, and *identities* represent long-term commitments. Youth, families, teachers, and community members can each report their views of students' futures.

Students' Aspirations and Expectations for Their Education and Careers

Sample Questions	Open-ended (aspirations): *What is the highest level of education you hope to attain?* *What job or career do you hope to have in the future?* Closed-ended (expectations): *Check the highest level of education you expect to attain.* *Of the jobs listed, which one comes closest to the one you expect to have in the future?*
Sample Coding	Students' reports of their educational and occupational aspirations and expectations can be coded as described above for parents' education and occupations.
Sample Findings	In a longitudinal study described in Chapter 7, as students progressed through school, some reconciled their career aspirations with their academic skills or with their personal or family challenges. For example, they changed from planning to attend medical school and become a doctor to planning to attend community college to become a medical assistant (Cooper, Cooper, Burciaga, Domínguez, & Su, 2008).

Parents' Aspirations and Expectations for
Their Children's Education and Careers

Sample Questions	Open-ended (aspirations): *What is the highest level of education you hope your son or daughter will attain?* Open-ended (expectations); note that we prefer to ask parents this question in an open-ended rather than closed-ended format: *Thinking about your child's abilities, interests, what he/she is like, how he/she is doing in school, and what he/she wants out of life, what is the highest level of education you actually expect him/her to attain?*
Sample Coding	Parents' educational and occupational aspirations and expectations for their children can be coded as described for parents' own education and occupations.
Sample Findings	In a study described in Chapter 5 with Mexican immigrant parents who held working-class jobs, most sustained aspirations for their children to work as doctors, lawyers, and teachers, although for some their expectations dimmed over time (Azmitia et al., 1996; Mena, 2005).

Students' Career Identities

Career identity development can be measured by asking youth about their exploration and commitment to their career plans (Bennion & Adams, 1986; Grotevant & Cooper, 1998).

Sample Questions	Closed-ended:
	On the Extended Objective Measure of Ego Identity Status (EOMEIS-2; Bennion & Adams, 1986), respondents rate their agreement or disagreement to items tapping the four identity statuses proposed by Marcia (1966), e.g.:
	Identity moratorium: *"I'm still trying to decide how capable I am as a person and what jobs will be right for me"*;
	Identity diffusion: *"I haven't chosen the occupation I really want to go into. Right now, I'm just working at what is available until something better comes along"*;
	Identity foreclosure: *"I might have thought about a lot of different jobs, but there's never really been any question since my parents said what they wanted"*; and
	Identity achievement: *"It took me a while to figure it out, but now I really know what I want for a career."*
	Open-ended (Grotevant & Cooper, 1981; 1985; adapted from Marcia, 1966):
	What are you going to do after high school?
	Are you planning to go to college?
	Do you know what you will major in?
	What do you plan to do with it?
	When did you come to decide on (career choice)?
	What people or experiences have been major influences on your plans for the future?
	What kinds of difficulties or problems do you see associated with your decision to _____ ?
	If these things were to become difficult, what would you do then?
Sample Coding	Responses on the EOMEIS-2 survey are scored quantitatively (Bennion & Adams, 1986). Responses to open-ended identity interview questions are coded by trained coders for breadth and depth of exploration and commitment (Grotevant & Cooper, 1984; Grotevant & Von Korff, 2008; in press).
Sample Findings	In a survey study of a school-based sample of Latino youth described in Chapter 4, those reporting greater exploration of their career identities on the EOMEIS-2 (Bennion & Adams, 1986), compared to those reporting less exploration, rated their families' communication as expressing relatively high levels of both individuality and connectedness (Lopez, 2001).

Students' Math and Language Pathways through School

Students' math and language pathways can be assessed from their school and college transcripts for classes, grades, and test scores; completing classes required for university eligibility; college enrollment and graduation; community college transfer; and graduate and professional school pathways (Cooper et al., 2002). Students' self-reported grades, which are highly correlated with transcript data, can also be collected. Longitudinal data can help track how students' math and language pathways predict their options for future careers.

Sample Questions	Closed-ended (transcript): *What grades did students make over time?* Open-ended (self-report): *What math and language classes did you take through school? Write in the class and grade.*
Sample Coding	Math and language grades can be graphed over time from school transcripts and coded as *high, increasing, declining, back on track,* and *persisting* pathways (Cooper et al., 2005).
Sample Findings	In a study of African American and Latino youth participating in highly selective bridging programs described in Chapter 4, those with higher math and English pathways were more likely to attend four-year colleges and universities directly from high school, but grades did not always predict where students enrolled (Cooper et al., 2002).

In a community college bridging program, students used the template shown in Figure A.1 to map their own math pathways toward their long-term goals (Cooper et al., 2005).

	Middle School			High School				Long-Term Goal
	6th	7th	8th	9th	10th	11th	12th	
College Prep Math Classes			(sample) PreAlgebra	Algebra	Geometry	Algebra II	Trigonometry/ Calculus	
My Math Classes								
My Future Agenda								

Example:

		6th	7th	8th	9th	10th	11th	12th
grades	A	X						
	B		X	X				X
	C					X	X	
	D				X			
	F							

		6th F	6th S	7th F	7th S	8th F	8th S	9th F	9th S	10th F	10th S	11th F	11th S	12th F	12th S
My grades	A														
	A-														
	B+														
	B														
	B-														
	C+														
	C														
	C-														
	D+														
	D														
	D-F														

Figure A.1 *Charting math pathways:* As part of *It's All About Choices/Se Trata de Todas las Decisiones—Activities to Build Identity Pathways to College and Careers,* students graph their math pathways toward their career goals (Domínguez et al., 2001).

Algebra 1 as a Gateway to College and Careers

In the U.S., passing Algebra 1 by 9th grade is used as an index of preparation for college and careers by researchers, policymakers, the business community, and educators working with students and families.

Sample Questions	Closed-ended: School transcript or report card.
	Open-ended:
	Have you taken Algebra 1? What year did you take it?
	What grade did you make?
Sample Coding	The year in school a student passed Algebra 1 with a grade of C or better.
Sample Findings	In a longitudinal study described in Chapter 7, students who took Algebra 1 after 9th grade had more difficulty passing it than those taking it earlier, and some left high school without it (Cooper et al., 2005).

University Eligibility, Application, Admission, and Enrollment

The term *college* can refer to a technical school, community college, or four-year university.

Sample Coding	In California, students' school transcripts are assessed to see if students passed, with a grade of C (2.0) or better, the classes required for eligibility for the University of California and California State Universities. These are called *a–g courses* from their listing as: a) history or social science, 2 years; b) English, 4 years; c) math, 3 years, 4 recommended, including Algebra 1, geometry, and Algebra 2; d) laboratory science, 2 years, 3 recommended; e) language other than English, 2 years, 3 recommended; f) visual and performing arts, one year; and g) college-prep electives.
Sample Findings	One partnership identified 10th grade students who were almost on track in completing their a–g requirements for university eligibility and supported their getting back on track to apply and enroll in college. Also, as discussed in Chapter 6, the Educational Partnership Center at the University of California, Santa Cruz, traced rising rates of university applications, admissions, and enrollment among underrepresented students in its partner schools (Moran et al., 2005).

BRIDGING RESOURCES AND CHALLENGES ACROSS WORLDS

The concept of *worlds* refers to cultural knowledge and behavior in families, peer groups, schools, work, community organizations, and other settings (Phelan et al., 1998). The questions shown below in Figure A.2 are from the Bridging Multiple Worlds Survey (Cooper et al., 2002).

What are your worlds?

Circle the worlds you participate in and write in important people you interact with in these worlds. You can add worlds. Write their relationship to you, such as mother, father, sibling, friend, coach, priest, counselor, or principal. These people can be positive influences in your life or may cause you difficulties.

Family   Myself

Neighborhood

Friends

Program   School   Church or Mosque

Music   Video games or Internet   Sports

What do people expect of you in your main worlds?

From the page above, think about the goals, expectations, and values that important people in your worlds have for you. Then from the list below, write inside each world you circled up to 6 expectations (you may write the numbers rather than the words).

Positive	Negative
1. Work hard	17. Be lazy
2. Stay in school	18. Drop out of school
3. Do well in Math	19. Do poorly in Math
4. Do well in English	20. Do poorly in English
5. Be a good student	21. Be a poor student
6. Be confident	22. Be unsure of myself
7. Go to college	23. Do not go to college
8. Work right after high school	24. Be unemployed
9. Be rich	25. Be poor
10. Have a family in the future	26. Have a family too soon
11. Help others financially	27. Not help others financially
12. Be successful	28. Fail
13. Be honest	29. Be dishonest
14. Have respect for others	30. Be disrespectful
15. Be responsible for my own actions	31. Be irresponsible
16. Other:_____(write inside world)	32. Other:_____(write inside world)

Figure A.2 *What are your worlds?:* These sample questions from the Bridging Multiple Worlds Survey ask students, "What are your worlds?" and "What do people expect of you from your worlds?" (Cooper, Jackson, Azmitia, & Lopez, 1994, 2002).

Sample Questions	*What are your worlds? Circle the worlds in which you participate.* Closed-ended: *Please rate the degree to which your worlds are positively or negatively connected (from +3 to –3).* Open-ended: *Write in the important people you interact with in your worlds. Write their relationship to you, such as your mother, father, sibling, friend, coach, priest, counselor, or principal. These people can be positive influences in your life or cause you difficulties.*
Sample Coding	Responses can be coded by worlds such as families, peers, or sports or by the people whom students list in each world.
Sample Findings	In one study, students wrote that their worlds included their families (often more than one), neighborhoods, pre-college programs, school, church, sports, friends' houses, clubs, shopping malls, band/music/dance, and arcade/video games (Cooper et al., 1995).

Expectations in Each World

Sample Questions	Closed-ended: *Think about the goals, expectations, and values the important people in your world have for you. From the list, write inside each of the worlds you circled up to 6 expectations (e.g., work hard or be lazy, stay in school or drop out of school).* Open-ended: *Please write in what people expect of you in your main worlds.*
Sample Coding	As shown in Figure A.2 above, students can select from positive and negative expectations that they experience in each of their worlds or write in expectations.
Sample Findings	In one study, youth reported that their families more often held positive expectations for them like "working hard" and "being smart", and their neighborhoods more often held negative expectations for them like "being a failure" and "being selfish" (Cooper et al., 1995).

Resources and Challenges: Who Helps You? Who Causes Difficulties?

Asking youth "Who helps you?" and "Who causes difficulties?" prompts them to list specific people in their lives who are resources or challenges to them. With further instructions, students can describe the nature of their help or difficulties in more detailed written narratives. We ask this question in an open-ended format only.

Sample Questions	Open-ended, short answer: *Who helps you in math? Schoolwork? Staying on track to college? Planning your future? With your problems? Write in their relation to you, like mother or friend, rather than their name.*
	Open-ended narratives (Holt, 2003): *Think about the person who helps you most with your schoolwork. Write about a specific situation in which this person helped you and explain how he or she helped you. Be as specific as possible.*
Sample Coding	Responses can be coded by who helps or causes difficulties or by worlds. Written narratives can be coded for who helps and also for how these people helped, such as by providing encouragement, advice, direct help, active listening, or offering examples of positive and negative modeling—what youth should and should not do (Holt, 2003).
Sample Findings	In written narratives, students participating in the selective program discussed in Chapter 7 described their Mexican immigrant parents and siblings as helping them with schoolwork, math, and thinking about college. Despite parents' unfamiliarity with U.S. schools and not having attended college, they could help their adolescents both emotionally and instrumentally (Holt, 2003).

Challenges and Resources

Asking youth about their challenges and resources leads them to list issues in their lives. The open-ended format can reveal personal details of students' lives.

Sample Questions	Open-ended: *What are your challenges to reaching your goals?*
	What are your resources?
Sample Coding	Challenges and resources can be coded by issues, such as financial problems or racism, and by world, such as family, peers, or school. The open-ended format can reveal vivid personal realities of students' lives.
Sample Findings	In a study of the challenges and resources of Australian college students from refugee backgrounds (primarily from Asia, the Middle East, and Africa), their most common challenges were the English language, money problems, families, school tasks, time management, and the future (Brooker & Lawrence, 2010; see also Lawrence, Dodds, & Brooker, 2010).

CULTURAL RESEARCH PARTNERSHIPS FROM CHILDHOOD TO COLLEGE

Cultural research partnerships reach across lines of national origin, ethnicity, social class, and gender to boost resources across students' worlds to support their college and career pathways. These P–20 (preschool through graduate school) or K–16 (kindergarten through college) partnerships also connect students, families, schools, community programs, business partners, and university researchers and help them ask better questions about these pathways.

Demographics of Attendance: Who Came? Who was Missing?

Sample Questions	Closed-ended: Based on attendance records of programs and community demographics: *Who came? Who was missing?* Open-ended questions for students: *Why do you think this (pattern of attendance) happened?*
Sample Coding	Attendance data can be coded for age, grade level, gender, national origin, home languages, ethnicity, or other variables of interest.
Sample Findings	In a community college program described in Chapter 7, more middle school than high school students and more girls than boys attended the Summer Institute (Cooper et al., 2005). In the Fall Saturday Academy, youth in the program discussed graphs of these patterns and wrote their views about why this happened and how the program could motivate boys and older youth to attend. One 7th grade girl wrote: "Boys might care more about being popular than smart and they don't know that they can be popular and smart at the same time." Students also suggested new Summer Institute activities that would attract boys; these were implemented at the following year's Summer Institute.

What Is Success? Partnership Goals for Students, Families, Schools, and Communities

Successful partnerships set and adapt their goals over time in local, regional, national, and international contexts. These partnerships monitor data over time to align their activities and overall capacity to attain their valued outcomes (Rodriguez, McCollum, & Villarreal, 2002; Rodriguez, Villarreal, & Cortez, 2002).

Successful Pathways

Sample Questions	*Did you graduate from high school? Did you attend college after high school? If yes, where?*
Sample Coding	As the partnership described in Chapter 7 followed students through the pre-college program from age 12 to 18 and beyond, the program director, scholarship donors, and community college leaders defined success broadly to include graduating from high school and entering the world of work; attending community college, university, or technical school; or entering military service (Cooper, et al., 2005)
Sample Findings	In the early years of the program, about half of the students enrolled in community college after graduating from high school. Just under half finished high school but did not attend college immediately, and some enrolled later. Five years later, a new pattern emerged. About one-fourth enrolled in community college, one-fourth went directly to four-year universities, and one-half finished high school.

CONCLUSIONS

These measures, coding systems, findings, and graphs have been useful for researchers, educators, and policymakers in forging common efforts to address the academic pipeline problem. Taken together, these tools can continue to strengthen partners' abilities to more clearly define their goals, communicate about them with others, and evaluative and improve their effectiveness.

Demographic Portraits: Comparing Home Languages of Language Learners Across Schools

Researchers, educators, and students can use this tool to ask questions about demographic and institutional variables in and across communities. This example compares schools in terms of the home languages of English learners, using the California Department of Education Web site. Demographic data available from other states and nations vary; this example shows a general pattern for using such data. As an illustration, the following schools in California can be compared and contrasted: Johnson High School in Sacramento, Skyline High School in Oakland, and Watsonville High School in Watsonville.

1 To start, go to www.cde.ca.gov.
2 On the top of the screen, find "Data and Statistics" and click on it.
3 On the next page, click on "DataQuest" under the "Highlights" section.
4 On the next page, under "Level," click on "School," and under "Subject" go to "Student Demographics" and choose "English Learners" or other topics of interest, then press "Submit."
5 On the next page, choose a timeframe, such as "2009–2010," type in the name of a school, and then press "Submit."
6 Select the school, click on "Number of English Language Learners by Language," and press "Submit." Print tables from search.
7 Compare demographic information for variation within each school as well as similarities and differences across schools in the home languages of English learners. The numbers of English learners in California, listed by language and grade level, can be found at: http://data1.cde.ca.gov/dataquest/LepbyLang1.asp?cChoice=LepbyLang1&cYear=2004-05

Making these kinds of data easily available can facilitate active questioning and participation by a variety of constituencies, including educators, families, and students, as well as researchers. The studies reviewed in this book demonstrate that demographic and institutional variables are relevant to students' pathways to college. Providing such information can serve as an invitation for educators, policymakers, and other partners to "unpackage" the meanings and processes related to these demographic dimensions and act on their insights.

REFERENCES

Abraham, K. G. (1986). Ego-identity differences among Anglo-American and Mexican-American adolescents. *Journal of Adolescence, 9,* 151–166.

Achieve, Inc. (2009a). *Closing the expectations gap 2009: An annual 50-state progress report on the alignment of high school policies with the demands of college and careers.* Retrieved from: http://www.achieve.org/closingtheexpecttionsgap2009.

Achieve, Inc. (2009b). *The expectations gap: A 50-state review of high school graduation requirements.* Retrieved from: http://www.achieve.org/dstore.nsf/Lookup/coursetaking/$file/coursetaking.pdf.

Adger, C. T. (2001). School-community-based organization partnerships for language minority students' school success. *Journal of Education for Students Placed at Risk, 6,* 7–25.

Alberts, C., Mbalo, N. F., & Ackerman, C. J. (2003). Adolescents' perceptions of the relevance of domains of identity formation: A South African cross-cultural study. *Journal of Youth and Adolescence, 32,* 169–184.

Allen, J. P., Hauser, S. T., Bell, K. L., & O'Connor, T. G. (1994). Longitudinal assessment of autonomy and relatedness in adolescent-family interactions as predictors of adolescent ego development and self-esteem. *Child Development, 65,* 179–194.

Alvarez, D., & Mehan, H. (2006). Whole school detracking: A strategy for equity and excellence. *Theory into Practice, 45,* 82–89.

Antonucci, T. C., Birditt, K. S., Akiyama, H., Bengston, V. L., Gans, D., Pulney, N. M., & Silverstein, M. (2009). Convoys of social relations: An interdisciplinary approach. *Handbook of theories of aging* (2nd ed., pp. 247–260). New York: Springer.

Aquilino, W. S. (2006). Family relationships and support systems in emerging adulthood. In J. J. Arnett & J. L Tanner (Eds.), *Emerging adults in America: Coming of age in the 21st century* (pp. 193–217). Washington, DC: American Psychological Association.

Archer, S. L. (1985). Identity and the choice of social roles. In A. Waterman (Ed.), *Identity in adolescence: Processes and contents* (pp. 79–99). San Francisco: Jossey-Bass.

Archer, S. L. (1994). *Interventions for adolescent identity development.* Thousand Oaks, CA: Sage.

Arnett, J. J. (2003). Coming of age in a multicultural world: Globalization and adolescent cultural identity formation. *Applied Developmental Science, 7,* 189–196.

Arnett, J. J. (2004). *Emerging adulthood: The winding road from the late teens through the twenties.* New York: Oxford University Press.

Arroyo, C. G., & Zigler, E. (1995). Racial identity, academic achievement, and the psychological well-being of economically disadvantaged adolescents. *Journal of Personality and Social Psychology, 69,* 903–914.

Auerbach, S. (2006). "If the student is good, let him fly": Moral support for college among Latino immigrant parents. *Journal of Latinos and Education, 5,* 275–292.

Ayers, M., Foseca, J. D., Andrade, R., & Civil, M. (2001). Creating learning communities: The "Build Your Dream House" unit. In E. McIntyre, A. Rosebery, & N. Gonzalez (Eds.), *Classroom diversity: Connecting curriculum to students' lives* (pp. 92–99). Portsmouth, NH: Heinemann.

Azmitia, M., & Brown, J. R. (2002). Latino immigrant parents' beliefs about the "path of life" of their adolescent children. In J. M. Contreras, K. A. Kerns, & A. M. Neal-Barnet (Eds.), *Latino children and families in the United States* (pp. 77–110). Westbrook, CT: Praeger.

Azmitia, M., & Cooper, C. R. (2001). Good or bad? Peers and academic pathways of Latino and European American youth in schools and community programs. *Journal for the Education of Students Placed at Risk, 6*, 45–71.

Azmitia, M., Cooper, C. R., & Brown, J. (2009). Support and guidance from families, friends, and teachers in Latino early adolescents' math pathways. *Journal of Early Adolescence, 29*, 142–169.

Azmitia, M., Cooper, C. R., Rivera, L., Martinez, R., Lopez, E., Ittel, A., et al. (1994). *The path of life interview*. Santa Cruz: University of California, Santa Cruz.

Azmitia, M., Cooper, C. R., García, E. E., & Dunbar, N. (1996). The ecology of family guidance in low-income Mexican-American and European-American families. *Social Development, 5*, 1–23.

Azmitia, M., Syed, M., & Radmacher, K. (2008). On the intersection of personal and social identities: Introduction and evidence from a longitudinal study of emerging adults. In M. Azmitia, M. Syed, & K. Radmacher (Eds.), *The intersections between personal and social identities. New Directions for Child and Adolescent Development, 120*, 1–16.

Baca Zinn, M. (1982). Familism among Chicanos: A theoretical review. *Humboldt Journal of Social Relations, 10*, 224–238.

Bachnik, J. M. (1992). *Kejime*: Defining a shifting self in multiple organizational modes. In N. R. Rosenberger (Ed.), *Japanese sense of self* (pp. 152–172). Cambridge, MA: Cambridge University Press.

Bakken, J. P., & Brown, B. B. (2010). Adolescent secretive behavior: African American and Hmong adolescents' strategies and justifications for managing parents' knowledge about peers. *Journal of Research on Adolescence, 20*, 1–30.

Barbarin, O. A., McCandles, T., Coleman, C., & Hill, N. E. (2005). Family practices and school performance of African American children. In V. C. McLoyd, N. E. Hill, & K. A. Dodge (Eds.), *African American family life: Ecological and cultural diversity* (pp. 227–244). New York: Guilford Press.

Barnhill, L. R. (1979). Healthy family systems. *Family Coordinator, 28*, 94–100.

Barrett, J. (2001). *When the yellow brick road doesn't lead to the Emerald City: Multiple worlds and identity among working class European American youth*. Unpublished senior thesis, University of California, Santa Cruz.

Baumrind, D. (1975). The contributions of the family to the development of competence in children. *Schizophrenia Bulletin, 14*, 12–37.

Baumrind, D. (1991). Effective parenting during the early adolescent transition. In P. E. Cowan & E. M. Hetherington (Eds.), *Family transitions: Advances in family research* (Vol. 2, pp. 111–163). Hillsdale, NJ: Erlbaum.

Beavers, W. R. (1976). A theoretical basis for family evaluation. In J. M. Lewis, W. R. Beavers, J. T. Gossett, & V. A. Phillips (Eds.), *No single thread: Psychological health in family systems* (pp. 46–82). New York: Brunner/Mazel.

Becker-Stoll, F., Fremmer-Bombik, E., Wartner, U., Zimmerman, P., & Grossman, K. (2008). Is attachment at ages 1, 6 and 16 related to autonomy and relatedness behavior of adolescents towards their mothers? *International Journal of Behavioral Development, 32*, 372–380.

Bell, L. G., & Bell, D. C. (2005). Family dynamics in adolescence affect midlife well-being. *Journal of Family Psychology, 19*, 198–207.

Bellah, R. N., Madsen, R., Sullivan, W. M., Swidler, A., & Tipton, S. M. (1985). *Habits of the heart: Individualism and commitment in American life.* Berkeley, CA: University of California Press.

Bennion, L. D., & Adams, G. R. (1986). A revision of the extended version of the Objective Measure of Ego Identity Status: An identity instrument for use with late adolescents. *Journal of Adolescent Research, 1*, 183–197.

Berry, J. W., Phinney, J. S., Sam, D. L., & Vedder, P. (2006a). *Immigrant youth in cultural transition: Acculturation, identity, and adaptation across national contexts.* Mahwah, NJ: Erlbaum.

Berry, J. W., Phinney, J. S., Sam, D. L., & Vedder, P. (2006b). Immigrant youth: Acculturation, identity and adaptation. *Applied Psychology: An International Review, 55*, 303–332.

Berry, J. W., & Sabatier, C. (2010). Acculturation, discrimination, and adaptation among second generation immigrant youth in Montreal and Paris. *International Journal of Intercultural Relations, 34*, 191–207.

Bettie, J. (2002). Exceptions to the rule: Upwardly mobile White and Mexican American high school girls. *Gender and Society, 16*, 403–422.

Beyers, W., & Goossens, L. (2003). Psychological separation and adjustment to university: Moderating effects of gender, age and perceived parenting style. *Journal of Adolescent Research, 18*, 363–382.

Beyers, W., & Ryan, R. M. (2007). Conceptualizing parental autonomy support: Adolescent perceptions of promotion of independence versus promotion of volitional functioning. *Developmental Psychology, 43*, 633–646.

Beyers, W., Goossens, L., Vansant, I., & Moors, E. (2003). Structural model of autonomy in middle and late adolescence: Connectedness, separation, detachment, and agency. *Journal of Youth and Adolescence, 32*, 351–365.

Bjornsen, C. A. (2000). The blessing as a rite of passage in adolescence. *Adolescence, 35*, 357–365.

Blos, P. (1979). *The adolescent passage: Developmental issues.* New York: International University Press.

Blustein, D. L., Devanis, L. E., & Kidney, B. A. (1989). Relationship between the identity formation process and career development. *Journal of Counseling Psychology, 36*, 196–202.

Bodilly, S. J., Chun, J., Ikemoto, G., & Stockly, S. (2004). *Challenges and potential of a collaborative approach to education reform.* Santa Monica, CA: RAND.

Booth, M. (2002). Arab adolescents facing the future: Enduring ideals and pressures to change. In B. B. Brown, R. W. Larson, & T. S. Saraswathi (Eds.), *The world's youth: Adolescence in eight regions of the globe* (pp. 207–242). Cambridge, UK: Cambridge University Press.

Bosma, H. A., & Kunnen, E. S. (2001). *Patterns of conflict as determinant of adult identity development.* Paper presented at the European Conference on Developmental Psychology, Spetses, Greece.

Bourdieu, P., & Passeron, C. (1986). *Reproduction in education, society and culture.* London: Sage.

Bowen, W. G., Chingos, M. M., & McPherson, M. S. (2009). *Crossing the finish line: Completing college at America's public universities.* Princeton, NJ: Princeton University Press.

Brewer, M. B., & Chen, Y.-R. (2007). Where (who) are collectives in collectivism? Toward conceptual clarification of individualism and collectivism. *Psychological Review, 114,* 133–151.

Brittain, C. V. (1963). Adolescent choices and parent-peer cross pressures. *American Sociological Review, 28,* 385–391.

Brody, G. H., Stoneman, Z., Flor, D., McCrary, C., Hastings, L., & Conyer, O. (1994). Financial resources, parent psychological functioning, parent co-caring, and early adolescent competence in rural two-parent African-American families. *Child Development, 65,* 590–605.

Bronfenbrenner, U. (1979). *The ecology of human development: Experiments of nature and design.* Cambridge, MA: Harvard University Press.

Brooker, A., & Lawrence, J. (2010). *Developing through challenges and opportunities: Educational pathways of young people from refugee and immigrant backgrounds.* Paper presented at the meetings of the International Society for the Study of Behavioral Development, Lusaka, Zambia.

Brown, B. B., Bakkan, J. P., Nguyen, J., & Von Bank, H. (2007). Sharing information about peer relations: Parent and adolescent opinions and behaviors in Hmong and African American families. In B. Brown & N. Mounts (Eds.), *Linking parents and family to adolescent peer relations: Ethnic and cultural considerations* (pp. 67–82). San Francisco: Jossey-Bass.

Brown, B. B., Larson, R., & Saraswathi, T. S. (Eds.) (2002). *The world's youth: Adolescence in eight regions of the globe.* Cambridge, UK: Cambridge University Press.

Bunch, G. C., & Panayotova, D. (2008). Latinos, language minority students, and the construction of ESL: Language testing and placement from high school to community college. *Journal of Hispanic Higher Education, 7,* 6–30.

Burciaga, R. (2008). *Aspiring to profess: Cultural wealth influences on persistence and aspirations of Chicana Ph.D. students in education.* Paper presented at the meetings of the Society for Research in Adolescence, Chicago, IL.

Buriel, R. (1984). Teacher-student interactions and their relationship to student achievement: A comparison of Mexican-American and Anglo-American children. *Journal of Educational Psychology, 75,* 889–897.

Buriel, R., Perez, W., DeMent, T. L., Chavez, D. V., & Moran, V. R. (1998). The relationship of language brokering to academic performance, biculturalism, and self-efficacy among Latino students. *Hispanic Journal of Behavioral Sciences, 20,* 283–297.

Business-Higher Education Forum. (2001). *Sharing responsibility: How leaders in business and higher education can improve America's schools.* Paper presented at the Business-Higher Education Forum, Washington, DC.

Business-Higher Education Forum. (2004). *Public accountability for student learning in higher education: Issues and options.* Paper presented at the Business-Higher Education Forum, Washington, DC.

Business-Higher Education Forum. (2005). *Handbook for a commitment to America's future: A toolkit for leaders of state-level P-16 councils.* Paper presented at the Business-Higher Education Forum, Washington, DC.

California Department of Education. (2005). *2004 Academic Performance Index base report: Information guide.* Retrieved from: www.cde.ca.gov/index.asp

Caplan, J., Hall, G., Lubin, S., & Fleming, R. (1997). *Literature review of school-family partnerships.* Retrieved from: www. ncrel.org/sdrs/pidata/pi0ltrev

Carjuzaa, J., Fenimore-Smith, K. J., Fuller, E. D., Howe, W. A., Kugler, E., London, A. P., Ruiz, I., & Shin, B. (2008). Drawing parallels in search of educational equity: A multicultural education delegation to China looks outside to see within. *Multicultural Perspectives, 10,* 35–40.

Carter, P. (2005). *Keepin' it real: School success beyond black and white.* New York: Oxford University Press.

Carter, P. (2006). Straddling boundaries: Identity, culture, and school. *Sociology of Education. 79,* 304–328.

Cass, J., & Curry, C. (2007). *America's cradle to prison pipeline: A Children's Defense Fund Report.* Washington, DC: A Children's Defense Fund. Retrieved from: www.childrensdefense.org/child-research-data-publications/data/cradle-prison-pipeline-report-2007-full-lowres.pdf

Catsambis, S. (2001). Expanding knowledge of parental involvement in children's secondary education: Connections with high school seniors' academic success. *Social Psychology of Education, 5,* 149–177.

Cazden, C. B. (2002). A descriptive study of six High School Puente classrooms. *Educational Policy, 16,* 496–521.

Ceja, M. (2004). Chicana college aspirations and the role of parents: Developing educational resiliency. *Journal of Hispanic Higher Education, 3,* 338–362.

Chaidez, S. (2007). *Parents, Children, and Computers Program.* Paper presented at Chicano Latino Intersegmental Convocation (CLIC), San Francisco, CA.

Chandler, M. (2006). *Self and cultural continuity as a hedge against suicide in Aboriginal communities in Canada.* Paper presented at the International Society for the Study of Behavioral Development, Melbourne, Australia.

Chandler, M., Lalonde, C. E., Sokol, B. W., & Hallen, D. (2003). Personal persistence, identity development, and suicide. *Monographs of the Society for Research in Child Development, 68,* 2.

Chang, E. S., Chen, C., Greenberger, E., Dooley, D., & Heckhausen, J. (2006). What do they want in life?: The life goals of a multi-ethnic, multi-generational sample of high school seniors. *Journal of Youth and Adolescence, 35,* 321–332.

Chang, J. M. (1995). LEP parents as resources: Generating opportunity to learn beyond schools through parental involvement. In L. L. Cheng (Ed.), *Integrating language and learning for inclusion* (pp. 265–287). San Diego, CA: Singular Publishing Group.

Chang, J. M. (2004). *Family literacy nights: Building the circle of supporters within and beyond school for middle school English language learners.* (No. 11). Washington, DC, and Santa Cruz, CA: Center for Research on Education, Diversity, and Excellence (CREDE).

Chao, R. K., & Aque, C. (2009). Interpretations of parental control by Asian immigrant and European American youth. *Journal of Family Psychology, 23,* 342–354.

Chao, R. K., & Kaeochinda, K F. (2010). Parental sacrifice and acceptance as distinct dimensions of parental support among Chinese and Filipino American adolescents. In S. T. Russell, L. J. Crockett, & R. K. Chao (Eds.), *Asian American parenting and parent–adolescent relationships: Advancing responsible adolescent development* (pp. 61–77). NY: Springer.

Chao, R., & Tseng, V. (2002). Parenting of Asian adolescents. In M. H. Bornstein (Ed.), *Handbook of parenting* (pp. 59–93). Mahwah, NJ: Erlbaum.

Chapman, D., & Austin, A. (Eds). (2002). *Higher education in the developing world: Changing contexts and institutional responses.* Westport CT: Greenwood Press.

Chavira, G. (2005). *Latino adolescents' academic achievement: The roles of family involvement and students' career and ethnic identities.* Unpublished doctoral dissertation, University of California, Santa Cruz.

Chavira, G., Mikolyski, D., Cooper, C. R., Domínguez, E., & Mena, D. D. (2003). *Career goals, knowledge, participation, and school achievement of diverse low-income youth in a community college outreach program.* Paper presented at the Society for Research in Child Development, Tampa, FL.

Chavkin, N. (1996). Involving migrant families in their children's education: Challenges and opportunities for schools. In J. L. Flores (Ed.), *Children of la frontera: Binational efforts to serve Mexican migrant and immigrant students* (pp. 325–339). Charleston, VA: Office of Educational Research and Improvement.

Chemers, M. (2009). Research and evaluation in the development of student support programs. Learning Interventions Institute, National Institutes of Health, Washington, DC.

Chemers, M. M., Syed, M., Goza, B. K., Zurbriggen, E., Bearman, S., Crosby, F., et al. (2010). *The role of self-efficacy and identity in mediating the effects of science enrichment programs for under-represented minority students.* Manuscript submitted for publication.

Chemers, M., Hu, L., & Garcia, B, F. (2001). Academic self-efficacy and first year college student performance and adjustment. *Journal of Educational Psychology, 93,* 55–64.

Chhuon, V., Hudley, C., & Macias, R. (2006). *Cambodian American college students: Cultural values and multiple worlds.* Paper presented at the meetings of the American Educational Research Association, San Francisco, CA.

Chisholm, L., Büchner, P., Kruger, H., & Brown, P. (1990). *Childhood, youth, and social change: A comparative perspective.* London: Falmer Press.

Chrispeels, J., & Gonzalez, M. (2006). *No parent left behind: The role of parent education programs in assisting families to actively engage in their children's education.* Unpublished manuscript, University of California, San Diego.

Civil, M., & Bernier, E. (2006). Exploring images of parental participation in mathematics education: Challenges and possibilities, *Mathematical Thinking and Learning, 8,* 309–330.

Clancy, P., & Goastellec, G. (2007). Exploring access and equity in higher education: Policy and performance in a comparative perspective, *Higher Education Quarterly, 61,* 136–154.

Clothey, R. (2005). China's policies for minority nationalities in higher education: Negotiating national values and ethnic identities. *Comparative Education Review, 49,* 389–409.

Coffman, J. (1999). Learning from logic models: An example of a family/school partnership program. Cambridge, MA: Harvard Family Research Project.

Cohn, K., Dowell, D., Kim, S., Lindahl, C., Maldonado, C., & Seal, J. (2004). *Raising student achievement through effective educational partnerships: Policy and practice.* Long Beach, CA: California Academic Partnership Program.

Cole, M. (2010). Education as an intergenerational process of human learning, teaching, and development. *American Psychologist, 65,* 796–807.

Coleman, J. S. (1988). Social capital in the creation of human capital. *American Journal of Sociology Supplement, 94,* 95–120.

Collignon, F. F., Men, M., & Tan, S. (2001). Finding ways in: Community-based perspectives on Southeast Asian family involvement with schools in a New England state. *Journal of Education for Students Placed at Risk, 6,* 27–44.

Compton Unified School District (2004). *Achieving college partnership: Leaving no child behind.* Compton, CA: Compton Unified School District.

Cooper, C. R. (1994). Cultural perspectives on continuity and change in adolescents' relationships. In R. Montemayor, G. R. Adams, & T. P. Gulotta (Eds.), *Advances in adolescent development. Vol. 6. Personal relationships during adolescence* (pp. 78–100). Newbury Park, CA: Sage.

Cooper, C. R. (1999). Multiple selves, multiple worlds: Cultural perspectives on individuality and connectedness in adolescent development. In A. Masten (Ed.), *Cultural processes in child development: Minnesota Symposium on Child Development* (pp. 25–57). Hillsdale, NJ: Erlbaum.

Cooper, C. R. (2001). Bridging multiple worlds: Inclusive, selective, and competitive programs, Latino youth, and pathways to college. Affirmative development of ethnic minority students. *The CEIC Review: A Catalyst for Merging Research, Policy, and Practice, 9,* 22.

Cooper, C. R. (2002). Five bridges along students' pathways to college: A developmental blueprint of families, teachers, counselors, mentors, and peers in the Puente Program. *Educational Policy: An Interdisciplinary Journal of Policy and Practice, 16,* 607–622.

Cooper, C. R. (2003). Bridging multiple worlds: Immigrant youth identity and pathways to college. *International Society for the Study of Behavioral Development Newsletter, 27,* 1–4.

Cooper, C. R. (2005). Bridging multiple worlds: Aligning science, policy, and practice across regional P-20 partnerships builds pathways to college and careers. Retrieved from: http://www.bridgingworlds.org/P-20

Cooper, C. R. (2008, April). *Diversity and adaptation in linking research, practice, and policy.* Conference on Migration and Integration as a Process: Exploring Diversity and Adaptation, European Foundation Network, Ruhr-University, Bochum, Germany.

Cooper, C. R. (2009, July). *Cultural brokers: Helping immigrant youth on their pathways to college identities in multicultural societies.* Paper presented at Conference on Identity and Participation: Cross-cultural and Muslim Youth in Europe, United Nations Alliance of Civilizations, Vienna, Austria.

Cooper, C. R., & Burciaga, R. (2011). Pathways to college, to the professoriate, and to a green card: Linking research, policy, and practice on immigrant Latino youth. In T. N. Maloney & K. Korinek (Eds.), *Migration in the 21st century: Rights, outcomes, and policy.* (pp. 177–191). London: Routledge Kegan Paul.

Cooper, C. R., & Denner, J. (1998). Theories linking culture and psychology: Universal and community-specific processes. *Annual Review of Psychology, 49,* 559–584.

Cooper, C. R., & Grotevant, H. D. (1987). Gender issues in the interface of family experience and adolescent peer relational identity. *Journal of Youth and Adolescence, 16,* 247–264.

Cooper, C. R., & Verma, S. (2009). The ISSBD Regional Workshop Study: Insights from 19 nations. *Bulletin of the International Society for the Study of Behavioral Development, 3,* 41–44.

Cooper, C. R., Azmitia, M., García, E. E., Ittel, A., Lopez, E., Rivera, L., et al. (1994). Aspirations of low-income Mexican American and European American parents for their children and adolescents. In F. A. Villaruel & R. M. Lerner (Eds.), *Community-based programs for socialization and learning: New Directions in Child Development, 63,* 65–81.

Cooper, C. R., Baker, H., Polichar, D., & Welsh, M. (1993). Values and communication of Chinese, European, Filipino, Mexican, and Vietnamese American adolescents with their families and friends. In S. Shulman & W. A. Collins (Eds.), *Father-adolescent relationships. New Directions in Child Development, 62,* 73–89.

Cooper, C. R., Behrens, R., & Trinh, N. (2009). Identity. In R. A. Shweder, T. R. Bidell, A. C. Dailey, S. D. Dixon, P. J. Miller, & J. Modell (Eds.), *The Chicago companion to the child* (pp. 474–477). Chicago: University of Chicago Press.

Cooper, C. R., Brown, J., Azmitia, M., & Chavira, G. (2005). Including Latino immigrant families, schools, and community programs as research partners on the good path of life-*el buen camino de la vida.* In T. S. Weisner (Ed.), *Discovering successful pathways in children's development: Mixed methods in the study of childhood and family life* (pp. 359–422). Chicago: University of Chicago Press.

Cooper, C. R., Chavira, G., & Mena, D. D. (2005). From pipelines to partnerships: A synthesis of research on how diverse families, schools, and communities support children's pathways through school. *Journal of Education for Students Placed at Risk, 10,* 407–430.

Cooper, C. R., Cooper, R. G., Azmitia, M., Chavira, G., & Gullatt, Y. (2002). Bridging multiple worlds: How African American and Latino youth in academic outreach programs navigate math pathways to college. *Applied Developmental Science, 6,* 73–87.

Cooper, C. R., Cooper, R. G., Burciaga, R., Domínguez, E., & Su, D. (2008). *Capital and challenge: Bridging cultural worlds on pathways to college and the professoriate by Latino immigrant youth.* Paper presented at the meetings of the Society for Research in Child Development, Denver, CO.

Cooper, C. R., Denner, J., & Lopez, E. M. (1999). Cultural brokers: Helping Latino children on pathways toward success. In M. B. Larner (Ed.), *When school is out: The Future of Children, 9,* 51–57.

Cooper, C. R., Domínguez, E., & Rosas, S. (2005). Soledad's dream: How immigrant children bridge their multiple worlds and build pathways to college. In C. R. Cooper, C. García Coll, T. Bartko, H. Davis, & C. Chatman (Eds.), *Developmental pathways through middle childhood: Rethinking contexts and diversity as resources* (pp. 235–260). Mahwah, NJ: Erlbaum.

Cooper, C. R., Domínguez, E., Azmitia, M., Holt, E., Mena, D., & Chavira, G. (2010). Staying on the path toward college: One boy at the crossroads. In H. B. Weiss, H. Kreider, M. E. Lopez, & C. Chatman-Nelson (Eds.), *Preparing educators to engage families: Case studies using an ecological systems framework* (2nd ed.) (pp. 134–142). Thousand Oaks, CA: Sage.

Cooper, C. R., Domínguez, E., Chavira, G., & Mena, D. (2002). *The Bridging Multiple Worlds Toolkit.* Retrieved from: www.bridgingworlds.org

Cooper, C. R., García Coll, C., Thorne, B., & Orellana, M. F. (2005). Beyond demographic categories: How immigration, ethnicity, and "race" matter for children's emerging identities at school. In C. R. Cooper, C. García Coll, T. Bartko, H. Davis, & C. Chatman (Eds.), *Developmental pathways through middle childhood: Rethinking contexts and diversity as resources* (pp. 181–206). Mahwah, NJ: Erlbaum.

Cooper, C. R., Gjerde, P. F., Teranishi, C., Onishi, M., Kosawa, Y., Shimizu, H., et al. (1994, July). *Multiple worlds of adolescent competence in Japan and the U S: Between- and within-cultural analyses.* Paper presented at the Western Psychological Association, Kona, HI.

Cooper, C. R., Grotevant, H. D., & Condon, S. M. (1983). Individuality and connectedness in the family as a context for adolescent identity formation and role taking skill. In C. R. Cooper & H. D. Grotevant (Eds.), *Adolescent development in the family: New directions in child development.* Vol. 22, (pp. 43–59). San Francisco: Jossey-Bass.

Cooper, C. R., Grotevant, H. D., Moore, M. S., & Condon, S. M. (1984). Predicting adolescent role taking and identity exploration from family communication patterns: A comparison of one- and two-child families. In T. Falbo (Ed.), *The single child family* (pp. 117–142). New York: Guilford.

Cooper, C. R., Jackson, J. F., Azmitia, M., & Lopez, E. M. (1998). Multiple selves, multiple worlds: Three useful strategies for research with ethnic minority youth on identity, relationships, and opportunity structures. In V. C. McLoyd & L. Steinberg (Eds.), *Studying minority adolescents: Conceptual, methodological, and theoretical issues* (pp. 111–126). Mahwah, NJ: Erlbaum.

Cooper, C. R., Jackson, J. F., Azmitia, M., Lopez, E. M., & Dunbar, N. (1995). Bridging students' multiple worlds: African American and Latino youth in academic outreach programs. In R. F. Macias & R. G. García-Ramos (Eds.), *Changing schools for changing students: An anthology of research on language minorities* (pp. 211–234). Santa Barbara, CA: University of California Linguistic Minority Research Institute.

Cooper, C. R., Jackson, J., Azmitia, M., & Lopez, E. (1994, 2002). *The Bridging Multiple Worlds Survey: Qualitative and quantitative versions.* Santa Cruz, CA: University of California, Santa Cruz.

Cooper, C. R., & Mehan, H. (2006). *P-20 alliances for equity in access to higher education: Scientific advances, policy accountability, and practices for regional-state systems.* Oakland, CA: University of California Office of the President.

Cooper, C. R., Mehan, H., & Halimah, E. (2006). *Advancing a common P-20 framework with regional theories of change for students, schools, and educational systems.* Oakland, CA: University of California Office of the President.

Cooper, M. (Ed.) (2008). *Crossing borders: Diversity in higher education (migration, integration and lifelong learning).* Papers from the 17th annual conference of the European Access Network. London, UK: European Access Network.

Coppens, A., Mejia Arauz, R., & Rogoff, B. (2010, April). *Children's views of child involvement in family household work in two communities near Guadalajara, Mexico.* Paper presented at meetings of the American Educational Research Association, Denver, CO.

Coulthard, M. (1977). *An introduction to discourse analysis.* Essex: Longman House.

Creswell, J., & Clark, V. L. P. (2007). *Designing and conducting mixed methods research.* Thousand Oaks, CA: Sage.

Crocetti, E., Rubini, M., Luyckx, K., & Meeus, W. (2008). Identity formation in early and middle adolescents from various ethnic groups: From three dimensions to five statuses. *Journal of Youth and Adolescence, 37,* 983–996.

Crul, M. (2002). Success breeds success: Moroccan and Turkish student mentors in the Netherlands. *International Journal for the Advancement of Counseling, 24,* 275–287.

Crul, M., & Schneider, J. (2009). *TIES Policy Brief: The second generation in Europe: Education and the transition to the labour market.* Amsterdam: TIES. Retrieved from: www.tiesproject. eu/component/option,com_docman/task,cat_view/gid,45/Itemid,142/

Crystal, D. S., Kakinuma, M., DeBell, M., Azuma, H., & Miyashita, T. (2008). Who helps you? Self and other sources of support among youth in Japan and the USA. *International Journal of Behavioral Development, 32,* 496–508.

Daniels, R. (1990). *Coming to America: A history of immigration and ethnicity in American life.* New York: HarperCollins.

Data Quality Campaign. (2009). *The next step: Using longitudinal data to improve student success.* Retrieved from: http://www.dataqualitycampaign.org/files/NextStep.pdf

Datnow, A., & Cooper, R. (1997). Peer networks of African American students in independent schools: Affirming academic success and racial identity. *Journal of Negro Education, 66,* 56–72.

Davey, M., Eaker, D., Fish, L., & Klock, K. (2003). Ethnic identity in an American White minority group. *Identity: An International Journal of Theory and Research, 3,* 143–158.

De Bresser, S. (2009, May). *Workshop: The long route.* TIES Stakeholders Conference, Amsterdam, The Netherlands.

Dean, D. R., & Levine, A. (2008). What's missing: Why foundations and policy analysis are impatient with the pace of school-college reform. *Metropolitan Universities, 18,* 10–27.

Delgado-Gaitan, C. (1990). *Literacy for empowerment: The role of parents in children's education.* New York: Falmer Press.

Delgado-Gaitan, C. (1991). Involving parents in the schools: A process of empowerment. *American Journal of Education, 100,* 20–46.

Denner, J., Cooper, C. R., Dunbar, N., & Lopez, E. M. (2005). Access to opportunity: Latinos in a college outreach program: Application, selection, and participation. *Journal of Latinos in Education, 4,* 21–40.

Denner, J., Cooper, C. R., Lopez, E. M., & Dunbar, N. (1999). Beyond "giving science away": How university-community partnerships inform youth programs, research, and policy. *Society for Research in Child Development Social Policy Report, 13,* 1–18.

Destin, M., & Oyserman, D. (2010). Incentivizing education: Seeing schoolwork as an investment, not a chore. *Journal of Experimental Social Psychology, 46,* 846–849.

Deyé, S. (2009). *Making a difference: Eight state legislative policy recommendations for improving America's high schools.* Denver, CO: National Conference of State Legislatures. Retrieved from: http://www.ncsl.org/?tabid=19252.

Domínguez, E. E., Cooper, C. R., Chavira, G., Mena, D., Lopez, E. M., Dunbar, N., et al. (2001). *It's all about choices/Se trata de todas las decisiones: Activities to build identity pathways to college and careers. Bridging Multiple Worlds Toolkit.* Retrieved from http://www.bridgingworlds.org

Dorner, L. M., Orellana, M. F., & Jiménez, R. (2008). "It's one of those things that you do to help the family": Language brokering and the development of immigrant adolescents. *Journal of Adolescent Research, 23,* 515–543.

Dorner, L. M., Orellana, M. F., & Li-Grining, C. P. (2007). "I helped my Mom and it helped me": Translating the skills of language brokers into improved standardized test scores. *American Journal of Education, 113,* 451–478.

Duffy, H. M. (2005). Se puede! Preparing teachers to build leadership among underserved students. *The English Journal, 95,* 71–76.

Dunnigan, T., McNall, M., & Mortimer, J. T. (1993). The problem of metaphorical non-equivalence in cross-cultural survey research: Comparing the mental health status of Hmong refugee and general population adolescents. *Journal of Cross-Cultural Psychology, 24,* 344–365.

Durán, R. (2007). *Parent and community involvement in Latino academic attainment.* Paper presented at Chicano Latino Intersegmental Convocation (CLIC), San Francisco, CA.

Durán, R., Durán, J., Perry-Romero, D., & Sanchez, E. (2001). Latino immigrant parents and children learning and publishing together in an after school setting. *Journal of Education for Students Placed at Risk, 6,* 95–113.

Durán, R., Fernandez, G., & Chaidez, S. (2008, April). *Qualitative study of parents' voices in family-school engagement programs.* Paper presented at the meetings of the American Educational Research Association, New York.

Eccles, J. S., & Gootman, J. A. (Eds.). (2002). *Community programs to promote youth development.* Washington, DC: National Academy Press.

Eccles, J. S., & Midgley, C. (1989). Stage-environment fit: Developmentally appropriate classrooms for early adolescents. In C. Ames & R. E. Ames (Eds.), *Research on motivation in education: Vol. 3. Goals and cognitions* (pp. 13–44). New York: Academic Press.

Eccles, J. S., Midgley, C., Wigfield, A., Buchanan, C. M., Reuman, D., Flanagan, C., et al. (1993). Development during adolescence: The impact of stage-environment fit on young adolescents' experiences in schools and in families. *American Psychologist, 48,* 90–101.

Eckert, P. (1995). *Jocks and burnouts: Social categories and identity in the high school*. New York: Teachers College Press.

Edgert, P., & Taylor, J. W. (1996). *Progress report on the effectiveness of collaborative student academic development programs*. (No. 96-11). Sacramento, CA: California Postsecondary Education Commission.

Education Trust. (2004). *Education in America*. Washington, DC: The Education Trust.

Education Trust-West. (2010). No time to delay: Delivering the statewide data systems California's students deserve. *Policy Brief*. Oakland, CA: Education Trust-West.

Edwards, L N., & Pasquale, M. K. (2003). Women's higher education in Japan: Family background, economic factors, and the Equal Employment Opportunity Law. *Journal of the Japanese and International Economies, 17*, 1–32.

Elicker, J., Englund, M., & Sroufe, L. A. (1992). Predicting peer competence and peer relationships in childhood from early parent-child relationships. In R. D. Parke & G. W. Ladd (Eds.), *Family-peer relationships: Models of linkages* (pp. 77–106). Hillsdale, NJ: Erlbaum.

Engle, J., & Lynch, M. (2009). *Charting a necessary path: The baseline report of the Access to Success Initiative*. Washington, DC: The Education Trust.

Engle, J., & O'Brien, C. (2007). *Demography is not destiny: Increasing the graduation rates of low-income college students at large public universities*. Washington, DC: The Pew Institute.

Engstrom, C., & Tinto, V. (2008). Learning better together: The impact of learning communities on the pesistence of low-income students. *Opportunity Matters: A Journal of Research Informing Educational Opportunity Practice and Programs, 1*, 5–21.

Epstein, J. L. (1990). School and family connections: Theory, research and implications for integrating sociologies of education and family. *Marriage and Family Review, 15*, 99–126.

Epstein, J. L. (2001a). Building bridges of home, school, and community: The importance of design. *Journal of Education for Students Placed at Risk, 6*, 161–168.

Epstein, J. L. (2001b). *School, family, and community partnerships: Preparing educators and improving schools*. Boulder, CO: Westview Press.

Epstein, J. L., & Dauber, S. L. (1991). School programs and teacher practices of parent involvement in inner-city elementary and middle schools. *The Elementary School Journal, 91*, 289–303.

Epstein, J. L., & Sanders, M. G. (2006). Prospects for change: Preparing educators for school, family, and community partnerships. *Peabody Journal of Education, 81*, 81–120.

Epstein, J. L., Sanders, M. G., Sheldon, S. B., Simon, B. S., Salinas, K. C., Jansorn, N. R., Van Voorhis, F. L., Martin, C. S., Thomas, B. G., Greenfield, M. D., Hutchins, D. J., & Williams, K. J. (2009). *School, family, and community partnerships: Your handbook for action* (3rd ed.). Thousand Oaks, CA: Corwin Press.

Erickson, R., & Shultz, J. (1982). *The counselor as gatekeeper: Social interaction in interviews*. New York: Academic Press.

Erikson, E. H. (1950). *Childhood and society*. Oxford, England: Norton.

Erikson, E. H. (1968). *Identity: Youth and crisis*. New York: Norton.

Erkut, S. (2010). Developing multiple language versions of instruments for intercultural research, *Child Development Perspectives, 4*, 19–24.

Ewell, P. T., Schild, P. R., & Paulson, K. (2003). *Following the mobile student: Can we develop the capacity for a comprehensive database to assess student progression?* Indianapolis, IN: Lumina Foundation for Education.

Fan, X., & Chen, M. (2001). Parental involvement and students' academic achievement: A meta-analysis. *Educational Psychology Review, 13*, 1–22.

Fann, A. J. (2005). *Forgotten students: American Indian high school student narratives on college access*. Unpublished doctoral dissertation, University of California, Los Angeles.

Fann, A. J., Jarsky, K. M., & McDonough, P. M. (2009). Parent involvement in the college planning process: A case study of P-20 collaboration. *Journal of Hispanic Higher Education, 8*, 374–393.

Flores-Gonzalez, N. (1999). Puerto Rican high achievers: An example of ethnic and academic identity compatibility. *Anthropology and Education Quarterly, 30*, 343–362.

Ford, D. Y., & Harris, J. J. (1996). Perceptions and attitudes of Black students toward school, achievement, and other educational variables. *Child Development, 67*, 1141–1152.

Fordham, S. (1988). Racelessness as a factor in Black students' school success: Pragmatic strategy or Pyrrhic victory? *Harvard Educational Review, 58*, 54–84.

Fordham, S., & Ogbu, J. U. (1986). Black students' school success: Coping with the "burden of acting White." *The Urban Review, 18*, 176–206.

Fredricks, J. A., & Eccles, J. S. (2010). Breadth of extracurricular participation and adolescent adjustment among African-American and European-American youth. *Journal of Research on Adolescence, 20*, 307–333.

Freire, P. (1970). *Pedagogy of the oppressed*. New York: Seabury Press.

Freud, A. (1958). Adolescence. *The Psychoanalytic Study of the Child, 13*, 255–278.

Fry, R. (2002). *Latinos in higher education: Many enroll, too few graduate*. Washington, DC: Pew Hispanic Center.

Fuligni, A. J. (1998). Authority, autonomy, and parent-adolescent conflict and cohesion: A study of adolescents from Mexican, Chinese, Filipino, and European backgrounds. *Developmental Psychology, 34*, 782–792.

Fuligni, A. J. (Ed.). (2007). *Contesting stereotypes and creating identities: Social categories, social identities, and educational participation*. New York: Russell Sage Foundation.

Gallimore, R., Goldenberg, C. N., & Weisner, T. S. (1993). The social construction and subjective reality of activity settings: Implications for community psychology. *American Journal of Community Psychology, 21*, 537–559.

Gándara, P. (2002). A study of High School Puente: What we have learned about preparing Latino youth for postsecondary education. *Educational Policy, 16*, 474–495.

Gándara, P. (n.d.). *The Puente Program*. Unpublished manuscript, University of California, Davis.

Gándara, P., & Bial, D. (2001). *Paving the way to postsecondary education: K-12 intervention programs for underrepresented youth*. Washington, DC: National Postsecondary Education Cooperative Access Working Group, National Center for Education Statistics, U.S. Department of Education.

Gándara, P., & Contreras, F. (2009). *The Latino education crisis: The consequences of failed social policies*. Cambridge, MA: Harvard University Press.

Gándara, P., & Mejorado, M. (2005). Putting your money where your mouth is: Mentoring as a strategy to increase access to higher education. In W. G. Tierney, Z. B. Corwin, & J. E. Colyar (Eds.), *Preparing for college: Nine elements of effective outreach* (pp. 89–110). Albany, NY: State University of New York Press.

Gándara, P., & Moreno, J. F. (2002). Introduction: The Puente Project: Issues and perspectives on preparing Latino youth for higher education. *Educational Policy, 16*, 463–473.

Gándara, P., Gutierrez, D., & O'Hara, S. (2001). Planning for the future in rural and urban high schools. *Journal for the Education of Students Placed at Risk, 6*, 73–93.

Gándara, P., Gutierrez, D., William-White, L., & O'Hara, S. (2001). *The changing shape of aspirations: Mexican American students and the influence of peers, family, and school on future plans.* Paper presented at the UC ACCORD (All Campus Consortium on Research on Diversity) meeting, San Jose, CA.

Gándara, P., Larson, K., Mehan, H., & Rumberger, R. (1998). *Capturing Latino students in the academic pipeline.* Paper presented at the Chicano/Latino Policy Project (CLPP) Report, Vol. 1, No. 1. from ERIC Document ED427094.

Gándara, P., O'Hara, S., & Gutierrez, D. (2004). The changing shape of aspirations: Peer influence on achievement behavior. In M. A. Gibson, P. Gándara, & J. P. Koyama (Eds.), *School connections: U.S. Mexican youth, peers, and school achievement* (pp. 39–62). New York: Teachers College Press.

García Coll, C., & Marks, A. K. (2009). *Immigrant stories: Ethnicity and academics in middle childhood.* New York: Oxford University Press.

García Coll, C., Szalacha, L. A., & Palacios, N. (2005). Children of Dominican, Portuguese, and Cambodian immigrant families: Academic attitudes and pathways during middle childhood. In C. R. Cooper, C. García Coll, W. T. Bartko, H. M. Davis & C. Chatman (Eds.), *Developmental pathways through middle childhood: Rethinking contexts and diversity as resources* (pp. 207–233). Mahwah, NJ: Erlbaum.

Gaskins, S. (1994). Integrating interpretive and quantitative methods in socialization research. *Merrill-Palmer Quarterly, 40,* 313–333.

Geiser, S. (1996). California's changing demographics: Implications for UC. In S. Golub (Ed.), *Academic outreach and intersegmental partnerships: Outreach forum proceedings.* (pp. 12–16). University of California, Irvine: Center for Educational Partnerships.

George, P., & Aronson, R. (2003). *How do educators' cultural belief systems affect underserved students' pursuit of postsecondary education?* Boston, MA: Pathways to College Network.

Gibson, M. A. (1988). *Accommodation without assimilation: Sikh immigrants in an American high school.* Ithaca, NY: Cornell University Press.

Gibson, M. A. (1995). Patterns of acculturation and high school performance. *Linguistic Minority Research Institute News, 4,* 1–3.

Gibson, M. A. (1997a). Ethnicity and school performance: Complicating the immigrant/involuntary minority typology. *Anthropology and Education Quarterly, 28,* 431–454.

Gibson, M. A. (1997b). Exploring and explaining the variability: Cross-national perspectives on the school performance of minority students. *Anthropology and Education Quarterly, 28,* 318–329.

Gibson, M. A., & Hidalgo, N. (2009). Bridges to success in high school for migrant youth. *Teachers College Record, 111,* 683–711.

Gibson, M. A., Bejínez, L., Hidalgo, C., & Rolón, C. (2004). Belonging and school participation: Lessons from a migrant student club. In M. A. Gibson, P. Gándara & J. Koyama (Eds.), *School connections: U.S. Mexican youth, peers, and school achievement* (pp. 129–149). New York: Teachers College Press.

Gjerde, P. F., Cooper, C. R., Azuma, H., Kashiwagi, K., Kosawa, Y., Shimizu, H., et al. (2000, July). *The role of gender in resources and barriers for Japanese, Japanese American, and European American youth.* Paper presented at the International Society for the Study of Behavioral Development, Beijing, China.

Gjerde, P. F., Cooper, C. R., Kosawa, Y., Onishi, M., Teranishi, C., Shimizu, H., et al. (1995). *Family relations and adolescent goals and values in Japan and the U.S.: Between- and within-cultural analyses.* Paper presented at the Society for Research on Adolescence, Boston, MA.

Goh, M., Dunnigan, T., Schuchman, K. M., & Chin, J. L. (2004). Bias in counseling Hmong clients with limited English proficiency. In *The psychology of prejudice and discrimination: Ethnicity and multiracial identity, Vol. 2. Race and ethnicity in psychology* (pp. 109–136). Westport, CT: Praeger.

Goldenberg, C., Gallimore, R., & Reese, L. (2005). Using mixed methods to explore Latino children's literacy development. In T. S. Weisner (Ed.), *Discovering successful pathways in children's development: Mixed methods in the study of childhood and family life* (pp. 21–46). Chicago: Chicago University Press.

Goldenberg, C., Gallimore, R., Reese, L., & Garnier, H. (2001). Cause or effect? A longitudinal study of immigrant Latino parents' aspirations and expectations and their children's school performance. *American Educational Research Journal, 38,* 547–582.

Goldscheider, F., & Goldscheider, C. (1999). *The changing transition to adulthood: Leaving and returning home.* Newbury Park, CA: Sage.

Gomez, M. N., Bissell, M., Danziger, L., & Casselman, R. (1990). *To advance learning: A handbook on developing K-12 postsecondary partnerships.* Lanham, MD: University Press of America.

Gonzalez, K., Stoner, C., & Jovel, J. (2003). Examining the role of social capital in access to college for Latinas: Toward a college opportunity framework. *Journal of Hispanic Higher Education, 2,* 146–170.

Gonzalez, M., & Chrispeels, J. (2008). *Mapping family-school partnership program evaluation: The PIQE and MALDEF logic models.* Paper presented at the American Educational Research Association Annual Meeting, New York.

González, N., & Moll, L. C. (2002). *Cruzando el puente*: Building bridges to funds of knowledge. *Educational Policy, 16,* 623–641.

González, N., Andrade, R., Civil, M., & Moll, L. (2001). Bridging funds of distributed knowledge: Creating zones of practices in mathematics. *Journal of Education for Students Placed at Risk, 6,* 115–132.

Goodnow, J. J. (in press). Refugees, asylum-seekers, displaced persons: Children in precarious positions. In A. Ben-Arieh, J. Cashmore, G. Goodman, & G. B. Melton (Eds.), *Handbook of child research.* Thousand Oaks, CA: Sage.

Goossens, L. (2006). The many faces of adolescent autonomy: Parent-adolescent conflict, behavioral decision-making, and emotional autonomy. In S. Jackson & L. Goossens (Eds.), *Handbook of adolescent development* (pp. 135–153). Hove, UK: Psychology Press.

Gordon, E. T., & Gordon, E. W. (2002). *The conversion of natural groups into high performance learning communities.* Paper presented at the National Invitational Conference on Closing the Achievement Gap, Racine, WI.

Graafsma, T. L. G., Bosma, H. A., Grotevant, H. D., & deLevita, D. J. (1994). Identity and development: An interdisciplinary view. In H. A. Bosma, T. L. G. Graafsma, H. D. Grotevant, & D. J. deLevita (Eds.), *Identity and development: An interdisciplinary approach* (pp. 159–174). Thousand Oaks: Sage.

Greenfield, P. M., Keller, H., Fuligni, A., & Maynard, A. (2003). Cultural pathways through universal development. *Annual Review of Psychology, 54,* 461–490.

Greenfield, P. M. (1994). Independence and interdependence as developmental scripts: Implications for theory, research, and practice. In P. M. Greenfield & R. R. Cocking (Eds.), *Cross-cultural roots of minority child development* (pp. 1–37). Hillsdale, NJ: Erlbaum.

Greenfield, P. M., & Cocking, R. R. (1994). *Cross-cultural roots of minority child development.* Hillsdale, NJ: Erlbaum.

Greenfield, P. M. (2010). Particular forms of independence and interdependence are adapted to particular kinds of sociodemographic environment: Commentary on "Independence and interdependence in children's developmental experiences", *Child Development Perspectives,* 4, 37–39.

Grolnick, W. S., & Slowiaczek, M. L. (1994). Parents' involvement in children's schooling: A multidimensional conceptualization and motivational model. *Child Development,* 65, 237–252.

Grotevant, H. D., & Cooper, C. R. (1981). Assessing adolescent identity in the areas of occupation, religion, politics, friendship, dating, and sex roles: Manual for administration and coding of the interview. *JSAS Catalog of Selected Documents in Psychology, 11,* 52.

Grotevant, H. D., & Cooper, C. R. (1985). Patterns of interaction in family relationships and the development of identity formation in adolescence. *Child Development, 56,* 415–428.

Grotevant, H. D., & Cooper, C. R. (1986). Individuation in family relationships: A perspective on individual differences in the development of identity and role-taking skill in adolescence. *Human Development, 29,* 82–100.

Grotevant, H. D., & Cooper, C. R. (1988). The role of family experience in career exploration: A life-span perspective. In P. B. Baltes, D. L. Featherman, & R. M. Lerner (Eds.), *Life-span development and behavior* (Vol. 8, pp. 231–258). Hillsdale, NJ: Erlbaum.

Grotevant, H. D., & Cooper, C. R. (1998). Individuality and connectedness in adolescent development: Review and prospects for research on identity, relationships and context. In E. Skoe & A. Von der Lippe (Eds.), *Personality development in adolescence: A cross national and life span perspective* (pp. 3–37). London: Routledge.

Grotevant, H. D., & McRoy, R. G. (1998). *Openness in adoption: Exploring family connections.* Thousand Oaks, CA: Sage.

Grotevant, H. D., & Von Korff, L. (2008). *Adoptive identity exploration in adolescence: Compartmentalization or concurrent exploration across domains?* Paper presented at the meetings of the International Society for the Study of Behavioral Development, Wurzburg, Germany.

Grotevant, H. D., & Von Korff, L. (in press). Adoptive identity. In S. J. Schwartz (Ed.), *Handbook of identity theory and research.* New York: Springer Science + Business Media.

Grotevant, H. D., Thorbecke, W. L., & Meyer, M. L. (1982). An extension of Marcia's identity status interview into the interpersonal domain. *Journal of Youth and Adolescence, 11,* 33–47.

Gupta, A. (2006). *Affirmative action in India and the U.S.: A study in contrasts.* University of California, Berkeley: Center for Studies in Higher Education. Retrieved from: http://cshe.berkeley.edu/publications/docs/ROP.Gupta.10.06.pdf

Gutiérrez, K. D. (2008). Developing a sociocritical literacy in the third space. *Reading Research Quarterly, 43,* 148–164.

Gutman, L. M., & McLoyd, V. C. (2000). Parents' management of their children's education within the home, at school, and in the community: An examination of African-American families living in poverty. *Urban Review, 32,* 1–24.

Haight, W. (2002). *African-American children at church: A sociocultural perspective.* Cambridge, MA: Cambridge University Press.

Halimah, E. (2005). *Policy and practice for University of California P-20 regional intersegmental alliances.* Oakland, CA: University of California Office of the President.

Hamilton, S. F. (1994). Employment prospects as motivation for school achievement: Links and gaps between school and work in seven countries. In R. K. Silbereisen & E. Todt (Eds.), *Adolescence in context: The interplay of family, peers, school, and work in adjustment* (pp. 267–283). New York: Springer-Verlag.

Hamm, J. V. (1994). Negotiating the maze: Adolescents' cross-ethnic peer relations in ethnically diverse schools. In L. H. Meyer, H. S. Park, M. Grenot-Scheger, I. S. Schwartz, & B. Harcy (Eds.), *Making friends* (pp. 243–261). Baltimore, MD: Brooks-Cole.

Hardway, C., & Fuligni, A. (2006). Dimensions of family connectedness among adolescents with Mexican, Chinese, and European backgrounds. *Developmental Psychology, 42*, 1246–1258.

Harkness, S., Super, C. M., & Keever, C. H. (1992). Learning to be an American parent: How cultural models gain directive force. In R. D'Andrade & C. Strauss (Eds.), *Human motives and cultural models* (pp. 163–178). Cambridge, UK: Cambridge University Press.

Harrison, A. O., Wilson, M. N., Pine, C. J., Chan, S. Q., & Buriel, R. (1990). Family ecologies of ethnic minority children. *Child Development, 61*, 347–362.

Haycock, K. (1996). Thinking differently about school reform: College and university leadership for the big changes we need. *Change, 28*, 12–18.

Hayward, G. C., Brandes, B. G., Kirst, M. W., & Mazzeo, C. (1997). *Higher education outreach programs: A synthesis of evaluations.* Stanford, CA: Policy Analysis for California Education (PACE).

Heath, S. B. (1983). *Ways with words: Language, life, and work in communities and classrooms.* Cambridge, MA: Cambridge University Press.

Heath, S. B., & McLaughlin, M. W. (1993). *Identity and inner-city youth: Beyond ethnicity and gender.* New York: Teachers College Press.

Helms, J. E., Jernigan, M., & Mascher, M. (2005). The meaning of race in psychology and how to change it: A methodological perspective. *American Psychologist, 60*, 27–36.

Henderson, R. W. (1997). Educational and occupational aspirations and expectations among parents of middle school students of Mexican descent: Family resources for academic development and mathematics learning. In R. D. Taylor & M. C. Wang (Eds.), *Social and emotional adjustment and family relations in ethnic minority families* (pp. 99–131). Mahwah, NJ: Erlbaum.

Hernandez, D. J. (2004). Demographic change and the life circumstances of immigrant families. *The Future of Children, 14*, 17–47.

Hernandez, D. J., & Charney, E. (1998). *From generation to generation: The health and well-being of children in immigrant families.* Washington, DC: National Academy Press.

Hidalgo, N., Siu, S. F., & Epstein, J. L. (2003). Research on families, schools, and communities: A multicultural perspective. In J. Banks (Ed.), *Handbook of research on multicultural education* (2nd ed., pp. 614–635). New York: Macmillan.

Hollingshead, A. B., & Redlich, F. C. (1958). *Social class and mental illness.* New York: Wiley.

Holt, E. (2002). *Comparing the role of culture within capital and challenge models: Educational and occupational goals of Japanese, Japanese American and European American adolescents.* Paper presented at the Society for Research in Adolescence, New Orleans, LA.

Holt, E. (2003). *Who's helping and what are they doing? Latino adolescents and their networks of help.* Unpublished manuscript, University of California, Santa Cruz.

Horn, L. J., & Chen, X. (2002). *Toward resiliency: At-risk students who make it to college.* Washington, DC: Office of Educational Research and Improvement, U.S. Department of Education.

Houck, J. W., Cohn, K. C., & Cohn, C. A. (Eds.). (2004). *Partnering to lead educational renewal: High-quality teachers, high-quality schools.* New York: Teachers College Press.

Howley, C., & Cowley, K. S. (2001). *West Virginia Department of Education GEAR UP Project: Year 1 baseline survey (2000-2001): Gaining Early Awareness And Readiness for Undergraduate Programs.* Charleston, WV: West Virginia State Department of Education.

Hume, S. E. (2008). Ethnic and national identities of Africans in the United States. *Geographical Review, 98,* 496–512.

Huntsinger, C. S., & Jose, P. E. (2009). Parental involvement in children's schooling: Different meanings in different cultures. *Early Childhood Research Quarterly, 24,* 398–410.

Hurrelmann, K. (Ed.). (1994). *International handbook of adolescence.* Westport, CT: Greenwood.

Hurtado, A., & Cervantez, K. (2009). A view from within and from without: The development of Latina feminist psychology. In F. A. Villarruel, G. Carlo, J. M. Grau, M. Azmitia, N. J. Cabrera, & T. J. Chahin (Eds.), *Handbook of U.S. Latino psychology* (pp. 171–190). Los Angeles, CA: Sage.

Hurtado, A., & García, E. E. (1994). *The educational achievement of Latinos: Barriers and successes (University of California Latino Eligibility Study).* Santa Cruz, CA: Regents of the University of California.

Hutchison, R., & McNall, M. (1994). Early marriage in a Hmong cohort. *Journal of Marriage and the Family, 56,* 579–590.

Immerwahr, J. (2002). *Great expectations: How the public and parents—White, African American, and Hispanic—view higher education*Stanford, CA: National Center for Public Policy and Higher Education, and Public Agenda. National Center Report #00-2. Retrieved from: http://www.highereducation.org/reports/reports_center_2000.shtml

Immigration and Naturalization Service. (2002). *Statistical yearbook of the Immigration and Naturalization Service.* Washington, DC: U.S. Department of Justice.

Ingoglia, S., Lo Coco, A., Inguglia, C., & Pace, U. (2006, July). *Patterns of autonomy and intimacy in the parent-adolescent relationship: A comparison between Italian and Tunisian adolescents.* Paper presented at the meetings of the International Society for the Study of Behavioral Development, Melbourne, Australia.

Ito, M., Horst, H. A., Bittanti, M., Boyd, D., Herr-Stephenson, B., Lange, P. G., et al. (2008). *Living and learning with new media: Summary of findings from the Digital Youth Project.* Chicago, IL: John D. and Catherine T. MacArthur Foundation.

Jackson, S., & Goossens, L. (2006). The many faces of adolescent autonomy: Parent-adolescent conflict, behavioral decision-making, and emotional distancing. *Handbook of adolescent development* (pp. 135–153). New York: Psychology Press.

Jacob, W. J. (2007). Social justice in Chinese higher education: Regional issues of equity and access. *International Review of Education, 52,* 149–169.

Jarrett, R. L. (1995). Growing up poor: The family experiences of socially mobile youth in low-income African American neighborhoods. *Journal of Adolescent Research, 10,* 111–135.

Jarsky, K. M., McDonough, P. M., & Núñez, A.-M. (2009). Establishing a college culture in secondary schools through P-20 collaboration: A case study. *Journal of Hispanic Higher Education, 8,* 357–373.

Josselson, R. (1994). Identity and relatedness in the life cycle. In H. A. Bosma, T. L. G. Graafsma, H. D. Grotevant, & D. J. deLevita (Eds.), *Identity and development: An interdisciplinary approach* (pp. 81–102). Thousand Oaks, CA: Sage.

Kagitçibasi, Ç. (2005). Autonomy and relatedness in cultural context: Implications for self and family. *Journal of Cross-Cultural Psychology, 36*, 403–422.

Kagitçibasi, Ç. (2007). *Family, self, and human development across cultures: Theories and applications* (2nd ed.). Mahwah, NJ: Erlbaum.

Kahne, J., & Bailey, K. (1999). The role of social capital in youth development: The case of "I Have a Dream." *Educational Evaluation and Policy Analysis, 21*, 321–343.

Kao, G., & Rutherford, L. T. (2007). Does social capital still matter? Immigrant minority disadvantage in school-specific social capital and its effects on academic achievement. *Sociological Perspectives, 50*, 27–52.

Kao, G., & Tienda, M. (1995). Optimism and achievement: The educational performance of immigrant youth. *Social Science Quarterly, 76*, 1–19.

Kao, G., & Tienda, M. (1998). Educational aspirations of minority youth. *American Journal of Education, 106*, 349–384.

Kashiwagi, K. (2007). Low birthrate and women: Viewed from women's psychological development. *Japan Spotlight: Economy, Culture, & History, 26*, 20–22.

Kelly, M. (2008). *Towards a better future for all in Europe: Lessons from Ireland.* Paper presented at the 16th European Access Network Annual Conference, Galway, Ireland.

Kelly, S. (2006). Are teachers tracked? On what basis and with what consequence? *Social Psychology of Education, 7*, 55–72.

Khalil, N., Morales, J. C., & Mehan, H. (2006). Going the distance: The challenges of traveling cultural and geographical space. Unpublished manuscript, University of California, San Diego.

Kiang, L., & Fuligni, A. J. (2009). Ethnic identity in context: Variations in ethnic exploration and belonging within parent, same-ethnic peer, and different-ethnic peer relationships. *Journal of Youth and Adolescence, 38*, 732–743.

Kiang, L., Harter, S., & Whitesell, N. R. (2007). Relational expression of ethnic identity in Chinese Americans. *Journal of Social and Personal Relationships, 24*, 277–296.

Kirst, M. W., & Venezia, A. (Eds.). (2004). *From high school to college: Improving opportunities for success in postsecondary education.* San Francisco, CA: Jossey-Bass.

Kitayama, S., Markus, H. R., Matsumoto, H., & Norasakkunkit, V. (1997). Individual and collective processes in the construction of the self: Self-enhancement in the United States and self-criticism in Japan. *Journal of Personality and Social Psychology, 72*, 1245–1267.

Ko, L. K., & Perreira, K. M. (2010). "It turned my world upside down": Latino youths' perspectives on immigration. *Journal of Adolescent Research, 25*, 465–493.

Kroger, J. (1993a). *Discussions on ego identity.* Hillsdale, NJ: Erlbaum.

Kroger, J. (1993b). *Identity and context: How the identity statuses choose their match.* Newbury Park, CA: Sage.

Kroger, J. (2007). *Identity development: Adolescence through adulthood* (2nd ed.). Thousand Oaks, CA: Sage.

Kruse, J., & Walper, S. (2008). Types of individuation in relation to parents: Predictors and outcomes. *International Journal of Behavioral Development, 32*, 390–400.

Kuh, G. D., Kinzie, J. Buckley, J. A., Bridges, B. K., & Hayek, J. C. (2006). *What matters to student success: A review of the literature. Commissioned report for the National Symposium on Postsecondary Student Success: Spearheading a Dialog on Student Success.* Washington, DC: National Postsecondary Education Cooperative.

Kurtz, V. (2009). *Tasha goes to university.* Long Beach, CA: California Academic Partnership Program. Retrieved from: http://www.calstate.edu/capp/publications/docs/TashaGoes ToUniversity-acc.pdf

Kurtz, V. (2010). *Tasha comes home.* Long Beach, CA: California Academic Partnership Program. Retrieved from: http://www.calstate.edu/capp/publications/docs/TashaComesHome-acc.pdf

Kyle, D. W., McIntyre, E., Miller, K. B., & Moore, G. H. (2006). *Bridging school and home through family nights: Ready-to-use plans, for grades K-8.* Thousand Oaks, CA: Corwin Press.

LaFromboise, T. D., & Lewis, H. (2008). The Zuni Life Skills Development Program: A school/community-based suicide prevention program. *Suicide and Life-Threatening Behavior, 38,* 343–353.

LaFromboise, T. D., Hoyt, D. R., Oliver, L., & Whitbeck, L. B. (2006). Family, community, and school influences on resilience among American Indian adolescents in the upper Midwest. *Journal of Community Psychology, 34,* 193–209.

Lager, C. A. (2006). Types of mathematics-language reading interactions that unnecessarily hinder algebra learning and assessment. *Reading Psychology, 27,* 165–204.

Lamborn, S. D., & Steinberg, L. (1993). Emotional autonomy redux: Revisiting Ryan and Lynch. *Child Development, 64,* 483–499.

Lamborn, S., & Groh, K. (2009). A four-part model of autonomy during emerging adulthood: Associations with adjustment. *International Journal of Behavioral Development, 33,* 393–401.

Lara, J. (2005). *Santa Ana Partnership Evaluation Master Planning: 2004–2005 Program Year.* Irvine, CA: University of California, Irvine.

Lareau, A. (1987). Social class differences in family-school relationships: The importance of cultural capital. *Sociology of Education, 60,* 73–85.

Lareau, A. (2003). *Unequal childhoods: Class, race, and family life.* Berkeley, CA: University of California Press.

Larson, R. W., Pearce, N., Sullivan, P. J., & Jarrett, R. L. (2007). Participation in youth programs as a catalyst for negotiation of family autonomy with connection. *Journal of Youth and Adolescence, 36,* 31–45.

Lawrence, J. A., Dodds, A. E., & Brooker, A. (2010). Constructing research knowledge with refugee young people: Using computer-assisted techniques. *International Society for the Study of Behavioral Development Bulletin, 34,* 26–29.

Le, H.-N., Ceballo, R., Chao, R., Hill, N. E., Murry, V. M., & Pinderhughes, E. E. (2008). Excavating culture: Disentangling ethnic differences from contextual influences in parenting. *Applied Developmental Science, 12,* 163–175.

Leadership Conference on Civil Rights. (2009). *Realize the dream: Quality education is a civil right.* Washington, DC. Retrieved from: www.realizethedream.org/programs/san-jose.html

Leaper, C., & Ayres, M. (2007). A meta-analytic review of moderators of gender differences in adults' talkativeness, affiliative, and assertive speech. *Personality and Social Psychology Review, 11,* 328–363.

Lee, C.-T., Beckert, T. E., & Goodrich, T. R. (2010) The relationship between individualistic, collectivistic, and transitional cultural value orientations and adolescents' autonomy and identity status. *Journal of Youth and Adolescence, 39,* 882–893.

Lerner, R. M., & Steinberg, L. (Eds.) (2009). *Handbook of adolescent psychology, Vol. 2, Contextual influences on adolescent development* (3rd ed). Hoboken, NJ: Wiley.

Levitt, M. J. (2005). Social relations in childhood and adolescence: The convoy model perspective. *Human Development, 48,* 28–47.

Levitt, M. J. (in press). Social networks. In L. C. Mayes & M. Lewis (Eds.), *The environment of human development: A handbook of theory and measurement.* New York: Cambridge University Press.

Lewig, K., Arney, F., & Scott, D. (2006). Closing the research-policy and research-practice gaps: Ideas for child and family services. *Family Matters, 74,* 12–19.

Liamputtong, P. (2007). *Researching the vulnerable: A guide to sensitive research methods.* London: Sage.

Linger, D. (2006). Identity. In C. Casey & R. Edgerton (Eds.), *A companion to psychological anthropology: Modernity and psychocultural change.* (pp. 185–200). Oxford: Blackwell.

Lloyd, C. B., & Hewett, P. (2009). Educational inequalities in the midst of persistent poverty: Diversity across Africa in educational outcomes. *Journal of International Development, 21,* 1137–1151.

López, A., Cooper, C. R., Schwab, N., & Moran, C. (2009, April). Latina/o immigrant adolescents' views of parents' changing involvement in their educational pathways. Paper presented at the meetings of the American Educational Research Association, Denver, Colorado.

López, A., Gonzalez, E., Domínguez, E., Cooper, C. R., & Cooper, R. G. (2011, March). How immigrant Latino youth in pre-college programs gain college knowledge: Navigating families, peers, and school. Paper presented at the meetings of the Society for Research in Child Development, Montreal, Canada.

Lopez, E. M. (2001). Guidance of Latino high school students in mathematics and career identity development. *Hispanic Journal of Behavioral Sciences, 23,* 189–207.

Lopez, E. M., Wishard, A., Gallimore, R., & Rivera, W. (2006). Latino high school students' perceptions of gangs and crews. *Journal of Adolescent Research, 21,* 299–318.

Lopez, E. M. (2010). Latino high school students' mathematics and science routines. Manuscript submitted for publication.

Lopez, M. E. (2000). *The National Coalition of Advocates for Students: Capacity building for Southeast Asian family-school partnerships.* Cambridge, MA: Harvard Family Research Project.

Lowe, E. D., Weisner, T. S., Geis, S., & Huston, A. (2005). Child-care instability and the effort to sustain a working daily routine: Evidence from the New Hope ethnographic study of low-income families. In C. R. Cooper, C. García Coll, T. Bartko, H. Davis, & C. Chatman (Eds.), *Developmental pathways through middle childhood: Rethinking contexts and diversity as resources* (pp. 121–144). Mahwah, NJ: Erlbaum.

Lundquist, S. (2006). *Padres Promontores de la Educación, Santa Ana Partnership.* Paper presented at the ENLACE Family-Community Networking and Best Practices Workshop, Santa Barbara, CA.

Lundquist, S., Martinez, C., & Harrizon, R. (2008, June). *California ENLACE: Engaging Latino communities for education.* California Postsecondary Education Commission (CPEC), Sacramento, CA.

Luning, R. J., & Yamauchi, L. (2008, March). *Learning a once-forbidden language at school: Influences on students and their families.* Paper presented at the American Educational Research Association, New York, NY.

MacLeod, J. (1995). *Ain't no makin' it: Aspirations and attainment in a low-income neighborhood.* Boulder, CO: Westview Press.

Marcia, J. E. (1966). Development and validation of ego-identity status. *Journal of Personality and Social Psychology, 3,* 551–558.

Marcia, J. E. (1994). The empirical study of ego identity. In H. A. Bosma, T. L. G. Graafsma, H. D. Grotevant, & D. J. de Levita (Eds.), *Identity and development: An interdisciplinary approach* (pp. 67–79). Thousand Oaks, CA: Sage.

Marcia, J. E., Waterman, A. S., Matteson, D. R., Archer, S. L., & Orlofsky, J. L. (1993). *Ego identity: A handbook for psychological research.* New York: Springer-Verlag.

Markstrom-Adams, C., & Adams, G. R. (1995). Gender, ethnic group, and grade differences in psychosocial functioning during middle adolescence. *Journal of Youth and Adolescence, 24,* 397–417.

Markus, H. R., & Kitayama, S. (1991). Culture and the self: Implications for cognition, emotion, and motivation. *Psychological Review, 98,* 224–253.

Martinez, C. (2007). *The Santa Barbara Pathways Program.* Santa Barbara, CA: University of California, Santa Barbara.

Mass, A. I. (1992). Interracial Japanese Americans: The best of both worlds or the end of the Japanese American community? In M. P. P. Root (Ed.), *Racially mixed people in America* (pp. 265–279). Newbury Park, CA: Sage.

Matsumoto, D. (1994). *Cultural influences on research methods and statistics.* Pacific Grove, CA: Brooks/Cole.

Matsumoto, D. (1999). Culture and self: An empirical assessment of Markus and Kitayama's theory of independent and interdependent self-construal. *Asian Journal of Social Psychology, 2,* 289–310.

Matsumoto, D., Kudoh, T., & Takeuchi, S. (1996). Changing patterns of individualism and collectivism in the United States and Japan. *Culture and Psychology, 2,* 77–107.

Matute-Bianchi, M. E. (1991). Situational ethnicity and patterns of school performance among immigrant and non-immigrant Mexican descent students. In M. A. Gibson & J. U. Ogbu (Eds.), *Minority status and schooling: A comparative study of immigrant and involuntary minorities* (pp. 205–248). New York: Garland Press.

Mayer, A. (2007). *Interrupting social reproduction: The implementation of an international baccalaureate diploma program in an urban high school.* Unpublished doctoral dissertation, University of California, Davis.

McClafferty, K. A., McDonough, P. M., & Núñez, A. M. (2002). What is a college culture? Facilitating college preparation through organizational change. Retrieved from: http://www.gseis.ucla.edu/faculty/pages/mcclafferty.html

McDonough, P. M. (1997). *Choosing colleges: How social class and schools structure opportunity.* Albany, NY: State University of New York Press.

McDonough, P. M. (2004a). Counseling matters: Knowledge, assistance, and organizational commitment in college preparation. In W. J. Tierney (Ed.), *Nine propositions relating to the effectiveness of college preparation programs.* (pp. 69–87). New York: State University of New York Press.

McDonough, P. M. (2004b, June). *What research tells us about college access: Assuring the success of all students.* Paper presented at the California K–16 Partnerships and Student Success Conference, Long Beach, CA.

McIntyre, E., & Kyle, D. (2001). *Stuck kids and leapers: Young children's academic development in the midst of mandated reform.* Research report to the Center for Research on Education, Diversity, and Excellence (CREDE). Santa Cruz, CA: University of California, Santa Cruz.

McIntyre, E., Kyle, D., Hovda, R., & Stone, N. (1999). Nongraded primary programs: Reform for Kentucky's children. *Journal of Education for Students Placed at Risk, 4,* 47–64.

McLoyd, V. C. (1991). What is the study of African-American children the study of? In R. J. Jones (Ed.), *Black psychology* (3rd ed., pp. 419–440). Berkeley, CA: Cobb and Henry.

McLoyd, V. C. (2005). Pathways to academic achievement among immigrant children: A commentary. In C. R. Cooper, C. García Coll, T. Bartko, H. Davis, & C. Chatman (Eds.),

Developmental pathways through middle childhood: Rethinking contexts and diversity as resources (pp. 283–293). Mahwah, NJ: Erlbaum.

Mead, M. (1970). *Culture and commitment: A study of the generation gap.* Garden City, NY: Natural History Press.

Meeus, W., Iedema, J., Helsen, M., & Vollebergh, W. (1999). Patterns of adolescent identity development: Review of literature and longitudinal analysis. *Developmental Review, 19,* 419–461.

Mehan, H. (2007). *Restructuring and reculturing schools to provide students with multiple pathways to college and career* (paper mp-rr006-0207). Los Angeles, CA: UCLA Institute for Democracy, Education, and Access (IDEA).

Mehan, H., Villanueva, I., Hubbard, L., & Lintz, A. (1996). *Constructing school success: The consequences of placing underachieving students in high track classes.* Cambridge, UK: Cambridge University Press.

Mejorado, M. (2000). *Navigating complex issues in a California statewide mentoring program for Mexican American high school students.* Unpublished doctoral dissertation. University of California, Davis.

Mello, S. (2005). The SAAGE program: Using data to help students get back on track for college. In C. E. Moran, J. M. Roa, B. K. Goza, & C. R. Cooper (Eds.), *Success by design: Creating college-bound communities. The work of the UC Santa Cruz Educational Partnership Center* (pp. 53–61). Sacramento, CA: California Academic Partnership Program.

Mena, D. D. (2002, April). *Testing the dimming hypothesis: Do Latino parents' and early adolescents' educational and career goals dim during the transition to junior high school?* Paper presented at the meetings of the Society for Research in Adolescence, Baltimore, MD.

Mena, D. D. (2005). *Beyond deficit views of low-income Mexican-descent families: Exploring variation in Mexican-descent high school students' and parents' aspirations and expectations, educational involvement practices, and college knowledge.* Unpublished doctoral dissertation, University of California, Santa Cruz.

Mertens, D. M. (2010). *Research and evaluation in education and psychology: Integrating diversity with quantitative, qualitative, and mixed methods.* (3rd ed.) Newbury Park, CA: Sage.

Miles, M. B., & A.M. Huberman, A. M. (1994). *Qualitative data analysis: An expanded sourcebook* (2nd ed.) Thousand Oaks, CA: Sage.

Minuchin, S., & Nichols, M. P. (1998). Structural family therapy. In F. M. Dattilio (Ed.), *Case studies in couple and family therapy: Systemic and cognitive perspectives* (pp. 108–131). New York: Guilford Press.

Mishler, E. G., & Waxler, N. E. (1968). *Interaction in families: An experimental study of family process and schizophrenia.* New York: Wiley.

Mitchell, B. A. (2005). *The boomerang age: Transitions to adulthood in families.* Piscataway, NJ: Transaction.

Moran, C., Cooper, C. R., Goza, B. K., & López, A. (2009). Developing effective P-20 partnerships to benefit Chicano/Latino students and families. *Journal of Hispanic Higher Education, 8,* 340–356.

Moran, C., Roa, J. M., Goza, B. K., & Cooper, C. R. (Eds.). (2005). *Success by design: Creating college-bound communities: The work of the UC Santa Cruz Educational Partnership Center.* Sacramento, CA: California Academic Partnership Program.

Moschkovich, J. (2007). Beyond words to mathematical content: Assessing English learners in the mathematics classroom. In A. Schoenfeld (Ed.), *Assessing mathematical proficiency* (pp. 345–352). Cambridge, UK: Cambridge University Press.

Mosqueda, E. (2010). Compounding inequalities: English proficiency and tracking and their relation to mathematics performance among Latina/o secondary school youth. *Journal of Urban Mathematics Education, 3,* 57–81.

Mott, T. E. (2006). *Pathways and destinations: African refugees in the U.S.* Unpublished doctoral dissertation, The Ohio State University.

Myers, D., & Schirm, A. (1999). *The impacts of Upward Bound: Final report for Phase 1 of the national evaluation.* Washington, DC: Mathematica Policy Research.

Nasir, N. S., Atukpawu, G., O'Connor, K., Davis, M., Wischnia, S., & Tsang, J. (2009).Wrestling with the legacy of stereotypes: Being African American in math class. In D. B. Martin, (Ed.), *Mathematics teaching, learning, and liberation in the lives of Black children.* (pp. 231–248) New York: Routledge/ Taylor & Francis.

National Mathematics Advisory Panel. (2008). *Foundations for success: The final report of the National Mathematics Advisory Panel.* Washington, DC: U.S. Department of Education.

National PTA. (1997). *National standards for parent/family involvement.* Chicago, IL: Author.

National PTA. (2009). *PTA National standards for family-school partnerships: An implementation guide.* Alexandria, VA: National PTA. Retrieved from: http://www.pta.org/2757.asp

NCLB: Public Law 107-110. (2002). *No Child Left Behind Act of 2001.* Washington, DC: Congressional Record.

Ngo, B., & Lee, S. J. (2007). Complicating the image of model minority success: A review of southeast Asian American education. *Review of Educational Research, 77,* 415–453.

Niemann, Y. F., Romero, A., & Arbona, C. (2000). Effects of cultural orientation on the perception of conflict between relationship and education goals for Mexican American college students. *Hispanic Journal of Behavioral Sciences, 22,* 46–63.

Norris, S. A., Roeser, R. W., Richter, L. M., Lewin, N., Ginsburg, C., Fleetwood, S. A., Taole, E., & van der Wolf, K. (2008). South African-ness among adolescents: The emergence of a collective identity within the Birth to Twenty Cohort Study. *Journal of Early Adolescence, 28,* 51–69.

Núñez, A.-M., & Oliva, M. (2009). Organizational collaboration to promote college access: A P-20 framework. *Journal of Hispanic Higher Education, 8.* 322–339.

Oakes, J. (1985). *Keeping track: How schools structure inequality.* New Haven: Yale University Press.

Oakes, J. (2003). *Critical conditions for equity and diversity in college access: Informing policy and monitoring results.* Los Angeles, CA: University of California All Campus Consortium on Research for Diversity (UC/ACCORD). Retrieved from: http://ucaccord.gseis.ucla.edu/ research/indicators/pdfs/criticalconditions.pdf

Ogbu, J. U. (1989). The individual in collective adaptation: A framework for focusing on academic underperformance and dropping out among involuntary minorities. In L. Weis, E. Farrar, & H. G. Petrie (Eds.), *Dropouts from school: Issues, dilemmas, and solutions* (pp. 181–204). Albany, NY: State University of New York Press.

Ogbu, J. U. (1991). Minority coping responses and school experience. *Journal of Psychohistory, 18,* 433–456.

Ogbu, J. U. (1993). Differences in cultural frame of reference. *International Journal of Behavioral Development, 16,* 483–506.

Ogbu, J. U. (1995). Origins of human competence: A cultural-ecological perspective. In N. R. Goldberger & J. Bveroff (Eds.), *The culture and psychology reader* (pp. 245–275). New York: New York University Press.

Ogbu, J. U. (2003). *Black American students in an affluent suburb: A study of academic disengagement*. Mahwah, NJ: Erlbaum.

Okagaki, L., Helling, M. K., & Bingham, G. E. (2009). American Indian college students' ethnic identity and beliefs about education. *Journal of College Student Development, 50*, 157–176.

Orbe, M. P. (2008). Theorizing multidimensional identity negotiation: Reflections on the lived experiences of first generation college students. In M. Azmitia, M. Syed, & K. Radmacher (Eds.), *The intersections between personal and social identities. New Directions for Child and Adolescent development, 120*, 81–96.

Orellana, M. F. (2009). *Translating childhoods: Immigrant youth, language, and culture*. Piscataway, NJ: Rutgers University Press.

Orfield, G., & Frankenberg, E. (2007). *Lessons in integration: Realizing the promise of racial diversity in America's public schools*. Charlottesville, VA: University of Virginia Press.

Otto, L. B. (2000). Youth perspectives on parental career influence. *Journal of Career Development, 27*, 111–118.

Oyserman, D., Bybee, D., & Terry, D. (2006). Possible selves and academic outcomes: How and when possible selves impel action. *Journal of Personality and Social Psychology, 91*, 188–204.

Oyserman, D., Coon, H. M., & Kemmerlmeier, M. (2002). Rethinking individualism and collectivism: Evaluation of theoretical assumptions and meta-analyses. *Psychological Bulletin, 128*, 3–72.

Passel, J. S. (2006). The size and characteristics of the unauthorized migrant population in the U.S.: Estimates based on the March 2005 Current Population Survey, Pew Hispanic Center. Retrieved from: http://pewhispanic.org/files/reports/61.pdf

Peña, D. C. (2000). Parent involvement: Influencing factors and implications. *Journal of Educational Research, 94*, 42–54.

Penuel, W. R., & Wertsch, J. V. (1995). Vygotsky and identity formation: A sociocultural approach. *Educational Psychologist, 30*, 83–92.

Perez, W., Espinosa, R., Ramos, K., Coronado, H. M., & Cotes, R. (2009). Academic resilience among undocumented Latino students. *Hispanic Journal of Behavioral Sciences, 31*, 149–181.

Perez-Huber, L., & Malagón, M. C. (2007). Silenced struggles: The experiences of Latina and Latino undocumented college students in California, *Nevada Law Journal, 7*, 841–861.

Perna, L. W. (2000). Differences in the decision to attend college among African Americans, Hispanics, and Whites. *Journal of Higher Education, 71*, 117–141.

Perna, L. W., & Swail, W. S. (2001). Pre-college outreach and early intervention. *Thought and Action: The NEA Higher Education Journal, 27*, 99–110.

Petersen, A. C. (2006). Conducting policy-relevant developmental psychopathology research. *International Journal of Behavioral Development, 30*, 39–46.

Peterson, G. W., Strivers, M. E., & Peters, D. F. (1986). Family versus nonfamily significant others for the career decisions of low-income youth. *Family Relations, 35*, 417–424.

Phelan, P., Davidson, A. L., & Yu, H. C. (1991). Students' multiple worlds: Navigating the borders of family, peer, and school cultures. In P. Phelan & A. L. Davidson (Eds.), *Cultural diversity: Implications for education* (pp. 52–88). New York: Teachers College Press.

Phelan, P., Davidson, A. L., & Yu, H. C. (1998). *Adolescents' worlds: Negotiating family, peer, and school*. New York: Teachers College Press.

Phinney, J. S. (1990). Ethnic identity in adolescents and adults: A review of research. *Psychological Bulletin, 180*, 499–514.

Phinney, J. S. (1992). The Multigroup Ethnic Identity Measure: A new scale for use with diverse groups. *Journal of Adolescent Research, 7,* 156–176.

Phinney, J. S. (2006). Acculturation is not an independent variable: Approaches to studying acculturation as a complex process. In M. H. Bornstein & L. R. Côtè (Eds.), *Acculturation and parent-child relationships: Measurement and development* (pp. 79–95). Mahwah, NJ: Erlbaum.

Phinney, J. S., & Ong, A. D. (2007). Conceptualization and measurement of ethnic identity: Current status and future directions. *Journal of Counseling Psychology, 54,* 271–281.

Phinney, J. S., & Rosenthal, D. A. (1992). Ethnic identity in adolescence: Process, context, and outcome. In G. R. Adams & T. P. Gullotta (Eds.), *Advances in adolescent development: Adolescent identity formation* (pp. 145–172). Thousand Oaks, CA: Sage.

Phinney, J. S., Dennis, J., & Osorio, S. (2005). Reasons to attend college among ethnically diverse college students. *Cultural Diversity and Ethnic Minority Psychology, 12,* 347–366.

Phinney, J. S., Kim-Jo, T., Osorio, S., & Vilhjalmsdottir, P. (2005). Autonomy and relatedness in adolescent-parent disagreements: Ethnic and developmental factors. *Journal of Adolescent Research, 20,* 8–39.

Pike, K. L. (1990). On the emics and etics of Pike and Harris. In T. N. Headland, K. L. Pike, & M. Harris (Eds.), *Emics and etics: The insider/outsider debate. Frontiers of anthropology* (Vol. 7, pp. 28–47). Thousand Oaks, CA: Sage.

Portes, A. (1998). Social capital: Its origins and applications in modern sociology. *Annual Review of Sociology, 24,* 1–24.

Portes, A. (2000). The two meanings of social capital. *Sociological Forum, 15,* 1–12.

Portes, A., & Fernández-Kelly, P. (2008). No margin for error: Educational and occupational achievement among disadvantaged children of immigrants, *The ANNALS of the American Academy of Political and Social Science, 620,* 12–36.

Portes, A., & Rumbaut, R. G. (2001). *Legacies: The story of the immigrant second generation.* Berkeley, CA: University of California Press.

Portes, A., & Rumbaut, R. G. (2006). *Immigrant America: A portrait* (3rd ed.) Berkeley: University of California Press.

Pradl, G. M. (2002). Linking instructional intervention and professional development: Using the ideas behind Puente high school English to inform educational policy. *Educational Policy, 16,* 522–546.

Public/Private Ventures. (1996). *Mentoring: A synthesis of P/PV's research: 1998–1995.* Philadelphia, PA: Public/Private Ventures.

Putnam, R. D. (2000). *Bowling alone: The collapse and revival of American community.* New York: Simon & Schuster.

Pyke, K. (2005). "Generational deserters" and "black sheep": Acculturative differences among siblings in Asian immigrant families. *Journal of Family Issues, 26,* 491–517.

Quigley, D. D. (2002). *How are the high school students faring in the college-prep curriculum: A look at the benchmark data for UC partner high schools.* Oakland, CA: University of California Office of the President.

Quijada, P. (2005). Whose reservations are legitimized? Understanding indigenous adult-youth relationships in home and school contexts. *Dissertation Abstracts International, Section A, 65*(8–A), 2899.

Raeff, C. (2010). Independence and interdependence in children's developmental experiences. *Child* Development Perspectives, 4, 31–36.

Reese, L., Balzano, S., Gallimore, R., & Goldenberg, C. (1995). The concept of *educación*: Latino family values and American schooling. *International Journal of Educational Research, 23,* 57–81.

Reese, L., Gallimore, R., Goldenberg, C., & Balzano, S. (1995). Immigrant Latino parents' future orientations for their children. In R. F. Macias & R. G. García Ramos (Eds.), *Changing schools for changing students: An anthology of research on language minorities, schools and society* (pp. 205–230). Santa Barbara, CA: University of California Linguistic Minority Research Institute.

Reis, O., & Buhl, H. M. (2008). Individuation during adolescence and emerging adulthood—Five German studies. *International Journal of Behavioral Development, 32,* 369–371.

Rendón, L., Jalomo, R., Jr., & García, K. (1994). The university and community college paradox: Why Latinos do not transfer. In A. Hurtado & E. E. García (Eds.), *The educational achievement of Latinos: Barriers and successes* (pp. 227–258). Santa Cruz: Regents of the University of California.

Rhodes, J. E., Grossman, J. B., & Resch, N. L. (2000). Agents of change: Pathways through which mentoring relationships influence adolescents' academic adjustment. *Child Development, 71,* 1662–1671.

Rivera, H., Tharp, R. G., Bird, C., Feathers, M., Epaloose, G., Eriacho, W., et al. (2001). *Key findings from the "Zuni community survey" on issues of education, teaching, and learning in Zuni schools.* No. 1. Santa Cruz, CA: Center for Research on Education, Diversity, and Excellence (CREDE).

Rodríguez, J. L., Jones, E. B., Pang, V. O., & Park, C. D. (2004). Promoting academic achievement and identity development among diverse high school students. *The High School Journal, 87,* 44–53.

Rodriguez, R. G., McCollum, P., & Villarreal, A. (2002). *Community engagement review and planning guide.* San Antonio, TX: Intercultural Development Research Association.

Rodriguez, R. G., Villarreal, A., & Cortez, J. D. (2002). *Family and community engagement survey.* San Antonio, TX: Intercultural Development Research Association. Retrieved from: http://www.idra.org/images/stories/survey.pdf

Roeser, R. W., Galloway, M., Casey-Cannon, S., Watson, G., Keller, L., & Tan, E (2008). Identity representations in patterns of school achievement and well-being among early adolescent girls: Variable- and person-centered approaches. *Journal of Early Adolescence, 28,* 115–152.

Rogoff, B. (1990). *Apprenticeship in thinking: Cognitive development in social context.* New York: Oxford University Press.

Rogoff, B. (2003). *The cultural nature of human development.* New York: Oxford University Press.

Rogoff, B., Moore, L., Najafi, B., Dexter, A., Correa-Chavez, M., & Solis, J. (2006). Children's development of cultural repertoires through participation in everyday routines and practices. (pp. 490–515). In J. Grusec & P. Hastings (Eds.), *Handbook of socialization: Theory and research.* New York: Guilford.

Romo, H. D., & Falbo, T. (1995). *Against the odds: Latino youth and high school graduation.* Texas: University of Texas Press.

Root, M. P. P. (Ed.), *Racially mixed people in America.* Newbury Park, CA: Sage.

Ross-Seriff, F., Taqi Tirmazi, M. & Walsh, T. R. (2007). Cultural and religious contexts of parenting by immigrant South Asian Muslim mothers. In J. E. Lansford, K. Deater-Deckard, & M. H. Bornstein (Eds.), *Immigrant families in contemporary society* (pp. 194–211). New York: Guilford.

Rothstein-Fisch, C., Turnbull, E., & Garcia, S. G. (2009). Making the implicit explicit: Supporting teachers to bridge cultures. *Early Childhood Research Quarterly, 24,* 472–486.

Ruble, D., Alvarez, J., Bachman, M., Cameron, J., Fuligni, A., & García Coll, C. (2004). The development of a sense of "we": The emergence and implications of children's collective identity. In M. Bennett & F. Sani (Eds.), *The development of the social self* (pp. 29–76). New York: Psychology Press.

Rumbaut, R. G. (2000). Profiles in resilience: Educational achievement and ambition among children of immigrants in southern California. In R. D. Taylor & M. C. Wang (Eds.), *Resilience across contexts: Family, work, culture, and community* (pp. 257–294). Mahwah, NJ: Erlbaum.

Rumbaut, R. G. (2006). *Immigrant America: Some patterns, puzzles, and paradoxes.* Paper presented at the symposium on immigration: What we know and what we need to learn, Meeting of the Society for Research in Adolescence, Chicago, IL.

Rumberger, R. W., & Lim, S. A. (2008). *Why students drop out of school: A review of 25 years of research.* University of California, Santa Barbara: California Dropout Research Project.

Ryan, R. M., & Lynch, J. H. (1989). Emotional autonomy versus detachment: Revisiting the vicissitudes of adolescence and young adulthood. *Child Development, 60,* 340–356.

Sabogal, F., Marin, G., Otero-Sabogal, R., Marin, B., & Perez-Stable, E. J. (1987). Hispanic familism and acculturation: What changes and what doesn't? *Hispanic Journal of Behavioral Sciences, 9,* 397–412.

Saenz, V. B., & Ponjuan, P. (2009). The vanishing Latino male in higher education. *Journal of Hispanic Higher Education, 8,* 54–89.

Salbi, Z. (2005). *Between two worlds: Escape from tyranny: Growing up in the shadow of Saddam.* New York: Gotham Books.

Salmela-Aro, K., Aunola, K., & Nurmi, J. E. (2007). Personal goals during emerging adulthood: A 10-year follow up. *Journal of Adolescent Research, 22,* 690–715.

Sanders, M. G., & Epstein, J. L. (2000). The National Network of Partnership Schools: How research influences educational practice. *Journal for the Education of Students Placed at Risk, 5,* 61–76.

Santa Ana Partnership. (2006). *Padre à padre (Parent to parent): Lessons to guide the path toward higher education.* Retrieved from: http://sac.edu/community/partnerships/sapartneship/

Santiago, P. (2008, July). *Equity in tertiary education: Findings of OECD's thematic review of tertiary education.* Paper presented at the 17th European Access Network Annual Conference, Berlin, Germany.

Santiago, P., Tremblay, K., Basri, E., & Arnal, E. (2008). *Tertiary education for the knowledge society. OECD thematic review of tertiary education: Synthesis report. Volume 2.* Paris, France: Organisation for Economic Co-operation and Development.

Saxe, G. B., & Gearhart, M. (Eds.) (1988). *Children's mathematics.* San Francisco: Jossey-Bass.

Schofield, J. W., & Anderson, K. (1987). Combining quantitative and qualitative components of research on ethnic identity and intergroup relations. In J. S. Phinney & M. J. Rotheram (Eds.), *Children's' ethnic socialization: Pluralism and development* (pp. 252–273). Newbury Park, CA: Sage.

Schwartz, S. J. (2001). The evolution of Eriksonian and neo-Eriksonian identity theory and research: A review and integration. *Identity: An International Journal of Theory and Research, 1,* 7–58.

Schwartz, S. J. (2002). In search of mechanisms of change in identity development: Integrating the constructivist and discovery perspectives on identity. *Identity: An International Journal of Theory and Research, 2,* 317–339.

Schwartz, S. J. (2008). Self and identity in early adolescence: Some reflections and introduction to the special issue. *Journal of Early Adolescence, 28,* 5–15.

Schwartz, S. J., Pantin, H., Prado, G., Sullivan, S., & Szapocznik, J. (2005). Family functioning, identity, and problem behavior in Hispanic immigrant early adolescents. *Journal of Early Adolescence, 25,* 392–420.

Seginer, R. (1992). Sibling relationships in early adolescence: A study of Israeli Arab sisters. *Journal of Early Adolescence, 12,* 96–110.

Seginer, R. (2008). Future orientation in times of threat and challenge: How resilient adolescents construct their future. *International Journal of Behavioral Development, 32,* 272–282.

Seginer, R. (2009). *Future orientation: Developmental and ecological perspectives.* New York: Springer.

Seginer, R., & Mahajna, S. (2004). How the future orientation of traditional Israeli Palestinian girls links beliefs about women's roles and academic achievement. *Psychology of Women Quarterly, 28,* 122–135.

Seginer, R., Shoyer, S., Hossessi, R., & Tannous, H. (2007). Adolescent family and peer relationships: Does culture matter? In B. B. Brown (Ed.), *Linking parents and family to adolescent peer relations: Ethnic and cultural considerations. New directions in child and adolescent development* (pp. 83–99). San Francisco: Jossey-Bass.

Sellers, R. M., Copeland-Linder, N., Martin, P. P., & Lewis, R. L. (2006). Racial identity matters: the relationship between racial discrimination and psychological functioning in African American adolescents. *Journal of Research on Adolescence, 16,* 187–216.

Serpell, R. (1993). *The significance of schooling: Life-journeys in an African society.* Cambridge, UK: Cambridge University Press.

Serpell, R. (2009). *Social responsibility as a dimension of intelligence and an educational goal: Insights from programmatic research in Africa.* Paper presented at Conference on Strengthening Africa's Contributions to Child Development Research, Victoria, British Columbia, Canada.

Shartrand, A. M., Weiss, H. B., Kreider, H. M., & Lopez, M. E. (1997). *New skills for new schools: Preparing teachers in family involvement.* Washington, DC: U.S. Department of Education.

Shavit, Y., & Blossfeld, H.-P. (1993). *Persistent inequality: Changing educational attainment in thirteen countries.* Boulder, CO: Westview Press.

Shonkoff, J. (2002). Science, policy, and practice: Three cultures in search of a shared mission. *Child Development, 71,* 181–187.

Siri, D. (2005, June). *Alliance for Regional Collaboration to Heighten Educational Success (ARCHES): A vision whose time is now.* Paper presented at the California K–16 Partnerships and Student Success Conference, Long Beach, CA.

Sirin, S. R., Ryce, P., & Mir, M. (2009). How teachers' values affect their evaluation of children of immigrants: Findings from Islamic public schools. *Early Childhood Research Quarterly, 24,* 463–473.

Skorikov, V., & Unritani, R. (2008). *Continuity and changes in adolescent career decision-making.* Paper presented at the meetings of the Society for Research on Adolescence, Chicago, IL.

Skorikov, V., & Vondracek, F. W. (1998). Vocational identity development: Its relationship to other identity domains and to overall identity development. *Journal of Career Assessment, 6,* 13–35.

Sneed, J. R., Schwartz, S. J., & Cross, W. E. (2006). A multicultural critique of identity status theory and research: A call for integration. *Identity: An International Journal of Theory and Research, 6,* 61–84.

So, A. (1987). The educational aspirations of Hispanic parents. *Educational Research Quarterly, 11,* 47–53.

Soenens, B., Vansteenkiste, M., Lens, W., Luyckx, K., Goossens, L., Beyers, W., et al. (2007). Conceptualizing parental autonomy support: Adolescent perceptions of promotion of independence versus promotion of volitional functioning. *Developmental Psychology, 43,* 633–646.

Solis, J. (2003). Re-thinking illegality as a violence *against,* not by Mexican immigrants, children, and youth. *Journal of Social Issues, 59,* 15–31.

Solorzano, D. (1992). An exploratory analysis of the effects of race, class, and gender on student and parent mobility aspirations. *Journal of Negro Education, 61,* 30–44.

Solorzano, D., Ceja, M., & Yosso, T. (2001). Critical race theory, racial microaggressions, and campus racial climate: The experiences of African American college students. *Journal of Negro Education, 69,* 60–73.

Sroufe, L. A. (1979). The coherence of individual development. *American Psychologist, 34,* 834–841.

Sroufe, L. A., Egeland, B., Carlson, E. A., & Collins, W. A. (2005). *The development of the person: The Minnesota study of risk and adaptation from birth to adulthood.* New York: Guilford.

Stanton-Salazar, R. D. (2004). Social capital among working-class minority students: Prospects for applying a new concept to peer influences on achievement. In M. Gibson, P. Gándara, & J. Koyama (Eds.), *School connections: U.S. Mexican youth, peers and academic achievement* (pp. 18–38). New York: Teachers College Press.

Stanton-Salazar, R. D. (2010). A social capital framework for the study of institutional agents and their role in the empowerment of low-status students and youth. *Youth & Society, 42.*

Stanton-Salazar, R. D., Vasquez, O. A., & Mehan, H. (1996). Engineering success through institutional support. In A. Hurtado (Ed.), *The Latino pipeline* (pp. 100–136). Santa Cruz, CA: University of California Regents.

Steinberg, L., & Silk, J. S. (2002). Parenting adolescents. In M. H. Bornstein (Ed.), *Handbook of parenting: Vol. 1: Children and parenting* (2nd ed., pp. 103–133). Mahwah, NJ: Erlbaum.

Stephan, C. W. (1992). Mixed-heritage individuals: Ethnic identity and trait characteristics. In M. P. P. Root (Ed.), *Racially mixed people in America* (pp. 50–63). Newbury Park, CA: Sage.

Stewart, D. W., & Shamdasani, P. N. (1990). *Focus groups: Theory and practice.* Newbury Park, CA: Sage.

Stipek, D. (2005). Children as unwitting agents in their developmental pathways. In C. R. Cooper, C. G. Coll, W. T. Bartko, H. M. Davis, & C. Chatman (Eds.), *Developmental pathways through middle childhood: Rethinking contexts and diversity as resources* (pp. 99–120). Mahwah, NJ: Erlbaum.

Streitmatter, J. L. (1988). Ethnicity as a mediating variable of early adolescent identity development. *Journal of Adolescence, 11,* 335–346.

Su, D. (2008). *Resources, religion, and refugees: Observations on hidden capital in two Cambodian American language schools.* Paper presented at the meetings of the Bridging Multiple Worlds Alliance, San Jose, CA.

Suárez-Orozco, C., & Suárez-Orozco, M. M. (2001). *Children of immigration.* Cambridge, MA: Harvard University Press.

Suárez-Orozco, C., Rhodes, J., & Milburn, M. (2009). Unraveling the immigrant paradox: Academic engagement and disengagement among recently arrived immigrant youth. *Youth & Society, 41,* 151–185.

Suárez-Orozco, C., Suárez-Orozco, M. M., & Todorova, I. (2008). *Learning a new land: Immigrant students in American society*. Cambridge, MA: Harvard University Press.

Sue, D., & Sue, S. (1987). Cultural factors in the clinical assessment of Asian Americans. *Journal of Consulting and Clinical Psychology, 55*, 479–487.

Sugimoto, Y. (2010). *An introduction to Japanese society*. (2nd ed.) Cambridge: Cambridge University Press.

Sugimura, K. (2001). A longitudinal study of relatedness in identity formation of female adolescents. *The Japanese Journal of Developmental Psychology, 12*, 87–98.

Sugimura, K., Phinney, J. S., Yamazaki, M., & Takeo, K. (2009). Compliance, negotiation, and self assertion in Japanese adolescents' disagreements with parents. *International Journal of Behavioral Development, 35*, 77–87.

Syed, M. (2010a). Memorable everyday events in college: Narratives of the intersection of ethnicity and academia. *Journal of Diversity in Higher Education, 3*, 56–69.

Syed, M. (2010b). Developing an integrated self: Academic and ethnic identities among diverse college students. *Developmental Psychology, 46*, 1590–1604.

Syed, M., & Azmitia, M. (2008). A narrative approach to ethnic identity in emerging adulthood: Bringing life to the identity status model. *Developmental Psychology, 44*, 1012–1027.

Tamis-LeMonda, C. S., Way, N., Hughes, D., Yoshikawa, H., Kalman, R. K., & Niwa, E. Y. (2007). Parents' goals for children: The dynamic coexistence of individualism and collectivism in cultures and individuals. *Social Development, 17*, 183–209.

Tanakeyowma, L. M. (2008, November). *Padres Promotores/Santa Ana Partnership*. Paper presented at the Family Involvement Forum: Pathways to College, Monterey, CA.

Tanakeyowma, L. M., & Castellanos, J. (2009, April). *Padres Promotores: Incorporating a psychosocio-cultural approach to parent involvement*. Paper presented at the meetings of the American Educational Research Association, New York.

Taopoulos-Chan, M., Smetana, J. G., & Yau, J. P. (2009). How much do I tell thee? Strategies for managing information to parents among American adolescents from Chinese, Mexican, and European backgrounds. *Journal of Family Psychology, 23*, 364–374.

Taylor, P. (Ed.). (2009). *Between two worlds: How young Latinos come of age in America*. Washington, DC: Pew Hispanic Center.

Taylor, R. D., Casten, R., Flickinger, S. M., Roberts, D., & Fulmore, C. D. (1994). Explaining the school performance of African-American adolescents. *Journal of Research on Adolescence, 4*, 21–44.

Teddlie, C., & Tashakkori, A. (2008). *Foundations of mixed methods research: Integrating quantitative and qualitative techniques in the social and behavioral sciences*. Thousand Oaks, CA: Sage.

Telzer, E., & Fuligni, A. J. (2009). Daily family assistance and the psychological well-being of adolescents from Latin American, Asian, and European backgrounds. *Developmental Psychology, 45*, 1177–1189.

Teranishi, C., Gjerde, P. F., Cooper, C. R., & Onishi, M. (1995). *Linking qualitative and quantitative analyses of Japanese American adolescents' ethnicity and identity*. Paper presented at the Western Psychological Association, Seattle, WA.

Tharp, R. G., & Gallimore, R. (1988). *Rousing minds to life: Teaching, learning and schooling in social context*. Cambridge, UK: Cambridge University Press.

Tharp, R. G., & Yamauchi, L. A. (1994). *Polyvocal research on the ideal Zuni Indian classroom*. Santa Cruz, CA: National Center for Research on Cultural Diversity and Second Language Learning.

Tharp, R. G., Estrada, P., Dalton, S. S., & Yamauchi, L. (2000). *Teaching transformed: Achieving excellence, fairness, inclusion, and harmony.* Boulder, CO: Westview Press.

Tharp, R. G., Lewis, H., Hilberg, T., Bird, C., Epaloose, G., Dalton, S. S., et al. (1999). Seven more mountains and a map: Overcoming obstacles to reform in Native American schools. *Journal of Education for Students Placed at Risk, 4,* 5–26.

Thompson, M., & Crul, M. (2007). The second generation in Europe and the United States: How is the transatlantic debate relevant for further research on the European second generation? *Journal of Ethnic and Migration Studies, 33,* 1025–1041.

Thorne, A. (2004). Putting the person into social identity. *Human Development, 47,* 361–365.

Tierney, W. G. (2002). Parents and families in pre-college preparation: The lack of connection between research and practice. *Educational Policy, 16,* 588–606.

Tierney, W. G., Bailey, T., Constantine, J., Finkelstein, N., & Hurd, H. (2009). *Helping students navigate the path to college: What high schools can do. Using student achievement data to support instructional decision making.* Washington, DC: National Center for Education Evaluation and Regional Assistance, Institute of Education Sciences, U.S. Department of Education.

Tierney, W. G., Corwin, Z. B., & Colyar, J. E. (2004). *Preparing for college: Nine elements of effective outreach.* Albany, NY: State University of New York Press.

Tornatzky, L. G., Cutler, R., & Lee, J. (2002). *College knowledge: What Latino parents need to know and why they don't know it.* Claremont, CA: Tomas Rivera Policy Institute.

Toshiaki, T. (2010). *The new paradox for Japanese women: Greater choice, greater inequality.* Tokyo: I-House Press.

Townsend, S. S. M., Markus, H. R., & Bergsieker, H. B. (2009). My choice, your categories: The denial of multiracial identities. *Journal of Social Issues, 65,* 185–204.

Triandis, H. C., & Suh, E. M. (2002). Cultural influences on personality. *Annual Review of Psychology, 53,* 133–160.

Trinh, N. M., & Cooper, C. R. (2009, April). *Good student, good child: Academics, gender, and conflict in Vietnamese-American college students and their parents.* Paper presented at the Society for Research in Child Development, Denver, CO.

Trinh, N., Tsai, K., & Cooper, C. R. (2007). *Cultural bridges to college: Mapping pathways to college in families' home languages,* University of California, Santa Cruz. Retrieved from: http://www.bridgingworlds.org/language/index.html

Tudge, J. R. H., & Doucet, F. (2004). Early mathematical experiences: Observing young Black and White children's everyday activities. *Early Childhood Research Quarterly, 19,* 21–39.

Tufte, E. (1994). *Envisioning information.* Cheshire, CT: Graphics Press.

Tupan-Wenno, M. (2009, May). *Retention programs in higher education.* Paper presented at TIES Conference, Amsterdam, The Netherlands.

U.S. Census Bureau. (2000). *Population projections,* Retrieved from: http://www.census.gov

U.S. Department of Education. (1997). *Getting ready for college early: A handbook for parents of students in the middle and junior high school years.* Washington, DC: U.S. Department of Education.

U.S. Office for Civil Rights. (2004). *Achieving diversity: Race-neutral alternatives in American education.* Retrieved from: http://www.ed.gov/about/offices/list/ocr/edlite-raceneutralreport2.html

UNICEF. (2002). A League table of educational disadvantage in rich nations. *UNICEF Report Card #4.* Florence, Italy: UNICEF.

University of California Board of Regents. (2003). Forging California's future through educational partnerships: Redefining educational outreach. Final report of the Strategic Review Panel on UC Educational Outreach to the President of the University of California. Oakland, CA: University of California Office of the President.

University of California Board of Regents. (2005). *Policy affirming engagement in the preschool through postsecondary education system, as fundamental to the University of California mission as a Land Grant Institution.* Oakland, CA: University of California Office of the President.

University of California Office of the President. (2010). *A report to the legislature on student academic preparation and educational partnerships for the 2008–09 academic year.* Oakland, CA: Office of the Vice President for Education Partnerships.

Useem, E. L. (1992). Middle schools and math groups: Parents' involvement in children's placement. *Sociology of Education, 65,* 263–279.

Valencia, R. R., & Black, M. S. (2002). "Mexican Americans don't value education!"—On the basis of the myth, mythmaking, and debunking. *Journal of Latinos and Education, 1,* 81–103.

Van Voorhis, F. L. (2003). Interactive homework in middle school: Effects on family involvement and students' science achievement. *Journal of Educational Research, 96,* 323–339.

Venezia, A., Kirst, M., & Antonio, A. (2004). *Betraying the college dream: How disconnected K-12 and postsecondary educational systems undermine student aspirations.* Stanford, CA: Stanford Institute for Higher Education Research.

Vernez, G., Krop, C., Vuollo, M., & Hansen, J. S. (2008). *Toward a K-20 student unit record data system for California.* Santa Monica, CA: Rand Corporation.

Vigil, J. D. (2004). Gangs, streets, and schooling: Peer dynamics. In M. A. Gibson, P. Gandara, & J. Koyama (Eds.), *School connections: U.S. Mexican youth, peers, and school achievement* (pp. 87–106). New York: Teachers College Press.

Vigil, J. D., & Yun, S. C. (1996). Southern California gangs: Comparative ethnicity and social control. In C. R. Huff (Ed.), *Gangs in America* (2nd ed., pp. 139–156). Thousand Oaks, CA: Sage.

Voelkl, K. E. (1993). Academic achievement and expectations among African-American students. *Journal for Research and Development in Education, 27,* 42–55.

Vygotsky, L. S. (1978). *Mind in society: The development of higher psychological processes.* Cambridge, MA: Harvard University Press.

Walker, E. N. (2006). Urban high school students' academic communities and their effects on mathematics success. *American Educational Research Journal, 43,* 43–73.

Warner, M. (2005). *Redesigning the American high school: Getting it done: Ten steps to a state action agenda: A guidebook of promising state and local practices.* Washington, DC: National Governors' Association. Retrieved from: http://www.nga.org/cda/files/05warnerguide.pdf

Waters, M. C. (1996). The intersection of gender, race, and ethnicity in identity development of Caribbean American teens. In B. Leadbetter & N. Way (Eds.), *Urban girls: Resisting stereotypes, creating identities* (pp. 65–81). New York: New York University Press.

Watzlawick, P. (1966). A structured family interview. *Family Process, 5,* 256–271.

Weisner, T. S. (1984). Ecocultural niches of middle childhood: A cross-cultural perspective. In W. A. Collins (Ed.), *Development during middle childhood: The years from six to twelve.* (pp. 335–369). Washington, D.C.: National Academy Press.

Weisner, T. S. (2002). Ecocultural understanding of children's developmental pathways. *Human Development, 45,* 275–281.

Weisner, T. S. (2010). Ecocultural understanding. In H. B. Weiss, H. Kreider, M. E. Lopez, & C. Chatman-Nelson (Eds.), *Preparing educators to engage families: Case studies using an ecological systems framework* (2nd ed.), (pp. 84–90). Thousand Oaks, CA: Sage.

Weisner, T. S. (Ed.) (2005). *Discovering successful pathways in children's development: Mixed methods in the study of childhood and family life.* Thousand Oaks, CA: Sage.

Weisner, T. S., Gallimore, R., & Jordan, C. (1988). Unpackaging cultural effects on classroom learning: Native Hawaiian peer assistance and child-generated activity. *Anthropology and Education Quarterly, 19,* 327–351.

Weiss, H. B., Kreider, H., Lopez, E., & Chatman, C. (Eds.). (2005). *Preparing educators to involve families: From theory to practice.* Thousand Oaks: Sage.

Weiss, H. B., Kreider, H., Lopez, M. E., & Chatman-Nelson, C. (2010). *Preparing educators to engage families: Case studies using an ecological systems framework* (2nd ed.). Thousand Oaks, CA: Sage.

Werner, E. E. (1993). Risk, resilience, and recovery: Perspectives from the Kauai Longitudinal Study. *Development & Psychopathology, 5,* 503–515.

Whiting, B. B. (1976). The problem of the packaged variable. In K. Riegel & J. Meacham (Eds.), *The developing individual in a changing world: Historical and cultural issues* (Vol. 1, pp. 303–309). The Hague, Netherlands: Mouton.

Wilson, A., & Cooper, C. R. (2011). *Exploring knowledge of racial discrepancies in college attendance among Latino adolescents.* Paper presented at the meetings of the Society for Research in Child Development, Montreal, Canada.

Winograd, K. W. (2007). Negotiating borders: Examining patterns of collaboration and conflict between high schools and higher education funding in New Mexico. *Dissertation Abstracts International, Section A: Humanities and Social Sciences, 68*(6–A), 2276.

Wohlwill, J. F. (1973). *The study of behavioral development.* New York: Academic Press.

Yamauchi, L. (1994). *Stakeholders' voices and polyvocal research in Zuni.* Unpublished manuscript, University of Hawaii at Manoa.

Yamauchi, L., & Tharp, R. G. (1995). Culturally compatible conversations in Native American classrooms. *Linguistics and Education, 7,* 349–367.

Yamauchi, L., & Wilhelm, P. (2001). *E ola ka Hawi'i i kona ōlelo:* Hawaiians live in their language. In D. Christian & F. Genesee (Eds.), *Case studies in bilingual education* (pp. 83–94). Alexandria, VA: TESOL.

Yamauchi, L., Billig, S. H., Meyer, S., & Hofschire, L. (2006). Student outcomes associated with service-learning in a culturally relevant high school program. *Journal of Prevention & Intervention in the Community, 32,* 146–164.

Yamauchi, L., Ceppi, A. K., & Lau-Smith, J. (1999). Sociohistorical influences on the development of Papahana Kaiapuni, the Hawaiian language immersion program. *Journal of Education for Students Placed at Risk, 4,* 27–46.

Yamauchi, L., Lau-Smith, J., & Luning, R. J. (2008). Family involvement in a Hawaiian language immersion program. *The School Community Journal, 18,* 39–60.

Yin, R. K. (2008). *Case study research: Design and methods* (4th ed.). Newbury Park, CA: Sage.

Yoder, A. E. (2000). Barriers to ego identity status formation: A contextual qualification of Marcia's identity status paradigm. *Journal of Adolescence, 23,* 95–106.

Yonezawa, S., Wells, A. S., & Serna, I. (2002). Choosing tracks: "Freedom of choice" in detracking schools. *American Educational Research Journal, 39,* 37–67.

Yoshikawa, H., Weisner, T. S., Kalil, A., & Way, N. (2008). Mixing qualitative and quantitative research in developmental psychology: Uses and methodological choices. *Developmental Psychology, 44*, 344–354.

Yosso, T. J. (2005). Whose culture has capital? A critical race theory discussion of community cultural wealth. *Race, Ethnicity and Education, 8*, 69–91.

Youniss, J. (1980). *Parents and peers in social development: A Sullivan-Piaget perspective.* Chicago, IL: University of Chicago Press.

Youniss, J., & Smollar, J. (1985). *Adolescent relations with mothers, fathers, and friends.* Chicago, IL: University of Chicago Press.

Youniss, J., & Yates, M. (1997). *Community services and social responsibility in youth.* Chicago, IL: University of Chicago Press.

Zarate, M. E., & Meyer, C. W. (2007). *Perceptions, expectations, and programs: Understanding Latino parental involvement.* Los Angeles, CA: Tomás Rivera Policy Institute.

Zhiyong, Z. (2007, March). *Cultural conflict or amalgamation? Higher education access and equity of ethnic minorities in China.* Paper presented at the Workshop on Higher Education, Hong Kong.

Zimmer-Gembeck, M. J., & Collins, W. A. (2003). Autonomy development during adolescence. In G. R. Adams & M. D. Berzonsky (Eds.), *Blackwell handbook of adolescence* (pp. 175–204). Malden, MA: Blackwell.

INDEX

Note: Page numbers followed by *f* and *t* denote figures and tables, respectively. Author surnames carry initials only; first names are provided for other individuals discussed in the text.